The Asbury Theological Seminary Series in

Christian Revitalization Studies

This volume is published in collaboration with the Center for the Study of World Christian Revitalization Movements, a cooperative initiative of Asbury Theological Seminary faculty. Building on the work of the previous Wesleyan/Holiness Studies Center at the Seminary, the Center provides a focus for research in the Wesleyan Holiness and other related Christian renewal movements, including Pietism and Pentecostal movements, which have had a world impact. The research seeks to develop analytical models of these movements, including their biblical and theological assessment. Using an interdisciplinary approach, the Center bridges relevant discourses in several areas in order to gain insights for effective Christian mission globally. It recognizes the need for conducting research that combines insights from the history of evangelical renewal and revival movements with anthropological and religious studies literature on revitalization movements. It also networks with similar or related research and study centers around the world, in addition to sponsoring its own research projects.

In this study, Dr. Brian Ebel offers two contrasting and influential methodological perspectives on the central issue of explicating the person and work of Jesus Christ. By addressing this important issue he provides grounding for assessing more adequately the Christological basis for understanding movements of Christian revitalization, which this series is designed to address.

J. Steven O'Malley
General Editor
The Asbury Theological Seminary Studies in Christian Revitalization

Studies in Philosophical/Systematic Theology

The purpose of this sub-series in Philosophical/Systematic Theology is to make available the results of recent scholarly research into the various issues that have relevance for the revitalization of Christian thinking and spiritual formation in the life of the Church.

This book provides a unique look into the work of two theologians from different periods of time in the history of Christian theology. Both theologians were seminal thinkers who were attempting to address the central theological issues of their times. Comparing the *a priori* methodology of Anselm of Canterbury with the *a posteriori* methodology of Wolfhart Pannenberg, the author shows how Anselm attempted to develop a Christology focused on the cross and incarnation and Pannenberg developed a Christology focused on the resurrection of Jesus from the dead. The results of this inquiry highlight the pros and cons of each methodology and shows how the different methodologies led to different emphases in developing a Christology.

Laurence W. Wood
Subseries Editor
Frank Paul Morris Professor of Systematic Theology
Asbury Theological Seminary

A Dialog in the Contrasting Christologies of Anselm of Canterbury and Wolfhart Pannenberg

Brian Ebel

Asbury Theological Seminary Series:
The Study of World Christian Revitalization Movements in
Philosophical/Systematic Theology

EMETH PRESS
www.emethpress.com

*A Dialog in the Contrasting Christologies of
Anselm of Canterbury and Wolfhart Pannenberg*

Copyright © 2016 Brian Ebel

Printed in the United States of America on acid-free paper. All rights reserved. No part of this book may be reproduced, or stored in a retrieval system or transmitted in any form or by any means, electronic, mechanical, photocopying, recording, scanning or otherwise, except as permitted by the 1976 United States Copyright Act, or with the prior written permission of Emeth Press. Requests for permission should be addressed to: Emeth Press, P. O. Box 23961, Lexington, KY 40523-3961. http://www.emethpress.com.

Library of Congress Cataloging-in-Publication Data

Names: Ebel, Brian.
Title: A dialog in the contrasting christologies of Anselm of Canterbury and Wolfhart Pannenberg / Brian Ebel.
Description: Lexington : Emeth Press, 2016. | Series: Asbury Theological Seminary series: the study of world Christian revitalization movements in systematic/philosophical theology
Identifiers: LCCN 2015037668 | ISBN 9781609470968 (alk. paper)
Subjects: LCSH: Theology--Methodology. | Jesus Christ--Person and offices. | Anselm, Saint, Archbishop of Canterbury, 1033-1109. | Pannenberg, Wolfhart, 1928-2014.
Classification: LCC BR118 .E235 2016 | DDC 232.092/2--dc23
LC record available at http://lccn.loc.gov/2015037668

Contents

Abbreviations / vii
Acknowledgments / ix
Introduction: Christology via the Cross or the Resurrection? / 1

Part One:
The Christology of Anselm of Canterbury via the Cross

Chapter 1. The Anselmian Milieu and His Christology / 7
Chapter 2. *Cur Deus Homo*: Presuppositions & Methodology / 19
Chapter 3. *Cur Deus Homo*: Soteriology / 51
Chapter 4. Conclusion of Part One / 85

Part Two:
The Christology of Wolfhart Pannenberg via the Retroactive Significance of the Resurrection

Chapter 5. Introduction to the Pannenbergian Milieu: A Survey of the Pannenbergian Context / 89
Chapter 6. The Pannenbergian Christological Methodology: A Theology from Below / 95
Chapter 7. The Pannenbergian Retroactive Significance of the Resurrection / 127

Part Three:
A Critique of Anselm from a Pannenbergian Perspective

Chapter 8. A Pannenbergian Engagement with Anselm and its Implications for the Contemporary Atonement Conversation / 167

Chapter 9. Concluding Observations / 205

Abbreviations

All Anselmian works in Latin are cited from Schmitt.

All Anselmian works in English are cited from Davies & Evans.

M = *Monologion*

P = *Proslogion*

DIV = *De Incarnatione Verbi*

CDH = *Cur Deus Homo*

CDH C = *Cur Deus Homo, Commendatio operis ad Urbanum Papum II*

CDH P = *Cur Deus Homo, Praefatio*

BQT = *Basic Questions in Theology* (followed by a volume number, i.e. 1 or 2)

JGM = *Jesus - God & Man*

ST = *Wolfhart Pannenberg Systematic Theology* (followed by a volume number, i.e. 1, 2, or 3)

Acknowledgments

I would like to express my love and gratitude to my wife Mandy whose tireless support and encouragement during this process has been a reminder of the faithfulness and grace of God that never grows weary. I am thankful to my children Sarah Margaret and Luke for their love and support, and for reminding me of keeping the childlike awe and wonder of God. I also wish to thank my advisor, mentor, and friend Dr. Larry Wood of the Asbury Theological Seminary for his constant help, guidance, and wisdom. Similar thanks are extended to Dr. Tony Lane of the London School of Theology for his great advice, encouragement, and careful eye for detail. Many thanks are extended to my parents Jerry, Carol, and my sister Marybeth, as well as my mother and father-in-law who are ministers of the Gospel, Ray and Joyce Townsend. Thanks to my mentor and friend, Reverend Tom Grieb who encouraged me to see this work to its completion. Also special thanks to my best friend Pete Marra for his constant encouragement and "calling me out" to finish this as I promised from the beginning. Similar thanks to my colleagues in ministry John, Neil, Scott, and Faron, whom I affectionately call my "delinquent brothers." Finally, a special thanks to the people of Revolution Church who challenge me every day to be more committed to the One who still raises humanity and creation itself from the dead.

Introduction

This thesis considers the work of two theologians from differing epochs and asks the question how each constructs their Christology. Anselm of Canterbury utilized an *a priori* methodology from above featuring the cross and incarnation, and Wolfhart Pannenberg utilized an *a posteriori* methodology from below featuring the resurrection. While the duration of time between Anselm of Canterbury (1033-1109 CE) and Wolfhart Pannenberg (1928-present) is extensive, the principles of Christology are not necessarily limited by time. If Christologies are not limited by time, there can be fruitful understanding from such a study. While Anselm and Pannenberg are situated in two distinct historical periods, their theological contributions can be brought together for the purposes of discovering how the composition of their Christologies affect their outcomes, and then Christology as a whole.

More specifically, Christologies have been crafted throughout history from a variety of approaches. These include but are not limited to focusing on the incarnation of Jesus Christ as the pre-existent Son and logos, soteriology and the work of Jesus Christ on the cross, or upon the resurrection of Jesus Christ from the tomb on the third day as the fulfillment of the promise of salvation. Unsurprisingly, these Christologies contrast in a variety of differing ways. Given the progressive nature of revelation in the biblical history of salvation, consideration that the incarnation, crucifixion, and resurrection are more typically the primary places from which one begins the construction of Christology, and that both *a priori* (from above) or *a posteriori* (from below) have been methodological considerations, much can be gleaned by such a study.[1] To undertake the Christological enterprise is to begin with either the pre-existent Son and logos and his way of incarnation in an *a priori* manner, the soteriological implications of humanity and their need for salvation in an *a priori* manner, or consideration *a posteriori* of the death and/or resurrection of Jesus Christ and how this is evidentiary of the incarnation and/or the human need for salvation. Reflection upon the principles and methods used to construct these Christologies is of relevance for the theological community as well, given the nature of theology is a conversation happening among a greater community of participants throughout history. If theology is advancing,

---

[1] This point is demonstrated throughout this work, as Anselm takes an a priori methodological principle and Pannenberg an a posteriori methodological principle. Moreover, Anselm begins with the incarnation/crucifixion and Pannenberg the resurrection. Interestingly enough, Pannenberg takes a view of "from ahead" andmethodological principle and Pannenberg an *a posteriori* methodological principle. Moreover, Anselm begins with the incarnation/crucifixion and Pannenberg the resurrection. Interestingly enough, Pannenberg takes a view of "from ahead" and looks to the future as part of his methodological principle while at the same time considering "from below." Progressive revelation is meant here in a Scriptural sense (and not a doctrinal one) from the perspective of God continually unfolding reality to humanity in space-time or history.

one can see the expression of such advancements in the theological enterprise in the eventuation of their outcomes. In short, if the Christological programs of the past eventuate the outcomes of the present, and if such outcomes are typically conversational matters for the present, then it stands to reason the present community would do well to consider these past Christological programs and the outcomes of such programs. In turn, these theological developments that eventuate in the present connect them to greater theological conversation unfolding throughout history.

For example, consider systematic theology in contemporary circles. Theological conversation in the present era develops through a process of considering the presuppositions and methodologies of not only the previous era but also the current one. This process deconstructs terms, considers semantics, hermeneutics, and the like. Accordingly, it seems appropriate to consider how the primary person and connection to Christian faith – Jesus Christ – has come to be expressed by means of Christological method and related processes. If the greater community can see the progression that eventuated its own plight, the greater community can discern from whence its own starting points and outcomes have come; this in turn begins to illumine the direction in which the greater community is moving. Given the challenges modernity poses against the bodily resurrection of Jesus Christ via David Hume and his argument against miracles, or the debate between Gerd Lüdemann and William Lane Craig concerning the bodily resurrection of Jesus Christ in more recent years, or even the current atonement conversation happening in theological circles that challenges the violent and penal imagery of penal substitutionary atonement in J. Denny Weaver and a host of others, this work considers an even more elemental and yet necessary issue.[2] That issue is namely this: how have the Christologies of two key voices – one who developed his Christology via the cross and the other who developed his via the resurrection – who have made significant contributions to Christology, whose works are still being discussed and debated in greater theological circles, driven their own Christological outcomes, and what might the present theological community glean from such a study in light of its own conversations?

Therefore this work shall offer a contrast of Christologies which utilize two different approaches from two different milieus. How then shall this work proceed? Unit one considers how Anselm of Canterbury constructs a Christology via the cross to answer the incarnational question of why the God-Man, and unit two considers how Wolfhart Pannenberg constructs a Christology via the resurrection which retroactively establishes the cross and

---

[2] These are only a minute sampling of endless possibilities. See Hume, David. *An Enquiry Concerning Human Understanding*, ed. by Tom Beauchamp, 169-186. See also Copan, Paul H., Tacelli, Lüdemann, and Craig. *Jesus' Resurrection: Fact or Fiction? A Debate between William Lane Craig and Gerd Lüdemann*. Downers Grove: InterVarsity Press, 2000. See also Weaver, J. Denny. *The Non-Violent Atonement*. Grand Rapids: William B. Eerdmans Publishing, 2001.

incarnation.³ Firstly, chapter one (1.0) shall offer the contextual factors lending influence to Anselm and his Christology. Chapter two (1.1) shall demonstrate that Anselm of Canterbury sought to answer the intellectual challenges of his day by maintaining an Augustinian presupposition of the previous era, but by offering a newer Aristotelian methodology that the monasteries and schools featured: suspending the utilization of the materials of the Church such as Scripture and doctrine. He utilized the Augustinian presuppositionary principle *credo ut intelligam* of the previous era, and the Aristotelian *remoto Christo a priori* methodology of his present milieu. This shaped his answer to the incarnational question that the European Jewish community had long been asking, and answered the key question of his work, *Cur Deus Homo*. Thirdly, chapter three (1.2) shall demonstrate an understanding of the Anselmian soteriology by considering how Jesus Christ as the God-Man offers a satisfactory penitential act of supererogation (his death) to restore the offended honor of God brought about by the disobedience of humanity, and through this act, extends the benefit of salvation to humanity. These commitments shaped the Christology of Anselm which emphasized crucifixion by satisfaction, which for all practical purposes moved resurrection toward the periphery, the outcome in chapter four.

Following the study of Anselm in unit one, chapters one through four, the second unit beginning in chapter five shall proceed to Pannenberg. Chapter five (2.0) shall also examine the Pannebergian milieu to identify contextual factors lending influence to Panneberg and his Christology. The sixth chapter (2.1) demonstrates how Pannenberg provided a significant voice to pressing challenges such as the death of God theology, historical-critical methodologies, and modernistic assumptions that had for some time shaped the theological landscape. To address these challenges, Pannenberg utilized an *a posteriori from below* methodology featuring history as the relation between God and humanity and the revelation of the very self-hood of God. Chapter seven (2.2), demonstrates how Pannenberg featured a Christology promoting the retroactive significance or force of the resurrection of Jesus Christ which both epistemologically and ontologically establishes the incarnation, ministry, and cross of Jesus Christ. This, of course, has not been without contestation by Karl Barth and others because of the modern challenges toward history and the importance of historical criticism in his argument especially in the resurrection of Jesus Christ and its centrality to his Christology.⁴ Similar to Anselm, while his presupposition and methodology are not altogether new, the manner in which he constructs a response to his milieu is a new alternative,

---

³ This work proceeds with both chapter orientation and a number orientation to help designate the specific sections of the work. The Anselmian work is unit one, followed by a unit chapter number, and then a section number within that specific chapter (e.g. 1.1.1). The Pannenbergian work is unit two followed by a unit chapter number, and then a section number within that specific chapter (e.g. 2.1.1).

⁴ See for example chapter four (2.2), as throughout there are examples of those who disagree with Pannenberg on this very central presuppositionary and methodological premise from which he constructs his Christology.

especially given the manner in which he claims the future eventuates the present to transform the past and this is the very manner in which the retroactivity of the resurrection establishes Jesus of Nazareth as the Christ of God. Finally, chapter eight (2.3) considers how Pannenbergian Christology from the resurrection is held in dialectical tension with the cross and incarnation, and offers a fruitful contrast with Anselmian Christology, especially respective to obedience, merit, and satisfaction, as Pannenberg himself has challenged in both *Jesus – God & Man*, and *Systematic Theology Volume Two*.[5] This feature might offer a fruitful voice in the present theological conversation regarding atonement, and more specifically from the perspective of how the resurrection enhances the cross.

Ultimately, while Anselm and Pannenberg may not have derived their Christologies *ex nihilo*, their commonality is an offering of nuance to Christological proposals that led to new alternatives for theology. While Anselm constructed his corpus well over 900 years ago, his voice continues to be heard today and is both challenged and followed. Similarly, Pannenberg has been a theologian whose voice has been challenged, followed, and at least referenced in most significant theological works for the past fifty years. As such, given the fact that both were key theologians of their respective communities who offered key voices and new alternatives to the questions and challenges of their milieu, it stands to reason that the two might be brought into conversation with one another. Whether by comparison or contrast, Anselm and Pannenberg are important to the theological community as it considers how contemporary theological conversations have been driven by the works of these two great theologians who are part of the greater theological community past, present, and even future.

---

[5] See, for example, Pannenberg, *JGM*, 42-43, and 277-279. See also Pannenberg, *ST II*, 403-436.

Part One

The Christology of Anselm of Canterbury via the Cross

Chapter 1

The Anselmian Milieu and His Christology

1.0 A Survey of the Anselmian Context

The period 1000-1066 CE during the Middle Ages is generally considered by most scholars as a time of advancement, conquest, innovation, economic expansion, theological development, educational reform, and marked transformations in church and society. While scholars have differing opinions on epochal divisions and what elements perpetuated the transformations during this period of time, they generally agree that these years mark a transition from previous years.[6] Thus, what is of interest at present to this study are the elements within what might be called the primitive medieval era, or those years preceding 1000-1066 CE.

Generally speaking, the primitive medieval era might be conceived of in terms of a battle between good above and evil below. This battle featured a state of ongoing political and social chaos. Society was kept in a constant state of uncertainty through lengthy wars, forced conversions, and changing leadership. During this era kings were anointed with oil used in the consecration of bishops. Relics, rituals, symbols, even the body of St. Peter were tangible forms of the supernatural power needed by a weak and finite

---

[6] For example, Tillich and Southern, or David Knowles contend the Middle Ages transition from Augustine to 1150 as one epoch and then from 1153 to the Renaissance. See David Knowles. "The Cultural Influence of English Medieval Monasticism." *Cambridge Historical Journal Vol. 7 No. 3*. Cambridge: Cambridge University Press, 1943, 147-148. It is possible to see that the dating of the Middle Ages, while having received some general consensus, are difficult to agree upon because of the lack of materials and proper dating procedures during years prior to 1000 CE. Joesef Pieper makes this point in his work. See Josef Pieper. *Scholasticism: Personalities and Problems of Medieval Philosophy*. New York: Pantheon Books, 1960, 15-24. "Phantom time hypothesis" and whether or not the Middle Ages existed at all is a fascinating study seen in the work of Heribert Illig as he claims the lack of historical evidences from 614-911 CE support the possibilities of a manufacturing of time. See Heribert Illig. *Wer Hat an der Uhr Gedreht?* Neuss: Ullstein TB Publishers, 2001. See Paul Tillich. *A History of Christian Thought: From Its Judaic and Hellenistic Origins to Existentialism*, ed. by Carl E. Braaten. New York: Touchstone Books, 1967. See R.W. Southern. *Western Society and the Church in the Middle Ages*. Middlesex: Penguin Books, 1970.

humanity.⁷ The superstitions of the masses gave clergy incredible power, and the desire to understand reality through reason was at times at odds with religious thought.⁸ The small and insignificant nature of human life required the necessity of supernatural intervention. Charlemagne unified clergy and monastic communities with the mandatory Rule of Benedict, and a Saxon Gospel developed among the conquered. After the end of the Carolingian kings in 911 CE, Western Europe was "well along the road of the political economic system known as feudalism."⁹ Essentially, three classes of persons existed, "clergy, warriors, and workers."¹⁰ Feudal lords supplied protection and a court system in exchange for oaths by the working class who provided inexpensive labor and protected the lands of the feudal lords. In the middle of the battle between good and evil stood the Roman Catholic Church and its clergy with its call to prayer, uniformity of belief and behavior, and a united language.¹¹

Prior to the Norman Conquest of 1066 CE, the primitive medieval era might be characterized by a primitive theological supernaturalism, a framework by which humanity understood itself to be a part of the realm below that was filled with chaos and in need of divine intervention by God who existed in a realm located above and outside such chaos. Accordingly, this primitive medieval framework purported that, "Man chiefly knew himself as a vehicle for divine activity."¹² This required humanity to look heavenward for help and support in the chaotic earthly realm. However, during this century

---

⁷ The work of Jacques Le Goff on symbolism in the Middle Ages is helpful, as he explains kingship rites and their inclusivity of symbols of power especially as they were often combined with biblical symbols. King David and Melchizedek are good examples of this. See Jacques Le Goff. *Time, Work, and Culture in the Middle Ages*, trans. by Arthur Goldhammer. Chicago: The University of Chicago Press, 1977, 237-248. See also Southern, *Western Society*, 29-33.

⁸ See Reginald L. Poole. *Illustrations of the History of Medieval Thought and Learning*. New York: Dover Publications, 1960, 69-94.

⁹ Dale T. Irvin and Scott W. Sunquist. *History of the World Christian Movement. Volume I: Earliest Christianity to 1453*. Mayknoll: Orbis Books, 2003, 341.

¹⁰ Le Goff, *Time, Work, and Culture in the Middle Ages*, 53.

¹¹ "Roman Catholic Church" distinguishes the tradition in which Anselm writes that is nuanced from other traditions, most notably the Eastern Orthodox Church. While it is true the schism between East and West was not until 1054 CE, there are differences in nuance. Anselm, in keeping Augustinian tradition as shall later be delineated, more clearly favors the West or Roman Church. It is also important to recognize that Anselm as part of the Roman Church differs from Pannenberg who is part of the Protestant Church (a much later schism). The term "Church" is derived from the one catholic (in the sense of universal) Church, but terms such as "Roman" offer indication of which tradition is in view.

¹² R.W. Southern. *Medieval Humanism and Other Studies*. Oxford: Basil Blackwell, 1970, 32. Powicke claims the abuses of superstitions in the Medieval Roman Church were a "price paid for, not obstacles to, its universality." These brought the Western Church to its abuses of people in the purgation of sin from those who defied it. F.M. Powicke. "The Christian Life." *The Legacy of the Middle Ages*, ed. by C.G. Crump and E.F. Jacob. Oxford: The Clarendon Press, 1926, 34.

of sweeping change, a once small and utterly sinful and helpless humanity that could not possibly know the pursuits of God, realized the great opportunity they possessed to know God through their own human experiences.[13] The Norman Conquest, and its subsequent innovations fueled a growing desire for deeper thought, pressing the Roman Catholic Church for a response to meet this desire:

> The specialized governmental role of the clerical order within society led to clergy becoming more fully organized, more distinctly aware of their rights and privileges, and better equipped for enforcing a fuller and more coherent body of doctrine and code of behavior to go with it than had ever been possible before.[14]

More specifically, other religious and intellectual communities throughout Europe had the ability to ask critical questions that went unanswered by the Roman Catholic Church.[15] The inquiries began to reveal something important about doctrines and their authority:

> Nevertheless the absence of fundamental enquiry into the credibility and coherence of the Christian religion as a whole was a weakness. In the course of time it made the basic doctrines of the Church increasingly formal, and it was then easy to allege that these doctrines were formal and irrational.[16]

The clerical celibacy struggles within the Roman Catholic Church necessitated the Roman Council of 1059, aided by the help of one budding leader in its ranks, Lanfranc. Lanfranc was a master of law, logic, and administration. He and his contemporaries systematically changed the Church landscape through updates to property and position. Pope Urban II called for a

---

[13] Edward Grant claims that the need for faith and reason is a key element of the changes happening in this era. See Edward Grant. *God and Reason in the Middle Ages*. Cambridge: Cambridge University Press, 2001, 17-30. See Robert S. Hoyt and Stanley Chodrow. *Europe in the Middle Ages, Third Ed.* New York: Harcourt, Brace, and Jovanavich Publishers, 1957, 303-304. Arno Borst claims the desire to remain Christian (and thus not heretical) is an important example of why persons would zealously claim belief or even law over coincidence. It is possible to see how Christian advancements through ecclesial unification and the eradication of heresies presented opposing viewpoints based upon superstitions of the previous era. See Arno Borst. *Medieval Worlds: Barbarians, Heretics, and Artists in the Middle Ages*, trans. by Eric Hansen. Chicago: The University of Chicago Press, 1991, xi.
[14] R.W. Southern. *Scholastic Humanism and the Unification of Europe, Vol. I, Foundations.* Oxford: Blackwell Publishing, 1995, 135.
[15] For example see the communities at Orleans in 1022 or Montfort in 1028. See Borst, *Medieval Worlds*, 92-93.
[16] Southern, *Medieval Humanism*, 11. The Cambridge Medieval History illumines how the fears of the millennium and the apocalypse of 1,000 years began to subside after the year 1,000 CE. Some of the superstitious terror in the Church began to give way to the need for clearer explanation. See J.B. Bury. *The Cambridge Medieval History, Vol. III: Germany and The Western Empire*. New York: The MacMillan Company, 1922, 455-457.

crusade in 1095, pushing holy war to liberate Christians from heretical and oppressive non-believers.

By the year 1100 CE there was an even great threat that was growing:

> It often happens at critical moments in history that ideas which have long held the field almost unchallenged are suddenly discovered, not to be wrong, but to be useless; then almost everyone can see they are absurd. So it was around the year 1100. Even men with very little ability suddenly knew that the religious pretensions of kings had no foundation. They could see right through them without difficulty.[17]

Challenges such as these prompted a response from the Roman Catholic Church requiring doctrines, organization, and rules of life and faith. The Church turned to dialectic and debate as prominent methods of learning in monasteries. The mystical desire for God combined with a longing to reach an understanding of the order of all things became a chief pursuit of the monastic community.[18] These advances led to ecclesiastical reform in a changing world.[19]

The reason this historical context is important to this study now becomes apparent, for it is in the midst of this period of great change that Anselm of Canterbury (1033-1109 CE), a monk who became one of the significant theologians of the Western Church, emerged.[20] It is generally accepted that Anselm originated from Northern Italy, was monastically trained at Bec in Normandy, became its abbot, and then eventually archbishop of Canterbury in 1093. Some claim his lifetime occurs during some of the pivotal moments in Western society insofar as they relate not only to religious issues but intellectual and social issues as well.[21] During his lifetime the millennium was

---

[17] Southern, *Western Society*, 36-37.

[18] See Powicke, *The Christian Life*, 40-42. See also See also Southern, *Medieval Humanism*, 30-57.

[19] Colish argues that monastic communities were not only the leading centers of intellectual life, but that they brought (especially at Cluny) spiritual and ecclesiastical reform to reinvent Benedictine Rule which was important not only to the monastic communities but to the intellectual development of the age. See Marcia L. Colish. *Medieval Foundations of the Western Intellectual Tradition*. New Haven: Yale University Press, 1997, 160-162.

[20] As indicated above, most scholars generally accept this dating. See esp. Eadmer. *The Life of St. Anselm, Archbishop of Canterbury* ed. R.W. Southern. Oxford: Clarendon Press, 1962.

[21] These points are held by Gilson, Southern, Fairweather, Holopainen, and others. They similarly contend that the changing political, religious, and social landscapes were being shaped and Anselmian writings are a reflection of this. See Etienne Gilson. *History of Christian Philosophy in the Middle Ages*. New York: Random House Publishers, 1955. See also R.W. Southern. *St. Anselm: A Portrait in a Landscape*. Cambridge: Cambridge University Press, 1990. See Eugene R. Fairweather. *A Scholastic Miscellany: Anselm to Ockham*. Philadelphia: Westminster Press, 1956. See *Anselm and Abelard: Investigations and Juxtapositions*, ed. By G.E.M. Gasper and H. Kohlenberger. Pontifical Institute of Medieval Studies No. 19. Toronto: Pontifical Institute of Medieval

hanging and in the midst of a changing world, Christendom split into East and West, the conquest of England occurred, and monasticism began to thrive, characterized as "the uncompromisingly Christocentric period of Western civilization."[22] The number of monastic communities and their influence grew, and scholasticism – at least in embryonic form – which was the "the determinative cognitive attitude of the whole middle ages," was beginning to form.[23] Since Augustine's death in 430:

> There had not really been a constructive religious philosopher in Western Christendom for six hundred years...That is to say, there had been no one who had systematically asked fundamental questions about the Christian religion, such as: How do we know the attributes of God are those affirmed by the Christian religion? How do we know that God exists? Did God become man in Jesus Christ? Was this necessary...What is the relation between our reasoning on these subjects and faith?[24]

The above contextual factors from which the writings of Anselm emerge are important, and perhaps of chief importance to his context is the monastic community. While monastic communities had existed long before Anselm, their primary purpose during the primitive era was spiritual contemplation, societal withdrawal, and devotion to God. However, the reforms of Pope Gregory VII and the Norman Conquest propelled monasticism throughout Western Europe so that during the years of 1050-1153 CE it became the dominant intellectual force, though primarily because it was virtually the only intellectual force.[25] Monastic communities specialized in the study of logic and dialectic. They utilized the *Trivium* (grammar, rhetoric, and dialectic), *Quadrivium* (music, arithmetic, geometry, and astronomy), Scripture, the corpus of Christian tradition, and the works of Aristotle, Plato, and other schol-

---

Studies, 2006, vii-16. See Toivo Holopainen. *Dialectic and Theology in the Eleventh Century*. New York: E.J. Brill Publishers, 1996.

[22] Jaroslav Pelikan. *The Christian Tradition: A History of the Development of Doctrine, Vol. 3: The Growth of Medieval Theology (600-1300)*. Chicago: University of Chicago Press, 1978, 106. Original Source: Ernst Hartwig Kantorowicz. *The King's Two Bodies: A Study in Medieval Political Theology*. Princeton, 1957, 61.

[23] Tillich, *A History of Christian Thought*, 135.

[24] Southern, *Medieval Humanism*, 10. It is noteworthy to mention that Southern claims Anselm mentions Augustine so as to seemingly appease his teacher Lanfranc. See Southern, *A Portrait*, 71. However, Katherin Rogers argues that Anselm is one of the most devoted disciples of Augustine, whose work is the foundation of Christian philosophy in the early Middle Ages. See Katherin A. Rogers. *Anselm on Freedom*. Oxford: Oxford University Press, 2008, 30. Gilson also holds that Anselm had an "excellent knowledge of Augustine." Etienne Gilson. *A History of Philosophy: Medieval Philosophy*. New York: Random House Publishers, 1962, 129.

[25] See Steven P. Marone. "Medieval Philosophy in Context." *The Cambridge Companion to Medieval Philosophy*. Cambridge: Cambridge University Press, 2003, 10-18. See Raffaello Morgan. "Monastic Reform and Cluniac Spirituality." *Cluniac Monasticism in the Central Middle Ages*. Hamden: Archon Books, 1971, 11-12. See also Knowles, *The Cultural Influence of English Medieval Monasticism*, 147-148.

ars and philosophers from antiquity.[26] One can also gain access into the training of Anselm by looking to monastic materials found in the Rule of St. Benedict, the Abbey of Cluny in the tenth century, the influence of the Norman Conquest in the eleventh century, and most importantly by considering the influence of Lanfranc, the mentor of Anselm.[27] Typical of the cultural landscape that was undergoing transformation, monks saw themselves at war, and Anselm was part of this war. This intellectual battle is an undercurrent in the *Monologion*, *Proslogion*, and especially the *Cur Deus Homo*. In all three above named works there is a sense of empowering monks with new artillery, battling the detractors and unbelievers, and doing so with new weapons of logic.[28]

Scholars have varying opinions of the Anselmian contribution respective to his inclusion in the scholastic era. Some regard Anselm as a precursor to scholasticism and others claim scholasticism is post Anselmian, as generally scholars date the rise of scholasticism as "a mental discipline en vogue near the end of the twelfth century."[29] Perhaps then the correct approach to Anselm is to recognize that while not of the scholastic era per se, he in many respects represents a key forerunner to the scholastic method, perhaps "something of a Melchizedek, without spiritual ancestry save his descent

---

[26] See Ruth Graham. "The Intellectual Influence of English Monasticism Between the Tenth and Twelfth Centuries." *Transactions of the Royal Historical Society, New Series*, Vol. 17. 1903, 33-34. See Philippe Delhaye. *Medieval Christian Philosophy, Volume Twelve*, trans. by S.J. Tester: *Twentieth Century Encyclopedia of Catholicism*. New York: Hawthorn Books, 1960, 60-78. See also Irvin and Sunquist, *History of the World*, 423.

[27] See Dom Cuthbert Butler. *Benedictine Monachism: Studies in Benedictine Life and Rule*. Eugene: Wipf and Stock, 2005. See also Knowles, D. *The Monastic Order in England: A History of Its Development from the Time of St. Dunstan to the Fourth Lateran Council*. Cambridge: Cambridge Press, 1950, 1-82. See Workman, H. *The Evolution of the Monastic Ideal*. Boston: Beacon Press, 1913.

[28] For example, consider the opening prologues and chapters to these works and the methodology employed. In the *Monologion*, Anselm appeals to his own monastic context and utilizes dialectic. In the *Proslogion*, he furthers this by showing only the fool can say there is no God, and by the time of the *Cur Deus Homo* Anselm addresses the unbelievers who have raised questions about the Christian faith.

[29] M.D. Knowles. "Some Recent Advances in the History of Medieval Thought." *Cambridge Historical Journal*, Vol. IX, No. 1, Cambridge: Cambridge Press, 1947, 31. Southern is inclusive of Anselm in early scholasticism but notes that Aquinas marks the high point of scholasticism. Southern, *Scholastic Humanism*, 42-43. Etienne Gilson claims that Anselm is the "Father of Scholasticism" although Aquinas is a good expression of it. This was a claim of Grabmann who said this of Anselm, but only on the grounds of his utilization of dialectic to matters of faith. See Gilson, *The History of Christian Philosophy in the Middle Ages*, 139, 235-265. Fairweather advocates scholasticism "bursts into flower" in the work of Anselm of Canterbury. See Fairweather, *A Scholastic Miscellany*, 19. Colish notes that Anselm of Canterbury when used as a "benchmark" provides contrast to the scholastic thinkers that follow, although it is possible to see the rise of scholasticism in the beginning of the twelfth century as in Anselm of Canterbury. See Colish, *Medieval Foundations*, 265.

across the ages from St. Augustine."[30] As such, Anselm is noted by others as one whose "reputation outstrips that, not only of his contemporaries, but of every philosopher in the early Middle Ages."[31] Others call him "the most important predecessor to the Scholastics,"[32] or even a bridge of sorts between "the Patristic and Scholastic centuries,"[33] primarily due to his ability to bridge logic and faith. Finally, some call him the "Father of Scholasticism," as he laid foundations for what was to come in the twelfth and thirteenth centuries, and (along with others) made logic normative for Western Europe.[34] While he maintained the Augustinian tradition in his theological methodology, he also employed elements of logic for the purposes of supporting faith claims.[35] This is the reason why the theological attitude with which he wrote *fides quaerens intellectum* follows Augustine who wrote *crede ut intelligas*, even though his theses utilize logical argumentation including methodologies which suspend the utilization of Scripture. While he is certainly known for treatises that debate the unbelievers of his milieu, he also writes as one who gives reason to the doctrines of the Church. Therefore his theology is both critical and constructive; doctrinally oriented and apologetically formulated. In a culture located in a war between good and evil, Anselm sought to offer reason beyond revelation, offering understanding beyond the religious authoritarianism of the Church.

During the Anselmian period medieval philosophers were concerned with how one knows truth: through belief and faith in revelation or understanding it by reason? While the above questions surfaced about Christendom, few had taken an approach that looked beyond Scripture and the tradition of the Church. This is why the Anselmian utilization of Aristotelian logic and dialectic in combination with Augustinian tradition was unique.[36] Answers to

---

[30] Knowles, *Cambridge Historical Journal Vol. IX*, 31.

[31] John Marenbon. *Early Medieval Philosophy, 480-1150: An Introduction.* New York: Routledge Press, 1983, 94.

[32] Irvin and Sunquist, *History of the World*, 426.

[33] Southern, *A Portrait*, 441.

[34] See Gilson, *The History of Christian Philosophy*, 139. See Grant, *God and Reason in the Middle Ages*, 56-57.

[35] It should be noted that Anselm does not mention Aristotle in any of his major works other than *De Grammatico* and then not again until *Cur Deus Homo*. Southern notes that this is likely due to the warnings of Lanfranc against relying so heavily upon Aristotelian thought. See Southern, *A Portrait*, 64-65.

[36] See Fairweather, *Scholastic Miscellany*, 17-32, 46. Hyman and Walsh claim Anselm was "sometimes called the 'second Augustine' because of his profound unwillingness to say anything inconsistent with Augustine's writings." Anselm did utilize the Augustinian tradition insofar as it was dedicated to *sapientia* and the contemplation of the divine order in human experience. However, as will later be shown, while Anselm in many ways maintained the Augustinian tradition in the sense of *sapientia* and the high regard for Scripture and the materials of the Church, his methodology which suspended these materials differed due to the higher regard for logic and dialectic - a point of contention in the Augustinian tradition and more consistent with an Aristotelian tradition. See *Philosophy in the Middle Ages*, ed. by Arthur Hyman and James J.

such questions in the primitive era were not constructed through well-reasoned arguments but rather, by events in salvation history. Thus, Anselm of Canterbury provided an important corpus in response to the historical context in which he was situated by attempting to maintain tenets of Augustinian methodology from the previous era, while utilizing logic of the present era that addressed the questions of his milieu. Accordingly, his work should not be construed as a systematic theology per se, but rather as writing addressed to specific situations.[37] This can easily be seen through the lens of his introductory statements, the historical materials in his writings, and even interlocutors such as Boso in the *Cur Deus Homo* who play the role of his opposition. Therefore the theology of Anselm can be stated in terms of the materials he produced and the theological statements contained therein, as he does not provide a complete systematic theology to articulate his entire theological schema. This shall be important in chapters two (1.1) and three (1.2) as Anselmian Christology is methodologically developed from the cross, relegating the resurrection to the periphery.[38]

Finally, a word with respect to feudalism and medieval penance is appropriate. In conjunction with monasticism, feudalism was a reform shaping Western Culture and medieval history. Fedualism is best expressed through the narrative of contract:

Walsh. Indianapolis: Hackett Publishing, 1974, 147-148. See Irvin and Sunquist. *History of the World Christian Movement*, 426. See Meyrick H. Carre. *Realists and Nominalists*. Oxford: Oxford University Press, 1946, 29-31. See also the work of Katherin Rogers whose work is helpful on comparisons between Anselm and Augustine. Katherin A. Rogers. *The Neoplatonic Metaphysics and Epistemology of Anselm of Canterbury*. Lewiston: The Edwin Mellen Press, 1997.

[37] While Anselm is not attempting to write a systematic theology but rather responses to specific situations, his corpus provides at the very least detailed thought into his theology. Therefore, while Anselm did not sit down to write a complete systematic theology that may have helped illumine his thinking on important issues, most notably the resurrection, he nonetheless provides throughout his entire corpus a rather well developed understanding of his theology. See David S. Hogg. *Anselm of Canterbury: The Beauty of Theology*. Burlington: Ashgate Publishing Company, 2004, 7-8.

[38] More shall be said of this later in chapters two (1.1) and three (1.2), but the overall thrust of unit one concerns the method by which Anselmian Christology is formed. While Anselm believed in the resurrection of Jesus Christ from the dead, the resurrection in Anselmian thought is methodologically expressed at the periphery with the cross being central. Thus, methodologically speaking, the resurrection is a more peripheral matter for him. For Anselm, his Christology emphasizes the cross through an incarnational "from above" methodology as the means of understanding the person and work of Jesus Christ. Deme is helpful here, as he notes that the resurrection is almost entirely ignored by Anselm in his work, although references to the resurrection are mentioned in his prayers and devotional material. While quick to contend that Anselm would not have denied the resurrection, he is also quick to admit that the cross and resurrection are presented in a separate fashion with different meanings. See Dániel Deme. *The Christology of Anselm of Canterbury*. Burlington: Ashgate Publishing, 2003, 227-235.

Of baronial and knightly contracts of service...military necessities of earlier centuries of the Middle Ages which called into existence the knights' fees with their baronial and honorial superstructures.[39]

The difficulty of this term "feudalism," is that just as scholasticism is resistant to definition, so too feudalism had a vast complexity and inability to receive one primary definition. Feudalism is a cultural and societal term that is used of the Middle Ages, concerning its structure, principles, and agreements that comprised life from "roughly the eighth century onwards."[40] At its heart was a society of vassals, fiefs, and justice, upon which fiefs or estates were held contractually in exchange for military service. This system of hierarchy influenced society in its entirety. The status of persons was tied to land and those who held land were those who held greater power.[41] More specifically, to speak of feudalism in post-Norman England is to speak of agreements between lords and vassals, of honor and dishonor, of protection from invaders, and of the division of land.[42] Perhaps most telling is the feudal imagery Anselm expresses in his *Similitudo de regno et villa et castello et dungione*:

> At the centre there is a castle, and within the castle a keep; around the castle there is a town, and outside this, the open country. Those who live in the open country are Jews and unbelievers: the enemy destroys them without difficulty. The faithful laity are the dwellers in the town: here the enemy breaks in without much difficulty and they will be fortunate if they escape. The monks are

---

[39] Marc Leopold Bloch. *Feudal Society*, trans. by L.A. Manyon. Chicago: University of Chicago Press, 1961, xiii. See also Christopher Dawson. *Religion and the Rise of Western Culture*. London: Sheed and Ward Publishers, 1950, 167-169. See also F.M. Stenton. *The First Century of English Feudalism, 1066-1166*. Oxford: Clarendon Press, 1932. See also Bury, *The Cambridge Medieval History*, Vol. III, 458-459. Important to this is the J.H. Round Thesis written in 1891 that describes English Feudalism as being instituted by William the Conqueror. This is considered the "orthodox" position in the argument, and is thus the position of this chapter and section (1.0). It is also important to see how elements before the Norman Conquest illustrate how feudal elements were at least recognizable, albeit in embryonic form. See J.H. Round. "The Introduction of Knight-Service into England." *English Historical Review VI*. Oxford: English Historical Review, 1891, 417-443. See also J.H. Round. *Feudal England*. London: 1892. The point of contestation is offered by F.W. Maitland who claims that feudalistic tendencies existed before feudalism was established by William the Conqueror. See F.W. Maitland. *Domesday Book and Beyond: Three Essays in the Early History of England*. 1897.

[40] G.O. Sayles. *The Medieval Foundations of England*. Philadelphia: University of Pennsylvania Press, 1950, 199.

[41] See Hoyt and Chodorow. *Europe in the Middle Ages*, 458.

[42] Hoyt argues that William the Conqueror established feudalism on the basis of the instillations of the "fief, vassalage, and justice." Robert Hoyt and C.W.H. "The Iron Age of English Feudalism." *The Journal of British Studies, Vol. 2, No. 2*. Chicago: University of Chicago Press, 1963, 28. Darlington argues that it "is hardly possible to speak of any trend toward feudalism in England before 1066." This point is contestable by looking to the pre-Norman raids by the Vikings and seeing how the necessity of survival brought with it a feudal element. See R.R. Darlington. "Last Phase of Anglo-Saxon History." *English Historical Review, Vol. 22*. Oxford: 1937, 2.

those within the castle walls: they have many alarms, but they are safe so long as they remain inside and keep out of sight...Within the walls they will be safe, and therefore free, but not yet with that inalienable freedom which cannot be lost. That is reserved for the elite who are within the keep inside the castle walls: these are the angels in Heaven, immune alike from danger and alarm.[43]

While these words were not in the *Cur Deus Homo,* or any of his other main works for that matter, this feudal, monastic, and well-ordered worldview thematically fits the purview of his writings, and will surface again in October 1097 concerning angels, monks, and secular men.[44]

Just as feudalism is important, so too medieval penance provides an important contextual backdrop to Anselm and his works. The medieval penance system frames not only correctives for sinful behavior which have offended the honor of God as Anselm claims, but also an understanding of God and interactions with God in his milieu. Penance (*poenitentia*), is the notion that Christians desired to:

> Atone for their sins through confession, through penitential acts which demonstrated their repentance, and through good works, in order to ensure their salvation at the Last Judgment.[45]

The penance system found its impetus from the monastic community that derived a code of behavior for its communities. These standards of behavior were not only important for the monastic communities, but in time became important to society in general: to break them was to break a code that brought both personal and social ramifications for individuals.[46] Anselm drew his understanding of sin and the need for penance not only from the monastic community, but also from his idea of beauty and an emulation of the will of God for their order of all things.

Important as well is the need for contrition, as it is contrition that enables the forgiveness of sin – a penitential act.[47] Katherin Rogers raises the question of how Anselm utilizes forgiveness within the *Cur Deus Homo* asking why he (Anselm) will not simply make the move that God can forgive humanity. In this regard, she points to how God will not forgive without a recompense or

---

[43] Southern, *A Portrait*, 223.

[44] See Southern, *A Portrait*, 224.

[45] Sarah Hamilton. *The Practice of Penance: 900-1050.* Suffolk: St. Edmunsbury Press, 2001, 2.

[46] See John T. McNeill and Helena M. Gamer. *Medieval Handbooks of Penance: A Translation of the Principal Libri Poenitentiales and Selections from Related Documents.* New York: Columbia University Press, 1938, 4-5.

[47] See, for example, Herbermann who notes Anselm had commentary on Luke 17:14 demonstrating his understanding of contrition. Herbermann and others (most notably Williams) claim this became accepted in the scholastic era. See *The Catholic Encyclopedia Volume I,* ed. by Charles G. Herbermann. New York: Robert Appleton Company, 1907, 63-64. See George H. Williams. *Anselm: Communion and Atonement.* St. Louis: Concordia Publishing House, 1960, 21-22.

payment from the offender.⁴⁸ Within the scope of the *Cur Deus Homo* satisfaction will be the key way that Anselm demonstrates the manner in which the eternal blessedness, harmony, and beauty for which humanity was created has been lost because of sin, and the offended honor of God must be satisfied. Moreover, Anselm contends that it is necessary and fitting for one who is without sin and yet of the same nature as humanity to make this satisfaction. The satisfaction of Jesus Christ in his death on the cross restores the honor of God, as well as the lost harmony, blessedness, beauty, and order of things for humanity. Given that penance is a combination of confession, repentant acts, and a desire to do good works that ensures salvation at the last judgment, it becomes a natural turn of events that the death of Jesus Christ satisfies the honor of God and restores humanity to its state of intended blessedness. This penitential act of supererogation calls people to take Christ as their own, that they may be redeemed.⁴⁹

Given this exploration of the Anselimian milieu, why is this important to the study at present? The answer is straightforward: the contextual factors play a role in the writigns of Anselm, most notably the methodology he uses, which is of key interest to this work. While it may be true that monasticism, pre-scholasticism, feudal, and penitential related imagery could be removed from the argument of the *Cur Deus Homo* allowing it to potentially remain intact, the argument is nonetheless influenced by these important sources.⁵⁰ If one looks beyond its logical argumentation, the image of *Cur Deus Homo*

---

⁴⁸ See CDH 1.11-1.15, 1.19-21. See Katherin A. Rogers. "Anselm on Forgiveness, Patience, and Free Will." *Anselm Journal 6.2*. Manchester: The St. Anselm Journal, 2009, 1-7. The Latin word here is *satisfactio* and this word forms the crux of the Anselmian doctrine of satisfaction concerning how it is necessary to provide a satisfaction to the offended honor of God. It is noteworthy to mention how this fits within the doctrine of penance as the offender is seeking to make a satisfaction for their sin through an act that has dishonored God and brought disharmony to the intentions for humanity and the created order which was intended to be one of beautiful harmony.

⁴⁹ See CDH 2.20.

⁵⁰ As this chapter has demonstrated, monastic, pre-scholastic, feudal, and penitential imagery are part of the Anselmian context. The utilization of logic and dialectic in a milieu that desired explanations independent of Scripture and the materials of the Church, even suspension of the knowledge of Christ himself (*remoto Christo*), are evidentiary of the monastic underpinnings of the work. More importantly, as will be revealed in chapter two (1.1), the CDH arises out of both questions of Western European Jews and the monastic communities. The feudal context that dominated the cultural landscape and influences relationships in the Anselmian context is also important, and one can find its influence within his corpus as well. Finally, the medieval penance system is found in the CDH as his understanding of *poenitentia* is found in the work and obedience of Jesus Christ in his death. See Sayles, *Medieval Foundations*, 201-203. See also Stenton, *The First Century of English Feudalism, 1066-1166*, 7-40. See also Hamilton, *The Practice of Penance*, 1-15. See also Southern, *A Portrait*, 221-222. See also Joel B. Green and Mark D. Baker. *Recovering the Scandal of the Cross: Atonement in New Testament and Contemporary Contexts*. Downers Grove: InterVarsity Press, 2000, 126-136. J. Denny Weaver. *Atonement and Violence: A Theological Conversation*, ed. by John Sanders. Nashville: Abingdon Press, 8-10.

remains that God is portrayed as the Feudal Lord and humanity as the vassals who have not shown honor to their Feudal Lord. Jesus Christ who by way of his act of penitential atonement to repay the dishonor done unto God, effects satisfaction, and salvation is the outcome for the once unfaithful vassals. So, by means of submission, the kind of submission in faith and repentance typical of monastic communities and their commitment to permanence and obedience as well as penance, one receives benefit of the atoning work of Christ. What shall ultimately become recognizable from this chapter concerns how the context of Anselm shapes the impetus of an *a priori* methodology by situating hearers in need of paying a magnanimous debt which they are unable to pay – a debt which Anselm will later say that only a God-Man who is one with God can satisfy. It is this restoration of honor to God via the cross of Jesus Christ that establishes the cross as central to Anselmian Christology, moving the resurrection toward the periphery.

Chapter 2

Cur Deus Homo: Presuppositions and Methodology

Given the landscape of Anselmian era, this study now turns to the specific document in question called *Cur Deus Homo*, which provides some of the strongest insight into the Christology of Anselm of Canterbury. The intentions of this chapter are four-fold: (1) To provide a general context for the *Cur Deus Homo* which includes two primary reasons for its historical construction: (a) a response to a theological debate which featured a deletion of previously oriented ransom theories of atonement involving payments made to the devil, and (b) a response to the Jewish questions in Europe (1.1.1); (2) To explore the Anselmian presupposition of *credo ut intelligam* by first demonstrating how this principle is inherent throughout three of his early and key writings, and then how this presupposition is evident in the *Cur Deus Homo* (1.1.2); then (3) To demonstrate how while the *credo ut intelligam* presupposition is held by Anselm as a feature of his seeking to uphold Augustinian tradition, the *remoto Christo* methodology built upon logic and dialectic compromises this presupposition representing an *a priori* "theology from above" which in turn shapes the theological commitments and outcomes of the *Cur Deus Homo* (1.1.3); and finally, (4) How given these findings, the *remoto Christo* methodology compromised the *credo ut intelligam* presupposition and juxtaposes it to *intelligo ut credam*. (1.1.4).[51] The combination of milieu, contextual factors

---

[51] This statement was raised as a potential juxtaposition by John McIntyre. This chapter contends the methodology compromises the presupposition thus juxtaposing it. The preceding material illumined this as the Augustinian tradition from the previous milieu and Aristotelian logic from the Anselmian milieu are concurrently employed. Essentially, the Anselmian presupposition is Augustinian while the methodology is Aristotelian. See John McIntyre. *St. Anselm and His Critics: A Re-Interpretation of the Cur Deus Homo*. Edinburgh: Oliver and Boyd Publishers, 1954, 5. Hopkins disagrees with this, claiming that McIntyre is suggesting that a discontinuity exists within the *Cur Deus Homo* itself. Hopkins points to the text where Anselm claims that the belief in order to understand formula will not be subjugated to understand to believe in CDH *Commendatio* and 1.1. Hopkins softens his position by claiming Anselm holds belief to understanding is for believers while unbelievers are brought to a position of belief through understanding. Contra Hopkins, Anselm does not make such a claim in his work but rather claims his argument is to help contemplate what is believed through the methodological suspension of belief for those who do not

for the writing of *Cur Deus Homo* (1.1.1), and the methodological commitments he makes that compromises his presupposition (1.1.2-1.1.3), shapes the Anselmian Christology by emphasizing the cross, thus relegating the resurrection to the periphery of his Christology, a feature brought into question in chapter two (1.2).

1.1.1 Setting the Stage for *Cur Deus Homo*

The year 1093 was a busy one for Anselm of Canterbury. He accepted his archbishopric, and more importantly, Anselm wrote the *Cur Deus Homo*.[52] The historical currents presented in chapter one (1.0) that developed prior to 1093 were important to the writing of the *Cur Deus Homo*. Theology is both critical and constructive, and in this fashion *Cur Deus Homo* rises in response to two primary issues of the Anselmian milieu—first, from the theological debates of the secular schools and secondly, from the criticisms of Christian doctrine coming from the growing Jewish communities in Western Europe.[53] Thus, both the schools and rising doctrinal challenges necessitated a response from the Western Church.

The Schools

Chapter one indicated that the monastic educational system utilized debate and dialectic as a method of educational growth. As such, it is not surprising that theological debates of significance would surface in the schools. The school at Laon under the direction of Anseau, more commonly known as Master Anselm, had a number of famous European pupils and within the scope of the various writings which the school produced, the *Sententiae* was best known for its provision of biblical and/or theological answers to a variety of questions.[54] The *Sententiae* features the work of Ralph, the brother of Master Anselm, who argues:

---

believe (CDH 1.1). See Hopkins, *A Companion to the Study of St. Anselm*, 63-65. See also Henry who notes the Augustinian-Aristotelian connection. See D.P. Henry. *The Logic of St. Anselm*. Oxford: Clarendon Press, 1967, 7-8.

[52] See Eadmer, *The Life of St. Anselm*. See also Southern, *St. Anselm: A Portrait*, 197-227.

[53] See Southern, *Saint Anselm: A Portrait*, 197. See CDH *Commendatio, Praefatio*, and 1.1.1 for the language regarding the Anselmian audience in the CDH. Hopkins agrees with the rejection of ransom oriented theories, a challenge which came from the schools. See Hopkins, *A Companion to the Study of St. Anselm*, 188. See also Asideu who describes the apologetic orientation of the *Cur Deus Homo* as Anselm seeks to refute Jews and unbelievers who are challenging the incarnation. See F.B.A. Asiedu. "Anselm and The Unbelievers: Pagans, Jews, and Christians in the *Cur Deus Homo*." *Theological Studies*, Vol. 62. Hanover: Theological Studies, 2001, 533-541.

[54] See Richard C. Dales. *The Intellectual Life of Western Europe in the Middle Ages*. Leiden: E.J. Brill Publishers, 1995, 261. A thorough delineation of these two issues is also offered in R.W. Southern. *St. Anselm and His Biographer*. Cambridge: Cambridge University Press, 1963, 82-91.

God became Man because Adam's sin had delivered mankind into the dominion of the Devil; and it was only by trapping the Devil into overstepping his authority, and subjecting a sinless man to the death which was the punishment for sin, that mankind could be rescued from the Devil's dominion. This sinless man was of course Christ.[55]

Boso, the star pupil of Anselm took issue with this logic, and Anselm formed a response.[56]

The finished *Sententiae* was similar to ransom oriented theologies of atonement that developed in Irenaeus, Origen of Alexandria, and Gregory of Nyssa in *The Great Catechism*:

> The Deity was hidden under the veil of our nature, that, as with ravenous fish, the hook of the Deity might be gulped down along with the bait of flesh, and thus, life being introduced into the house of death, and light shining in darkness, that which is diametrically opposed to light and life might vanish; for it is not in the nature of darkness to remain when light is present, or of death to exist when life is active.[57]

Overcoming the rights of the devil was an important issue for theology, especially in 1093; the supernaturalism of the previous era that posited humanity in a war between God and the devil was being challenged by transformations of the Roman Catholic Church in Western Europe. Anselm addressed the issue, taking it a step further by arguing that the devil had no rights to humanity at all. Rather, the issue was a loss of honor which humanity owed God that could not be repaid by humanity.[58] This step eventuated into a focus of restoration of the honor of God and by means of that restoration, salvation for humanity, who now owes submission to the will of God. While Anselm sought to maintain the Augustinian tradition, he also made a

---

[55] See Southern, *A Portrait*, 204.

[56] See CDH 1.6: *Hoc est quod valde mirantur, quia liberationem hanc redemptionem vocamus.* See also the response of Anselm in CDH 1.7 which concerns how God did not have to act against the devil, but rather against the decree of God, essentially pointing to how God was not obligated to act against the devil to liberate humanity. All Latin Anselmian translations are from Schmitt throughout this corpus. See Schmitt, F.S. *S. Anselmi Opera Omni: Vol. II.* Edinburgh: Thomas Nelson Publishers, 1946. See also Lottin, O. *Psychologie et morale aux XIIe et XIIIe siecles, 5: L'ecole d' Anselme de Laon et de Guillaume de Champeaux.* Paris: Publishers, 1959, 185-186. Quoted from Southern, *Saint Anselm: A Portrait*, 204.

[57] Gregory of Nyssa. "The Great Catechism." *Readings in the History of Christian Thought*, ed. Robert L. Ferm. New York: Holt, Rinehart, and Winston, 1964, 24. Quoted from Joel B. Green and Mark D. Baker. *Recovering the Scandal of the Cross: Atonement in New Testament and Contemporary Contexts.* Downers Grove: InterVarsity Press, 2000, 123.

[58] See CDH 1.6-1.7 and 1.20-1.25. All Anselmian English quotations and other references to his work without notation of citation in Latin from here forward are from Davies and Evans. See Anselm of Canterbury. *Anselm of Canterbury: The Major Works*, ed. by Brian Davies and Brian Evans. Oxford: Oxford University Press, 1998.

break from it.⁵⁹ This is an interesting move for a scholar whose mentor (Lanfranc) when debating with Berengar of Tours challenged the utilization of logic alongside or above that of the authority of the Church. While Anselm of Canterbury responded to the *Sententiae*, it is also important to realize that the educational system made its own response to the *Cur Deus Homo*:

> The monks…were unwilling to abandon the rights of the Devil. In the schools the tendency was to ignore Anselm's argument altogether, insisting on those elements in the case which had been made familiar by the school of Laon. The only school of thought which whole-heartedly accepted the refutation of the traditional account of the Devil's rights was that of Abelard.⁶⁰

The Jewish Challenge

Secondly, there was an even more important source fueling the *Cur Deus Homo*: a Jewish challenge necessitating an eccleisial response. Whether one looks to the arrival of Jews to London who were well trained, their debates with Gilbert Crispin (a friend of Anselm) respective to the incarnation, the reports of apologists feeling unprepared to confront the growing intellectual attacks upon Christianity, his own reflections on the atonement when he arrived in 1092 to Westminster, or the growing intellectual frontier and the fading views of a finite humanity and an overabundant supernatural worldview, it is not surprising that Anselm desired to make a response to the challenge.⁶¹ These elements in conjunction with the challenges and debates from the

---

⁵⁹ The key point here is found in CDH 1.1 where Anselm agrees with the Holy Fathers but looks to undertake the enquiries of the attackers regarding the subject by means of a new methodology. See CDH 1.1: *quamvis a sanctis patribus inde quoad sufficere debeat dictum sit, tamen de ilia verba quod deus mihi dignabitur asperire, petentibus ostendere.* Schmitt, Vol. II, 48. Rigg believed Anselm limited God too much in his argument which led to some level of rejection by the "schoolmen and doctors of the Church." See Rigg, *St. Anselm of Canterbury*, 176. Southern contends that there was a shift between Augustinian tradition and Aristotelian methodology here as he makes a "conscious break with tradition." (204). See Southern, *A Portrait*, 204-205. This is contested by Hopkins who notes the Aristotelian utilization in Anselm but attempts to demonstrate the continuity between Anselm and Augustine. Hopkins does agree that Anselm provides some level of update to the shortcomings of the argument of Augustine while maintaining a "traditional Christology." See Hopkins, *A Companion to the Study of St. Anselm*, 187-212.

⁶⁰ Southern, *A Portrait*, 210. See also G.R. Evans. *Anselm and A New Generation*. Oxford: Clarendon Press, 1980, 34-41. Perhaps the reason for the unwillingness to abandon the rights of the devil concerned a milieu at a crossroads between the supernatural battle between God and the devil and logic as the means of doing theology. See chapter one (7-9).

⁶¹ See Poole, *Illustrations of the History of Medieval Thought and Learning*, 69-94. See also, Southern, *A Portrait*, 198-199. See also Southern, *Western Society and the Church in the Middle Ages*, 29-33. See also G.R. Evans. *Anselm and Talking About God*. Oxford: Oxford University Press, 1978, 127. Hogg admits the audience of the *Cur Deus Homo* is Christian so that they might give a reason for the hope within them (See CDH 1.1). See Hogg, *Anselm of Canterbury*, 156.

schools, as well as the specific Jewish challenge stating the Christian position on the incarnation was an offense to the dignity of God became the main issue. This issue was formulated as such:

> How can the Incarnation, with all its indignity of human contact, insult, injury, and shameful death be reconciled with the supreme dignity and stability of God? To the Jew, this issue of God's transcendent majesty was of immense importance.[62]

Given the challenge from the schools and the Jewish community, a response was needed and Anselm wrote the *Cur Deus Homo* as a response to believers as well as "unbelievers."[63] His style for responding to these challenges was through dialectic, in the form of a conversation between Anselm and his star pupil Boso. Boso challenged the positions Anselm took in the work and raised significant questions throughout the work so Anselm could provide clarification.

A Brief Survey of the Cur Deus Homo

Finally, consider in this brief survey a summary of the contents of the material in question. The *Cur Deus Homo* is divided into two books, and it is helpful to briefly outline each of these two books and the thrust of the argument for each book. Book One concerns humanity and the intention of God for eternal human blessedness, set in contrast with the fallenness of humanity and its need for salvation. The flow of the argument might be summarized as such: (1) a consideration of common objections to faith present in his contextual milieu and the need for an understanding of redemption;[64] (2) a logical argument for the fallenness of humanity and its sin, including the meaning of sin and the inescapable ability for humanity to provide a satisfactory response of recompense to God; (3) and finally the necessity for a response to the heavy weight of sin is for humanity to be saved by Christ because of its inability to retain the blessedness for which they were created. Book Two concerns the logic of the incarnation of Jesus Christ for the salvation of humanity, and the flow of the argument may be summarized as such: (1) humanity was created to be "blessedly happy" although sin destroyed the possibility of immortality and the restoration needed to arrive at the proper intended state; (2) God was able to bring about the necessary recompense for the salvation of humanity through a God-Man; and finally, (3) the death of the God-Man brought about the salvation of humanity insofar as humanity

---

[62] Southern, *St. Anselm and His Biographer*, 89.
[63] This address is made in the *Praefatio*: *Quorum prior quidem infidelium Christian fidem, quia rationi putant illam repugnare, respuentium continet obiectiones et fidelium responsiones*. Schmitt, *Vol. II*, 42-43.
[64] See McIntyre, *St. Anselm and His Critics*, 56-61, as he demonstrates how the first ten chapters are important to understanding the *Cur Deus Homo* for they deal with his reason for writing about views of the atonement to even objections of the atonement by unbelievers.

takes him and is redeemed.[65] In essence the argument, if summarized, looks as such:

> Humanity, created for blessedness,[66] has stolen away our whole selves from God, depriving God of the honor due unto God,[67] and depriving God of whatever he proposed to make of human nature;[68] the only means of God completing what he designed human nature for[69] is through the satisfaction of the dishonor of sin toward God. The payment of this satisfaction can only be made by one who is fully God and fully human[70] – Jesus Christ.[71] Through this death, thus paying a complete recompense for sin, God can bring to completion the nature of humanity, so that humanity should and can rejoice in God.[72]

The thrust of the argument emphasizes satisfying the offended honor and necessity of justice for God, by means of satisfaction.[73] Satisfying a just God is of chief importance, and the death of Jesus whose life is of infinitely greater value than the sins of humanity provides this satisfaction.[74]

---

[65] For a helpful synopsis see Davies and Evans, *Anselm of Canterbury*, 262-265.
[66] See CDH 1.3, 268-269.
[67] See CDH 1.6, 270-271.
[68] See CDH 1.23, 308-309.
[69] See CDH 2.4, 317.
[70] See CDH 2.5-2.6, 318-320.
[71] While Anselm uses terms such as "he" for God, this writer chooses to utilize "God" without personal pronouns. Moreover, rather than utilizing "man," this writer chooses to utilize inclusive language "humanity" to maintain that the scope of all humanity was affected through the work of Jesus Christ, not just the male species. The only exception taken is the use of the term "God-Man" given that Jesus Christ was a human being of male gender, and this is specifically the terminology that Anselm utilizes.
[72] See CDH 2.4, 317.
[73] The word "satisfaction" contains the Anselmian understanding of atonement. Satisfaction comes from the Latin *satisfactio*, a word utilized for making amends, reparations, or a satisfaction derived from punishment. Its origins are demonstrated in the feudal system by looking to the court system and how when honor due the feudal lord was not offered, there was a satisfaction due as a means of reparation. One clear textual example of this is found in CDH 2.16 when Anselm references those who sin against the king as being unable to make restitution. *Satisfactio* also is found in the medieval penance system that emphasizes personal and private penance for sins and making an amends for sin through the doing of works. See Kevin A. McMahon. "The Cross and the Pearl: Anselm's Patristic Doctrine of the Atonement." *Saint Anselm – His Origins and Influence* ed. by John R. Fortin. Lewiston: The Edwin Mellen Press, 2001, 58. See McNeill and Gamer, *Medieval Handbooks of Penance*, 3-12. See also Southern, *A Portrait*, 214-216, 221-227. See also Hogg who includes Old Testament theology in his analysis of satisfaction. See Hogg, *Anselm of Canterbury*, 163-165. See also McIntyre, *St. Anselm and His Critics*, 45-46.
[74] See CDH 2.6, 2.7, and 2.14, 318-335.

It is significant to mention that with the exception of his reference to the general resurrection of humanity,[75] the resurrection of Jesus is absent and an almost peripheral issue. While Anselm certainly believed in the resurrection, it is not a part of his methodological presentation. Mentioned in chapter one, this is due to a methodological proposal that posits soteriology with the cross to be the focal point of his Christology at the expense of the resurrection, thus relegating it to the periphery. To be sure, Anselm believed in the resurrection of Jesus Christ as one finds some evidences in his devotional materials, although resurrection is not a primary source of reflection throughout his key works.[76] Rather, the salvation Jesus Christ offers is a satisfaction of the offended honor of God by means of the cross of Jesus Christ who was made incarnate for the sake of humanity. Thus the cross and subsequently the incarnation, is the central Christological element in his argument. While perhaps not the intention of Anselm, his contextual factors, presupposition, and methodology in the *Cur Deus Homo*, shape his Christology as being derived from the cross with the resurrection as a peripheral issue. This shall be discussed later in chapter three.

1.1.2 *Cur Deus Homo*: Presupposition

This chapter now moves to explore the *credo ut intelligam* principle summarily, then through three principal writings (*Monologion, Proslogion, De Incarnatione Verbi*), and finally by means of its operation in the *Cur Deus Homo*. What might be generally said is that the *credo ut intelligam* principle operates in the *Monologion* (*de ratione fidei*), more specifically in the *Proslogion* (*credo ut intelligam*), and then more thoroughly in the *De Incarnatione Verbi*. The manner in which this presuppositionary principle of Augustinian origin operates within the scope of the first three writings created a continuity Anselm sought to maintain in the *Cur Deus Homo*. This continuity was typical of the materials of the Roman Catholic Church. These findings shall later demonstrate that while Anselm sought to hold to this traditional Augustinian presupposition of believing first and on the basis of believing then understanding, Anselm utilizes an Aristotelian methodology which pushes the bounda-

---

[75] The thrust of 2.3 concerns the restoration of humanity to perfection through the resurrection of the dead, a state of being "reconstituted as the sort of being he would have been if he had not sinned." See CDH 2.3, 316.

[76] Stated in chapter one and as shall later be explicated, while Anselm was not a systematic theologian, nor did Anselm intend on writing a complete systematic theology, and while he believed in the resurrection of Jesus Christ from the dead, the resurrection is methodologically expressed separate from the cross and is thus, methodologically speaking, a more peripheral matter for him. The Christology of Anselm emphasized cross and incarnation through a "from above" methodology as the means of understanding the person and work of Jesus Christ. Deme is helpful here, as he notes that the resurrection is almost entirely ignored by Anselm in his work. While quick to contend Anselm would not have denied the resurrection, he is quick to admit the cross and resurrection are presented separately with different meanings. See Deme, *The Christology of Anselm of Canterbury*, 227-235.

ries of the Augustinian presupposition into newfound territory, moving understanding as the avenue to believing. Thus, Anselm will utilize a *remoto Christo* methodology which offers logic a higher position than his predecessors to address an important apologetic need for those outside the Christian Community, although there is intent for his corpus to be instructive for the Roman Catholic Church. More specifically, Anselm will utilize a methodology which seeks to demonstrate independent of the knowledge of Jesus Christ that his death is necessary to satisfy the offended honor of God. This in turn compromises his presupposition of believing in order to understand. This shall be the important issue for how Anselm does Christology by means of the cross, relegating the resurrection to the periphery.[77]

Credo ut Intelligam: The Underlying Presupposition

According to his presupposition, Anselm sought to convey the logic of what is believed by faith. This was, as has already been demonstrated, of Augustinian origin, as belief comes before understanding. Whether one considers *de ratione fidei*, *fides quaerens intellectum*, or *credo ut intelligam*, these statements represent guiding Augustinian presuppositions of a tradition in which Anselm desires to do theology. Inherent in these presuppositions is a longing for faith to be supported by reason so that what is believed is understandable and therefore more easily believed, holding faith and reason in dialectical tension.[78] While apparent in his earlier writings, this position of Anselm re-

---

[77] Deme is helpful here as he describes a "hermeneutic circle" by which Anselm utilizes the *credo ut intelligam* principle as a presupposition in conjunction with the *remoto Christo* principle. He also notes that the "previous presupposition (i.e. *credo ut intelligam*) become partially and temporarily removed in the thought process." See Deme, *The Christology of Anselm of Canterbury*, 13. Visser and Williams argue that the "central discussions of the *ratio fidei* are founded in the *Monologion*, *Proslogion*, *De Incarnatione Verbi*, and *Cur Deus Homo*. See Sandra Visser and Thomas Williams. *Great Medieval Thinkers: Anselm*. Oxford: Oxford University Press, 2009, 14. Hopkins claims that the principle is certainly part of the *Proslogion* but claims that one cannot demonstrate the specific instances of the influence of Augustine upon Anselm even though Anselm is Augustinian. He then later points to the *Monologion* and its utilization of *de ratione fidei* from *De Trinitate* and how the *Cur Deus Homo* also looks to this necessity of belief, which seemingly undoes his claim that one cannot demonstrate the Augustinian influence in Anselm. Moreover, as mentioned in this chapter above (1.1.1), Hopkins disagrees with McIntyre who suggested the potentiality for discontinuity to exist between presupposition and methodology, claiming this would suggest a discontinuity in the whole of the *Cur Deus Homo* itself. See Hopkins, *A Companion to the Study of St. Anselm*, 26-41, and 63-65. Hogg also disagrees with McIntyre as he claims that Anselm contends "belief and experience are necessary for genuine knowledge." Hogg agrees with Barth in his treatment of the work. Hogg also claims that Aristotelian thought is in contradiction with Anselm who holds too much of a theological-aesthetic unity for Aristotelian thought. See Hogg, *St. Anselm of Canterbury*, 158-163.

[78] While there is indeed a dialectical tension of sorts, Gilson demonstrates Anselm goes against the excesses of dialecticians because he believes faith comes first and

garding faith and reason might have likely received its greatest development out of his defense to a challenge made by Roscelin in 1089 concerning his orthodoxy. This development is not without irony as his presupposition developed out of apologetic desires in the beginning of his work, and then from the challenge in 1089, it required he develop it further so he could defend it. The response Anselm offered to Roscelin purported that reason is used to defend faith against unbelievers, but as for Christians, they were to hold to the faith they professed in baptism and understand the deeper meaning of faith.[79]

The expression of this language of faith and reason eventuated for Anselm a primary presuppositionary principle undergirding his writing, *credo ut intelligam*. Some have noted Anselm is the "first theist really to put the *credo ut intelligam* principle explicitly and continuously into action,"[80] and one can easily find the expression of this presuppositionary principle in four important writings of Anselm including the *Monologion, Proslogion, De Incarnatione Verbi*, and *Cur Deus Homo*.[81] This presuppositionary principle is not anything altogether new as these statements are of Augustinian origin (*intelligo ut credam*).[82] Thus, Anselm sought to maintain the previously utilized Augustinian tradition by including it in his own corpus. This is significant as Lanfranc, his mentor, believed this tradition was important for doing theology, and the Roman Catholic Church had utilized this methodology for quite some time. Anselm indicates for him, faith is the beginning or starting point of truth. This is intended to demonstrate his desire to hold to belief stemming from the authority of Scripture as primary, giving logic and reason a

---

reason as the means to uphold and prove faith to be true. See Gilson, *History of Christian Philosophy in the Middle Ages*, 129. Although Barth and Gilson are often seen in opposition respective to the Anselmian faith and reason issue, Barth holds a similar position offering that the "dominating factor in Anselm's mind is that even the Church Fathers wrote about it (*intelligere*) in order to give the faithful joy in believing by a demonstration of the *ratio* of their faith." See Karl Barth. *Anselm: Fides Quaerens Intellectum*. London: SCM Press LTD, 1960, 15. This work shall demonstrate that while there is a dialectical tension of sorts, the methodology compromises his presupposition of belief in order to understand.

[79] See Southern, *A Portrait*, 123. In this regard, Hopkins position of belief-understanding for believers vs. understanding-belief for unbelievers might be strengthened. However, it is also possible to see how while Anselm in the *Commendatio* points to belief-understanding, his point to the Pope Urban II is that the encouragement of Isaiah is to "pay more attention to understanding." CDH C, 260. The spirit of this is upheld in the *Praefatio* when he points to his *remoto Christo* methodology and his desire to demonstrate with reason and truth even if nothing is known of Christ that the God-Man is necessary. See CDH P, 261-262. Also see CDH, 42 for Latin.

[80] McIntyre, *St. Anselm and His Critics*, 1-2. This point is also most made by Grant, Barth, Southern, and Deme.

[81] See Visser and Williams. *Anselm*, 14-25. See also McIntyre. *St. Anselm and His Critics*, 7-55.

[82] See Augustine Sermon 212.1. See also Augustine *De Trinitate* 1:1-2.

supporting role.⁸³ Given the importance of reason and logic in his milieu, this distinction Anselm crafts further demonstrates his relevance within his milieu in utilizing logic, while concurrently maintaining continuity with the tradition of the Church and the Scriptures as primary sources of authority. For Anselm, while belief is primary, understanding is its close counterpart, as belief should seek understanding or confirmation. He sees this longing for understanding as the proper obligation of Christians.⁸⁴ Ultimately, Anselm utilized a strong reliance on the *ratio fidei* as an important expression of the presuppositionary principle, and utilized rational structures to bridge faith and understanding.⁸⁵

So, for Anselm, understanding is a mature expression of belief and he sees his work as bridging faith and understanding by means of reason. Without belief and participation in that belief – without *credo ut intelligam* – one cannot understand. Anselm seeks to prove this in three of his major works:

> That God exists (*Proslogion*), that God is supreme Goodness and Justice (*Monologion*), and that he has made provision for humanity's salvation in the only way possible (*Cur Deus Homo*).⁸⁶

Anselm quotes 1 Peter 3:15 and Isaiah 7:9 as important Scriptural truths for the necessity of understanding what one believes in the Cur *Deus Homo*,⁸⁷ although his presuppositionary principle might be better understood from the perspective of Colossians 1:28: "We proclaim him, admonishing and teaching everyone with all wisdom, so that we may present everyone perfect in Christ."⁸⁸ One finds an underlying purpose that naturally develops throughout his corpus of helping people to understand what they believe, eventuating the possibility for helping those who do not believe to come to a juncture where they see the reason they should believe. Therefore Anselm had both a catechismal and apologetically oriented purpose in his writings, and he clearly struggles with this outcome by encouraging people not to believe out of their own will so that they may gain understanding; rather he tells them to believe so they may understand.⁸⁹

---

⁸³ Lanfranc held this position and this was part of his debate with Berengar. See Holopainen, *Anselm and Lanfranc's Heritage*, 4-9. See also Gilson, *A History of Philosophy: Medieval Philosophy*, 49.

⁸⁴ See Barth, *Anselm: Fides Quaerens Intellectum*, 15-21. See McIntyre, *St. Anselm and His Critics*, 4. See Southern, *A Portrait*, 125-127. See Visser and Williams, *Anselm*, 13-25. See Hopkins, *A Companion to the Study of St. Anselm*, 38-66.

⁸⁵ See Deme, *The Christology of Anselm of Canterbury*, 13. Original Source: L. Karfikova. *Anselm z Canterbury: Fides Quaerens Intellectum*. Prague: Kalich Publishers, 1990, 3.

⁸⁶ Hopkins, *A Companion to the Study of St. Anselm*, 43.

⁸⁷ See CDH 1.1, 265-266.

⁸⁸ Colossians 1:28, NIV.

⁸⁹ For example, see CDH 1.1, 265-266. Anselm found tension between his methodology and presupposition. His desire to hold to the Augustinian tradition while writing for the milieu through an Aristotelian methodology created a tension

What intial findings can be made respective to the Anselmian *credo ut intelligam* presuppositionary principle? First, Anselm wanted belief or faith to be the cornerstone or central response of humanity with understanding as the necessary consequent so persons become mature in their belief.[90] This sets him in strong continuity with the Augustinian tradition that the Roman Church leadership longed for. Second, the purpose of logical arguments was to aid in the process of maturation so that persons may come to understand what it is they believe. This places him squarely within the Aristotelian methodology that his milieu desperately wanted as part of the argument. Thirdly, while his presuppositionary principle intended for belief to be primary, there is at least a possibility that his arguments are equally (if not more) toward helping those who do not presently believe. And fourthly, it is possible to see how Anselm realized an important apologetic purpose, which gives impetus to his encouragement of people believing not out of their own will to gain understanding but beleiving so that they may understand. One final note should be made here with respect to Anselm: he most likely did not think understanding ever transcended the mystery of God.[91] This reality held Anselm to an epistemic humility of sorts, and did not allow him to move into rational philosophies and theologies that later developed in Descartes, Kant, and the like. Now that the presuppositionary principle has been explained, this present work turns to the application of the principle in three primary works, and then in the *Cur Deus Homo*.

The *Credo ut Intelligam* Principle throughout Three Primary Works

The *Monologion* is typically treated as the first writing of Anselm. It is critical to recognize his presuppositionary principle comes into existence due to the desires of his monks who longed for an argument for the existence of God that did not presuppose belief. The monks desired the "plain truth," and this is evidenced by the original title of the *Monologion*, "*Exemplum meditandi de ratione fidei.*" The scope of the argument features the suspension of Scripture for reason alone (*sola ratione*) although Anselm claimed the overarching pur-

---

against logic taking a position over belief. This being said, his method pushed believers past belief toward understanding.

[90] Barth holds a similar position positing that Anselm believed "*fides* is essentially - *quaerens intellectum.*" See Barth, *Anselm: Fides Quaerens Intellectum*, 21. McIntyre is somewhat similar to Barth here in that for the believer, a more complete understanding comes to pass. For the unbeliever, they are brought to a place of understanding and the possibility for faith. See McIntyre, *St. Anselm and His Critics*, 53-55.

[91] See Gilson, *A History of Philosophy*, 130. Gilson contends even though Anselm may have proved the logical necessity of the existence of God, redemption, incarnation, etc., that this is far from explaining the divine mysteries themselves. Considering Lanfranc had high regard for epistemic humility, it would not be surprising that Anselm would be similar. One also sees this in the tensions within his work between logic and belief.

pose was for reason to make faith reasonable, which held his presupposition intact. One immediately recognizes that while the *credo ut intelligam* presuppositionary principle is not mentioned explicitly in the *Monologion*, it nonetheless governs the argument.

Anselm claims affinity with his tradition by stating that he will not contradict Augustine in *De Trinitate*,[92] although the very methodology he utilizes suspends Scripture[93] and the traditions and doctrines of the Roman Church in the *Monologion*. In fact, as some have argued, Anselm relied upon the Platonic Doctrine of the Forms, and logic to make his point.[94] This potential contradiction between the presuppositionary principle and the methodology of *auctoritate scripturae...nihil* or *sola ratione* is an important distinction to make. McIntyre raises a similar point as he claims:

> If the Monologion is properly interpreted as *fides quaerens intellectum*, then the previously mentioned dual character of St Anselm's method reappears.[95]

The previously mentioned dual character of this method which Anselm utilizes is, as McIntyre calls it, "an unresolved contradiction" between the letter and spirit of the work, or better stated between faith (*fides*) and reason (*ratione*).[96] Thus, the method by which Anselm achieves his argument (*sola ratione*) is independent of the methodology of Augustine, but only for the purposes of understanding that which he already believes.[97] McIntyre notes Anselm does not mention the name of God until later in his argument – long after the non-believing person is brought to a place of logical outcomes in which they must accept the logic of a supreme being.[98]

---

[92] See McIntyre, *St. Anselm and His Critics*, 12.

[93] The terminology Anselm utilizes is *auctoritate scripturae...nihil*. See Monologion, *Prologus*. Schmitt, Vol. I, 7. Hogg and Barth have contested this, claiming principles of Scripture are evident in CDH. One can also make the case that his cultural milieu is also as evident, although Hogg attempts to refute this. It seems that while there are Scriptural principles at play to support his arguments in CDH, the whole of Scripture and especially the whole of the history of Jesus Christ are methodologically suspended *remoto Christo*. See Hogg, *St. Anselm of Canterbury*, 163-165. See Barth, *Anselm: Fides Quaerens Intellectum*, 53-54.

[94] Evans claims that the utilization of climbing a ladder to God is a Platonic concept that is founded in the concept of the Supreme Being. See Evans, *Anselm*, 17. Here Anselm points to *sola ratione* as the means of making his point. See Monologion, *Prologus*. Schmitt, Vol. I, 13. McIntyre, *St. Anselm and His Critics*, 12-13.

[95] McIntyre, *St. Anselm and His Critics*, 13.

[96] See McIntyre, *St. Anselm and His Critics*, 6-7.

[97] This is an interesting issue which Barth comments on as part of both the *Monologion* and *Proslogion*. Barth holds that the issue is an open question to be discerned by faith and understood by reason. It is the meaning of the existence of God as a concept or as reality of truth which is the origin of all truth – this is the very question Anselm seeks to answer. Ironically, the means by which he attempts to go about it is by the reason of faith rather than from the basis of faith upheld by reason. See Barth, *Anselm: Fides Quaerens Intellectum*, 95-100.

[98] See McIntyre, *St. Anselm and His Critics*, 14.

McIntyre raises an important question this chapter has to reflect upon: are the letter and spirit of the work of Anselm at odds? Does his method match his presuppositionary principle? What might be said of the *Monologion* at this juncture is that while Anselm intends belief to be the presupposition for understanding, the methodology he employs begins with understanding so as to gain elementary belief or further garner greater belief. The methodology by which he achieves this is through the use of logic, and without primary appeals to Scripture or doctrine, or the tradition of the Church.[99] This in turn raises another question, namely, is Scripture a primary source for belief in Anselm, and more importantly, are the Scriptures (and doctrines of the Church for that matter) the corpus that enables belief, or is belief solely the gift of God? One immediately has to question how the methodology of *sola ratione* could match a presuppositionary principle of *credo ut intelligam*. The two would more likely be at odds if Scripture or the doctrines of the Church enable belief, and the presuppositionary principle under his methodology of suspending Scripture would become *intelligo ut credam*. If belief is a condition requiring no sources at all, then further issue arises – why believe at all?[100]

Fortunately, it is possible to consider Lanfranc, the teacher of Anselm to resolve this issue. Lanfranc held Scripture as being the primary source enabling belief. One can recognize this by looking to his debates with Berengar in which he (Lanfranc) challenges the emphasis of Berengar toward logic and reason over Scripture and the works of the Early Fathers. Perhaps this is the reason why Lanfranc, the mentor of Anselm did not meet the *Monologion* with much response at all, and perhaps this is the reason why the *Proslogion* begins with an intensely devotional chapter emphasizing the necessity of belief and the desire to know God more fully. Visser and Williams even go so far as to comment:

> We do not have the texts of Lanfranc's assessment, but we do know that he took a dim view of Anselm's avoidance of Scriptural authority. One can imagine that he was especially put off by the way in which Anselm occasionally gives reason the job of approving the text of Scripture.[101]

Thus, it is possible to glean that the methodological suspension of Scripture for the utilization of reason (i.e. an exploration of Christian faith without belief) is one important way in which the presuppositionary principle of *credo ut intelligam* seems to be compromised. While the argument is addressed to and written for those who believe, it would be incredibly naïve to think it is only for believers. It may have had a purpose for helping people to

---

[99] To be fair there is not necessarily anything that contradicts Scripture. This is the point Evans makes with regard to Anselm, namely that he utilizes reason insofar as it does not contradict Scripture. See Evans, *Anselm*, 40-41.

[100] On this point, Hogg is in agreement as there "is a lack of attention to the life of Jesus." See Hogg, *St. Anselm of Canterbury*, 180.

[101] Visser and Williams. *Anselm*, 17.

understand, but perhaps an even a greater purpose for those who do not believe – especially given the milieu.

Secondly, this investigation turns to the *Proslogion*, a well-received work by the Roman Catholic Church that has been utilized and scrutinized by scholars and clergy for hundreds of years.[102] The work is intended to be of a devotional character to God, expressed in this statement capturing the essence of the *credo ut intelligam* presuppositionary principle:

> For I do not seek to understand so that I may believe; but I believe so that I may understand. For I believe this also, that unless I believe, I shall not understand.[103]

This devotionally and Scripturally oriented beginning to the *Proslogion* contrasts with the first chapter of the *Monologion* by claiming from the outset that reason helps people toward what they do not know, and begins from the example of persons who have never heard of, or do not believe in God.[104] Moreover, whereas the first chapter of the *Monologion* occurs after a prologue revealing the monks desire for the *ratio fidei*, the *Proslogion* fits better with the *credo ut intelligam* presuppositionary principle as Anselm reveals his deep faith and devotion to God – his belief – before he undertakes the task of proving that the fool who claims there is no God is indeed foolish.

Given this beginning, the *Proslogion* begins its second chapter by setting the stage for how belief and understanding prove that those who claim there is no God are indeed foolish. Anselm utilizes logical statement that he draws from the Scriptural authority of Psalm 13. The *credo ut intelligam* principle is intended then to prove the one who says there is no God is indeed foolish, and Anselm derives his proof by making the statement "(God is) that than which no greater can be thought."[105] McIntyre claims:

> He has been seeking to understand (*intelligere*) what is involved in believing (*credere*) that God is such, and this understanding has led to fuller faith.[106]

Amazingly, the *Proslogion* morphs from an intensely devotional and Scripturally pregnant first chapter to a second chapter with a more logically oriented thesis featuring Scripture, to a third chapter that includes a penultimate sentence when Anselm claims that the existence of God "is so evident

---

[102] Perhaps the greatest evidence of this is the acceptance of Lanfranc, the long-standing survival of the document within the Roman Catholic Church, and the appointment of Anselm some 15 years later to the archbishopric. See Southern, *A Portrait*, 119-120, 127-128.

[103] The origins of this statement are of Augustinian origin and a paraphrase of Isaiah 7. See P 1, 84-87.

[104] See M 1, 11-12.

[105] See P 3, 88.

[106] McIntyre, *St. Anselm and His Critics*, 10. Visser and Williams are very critical of the *Proslogion* because of the manner in which Anselm utilizes terminology that could be construed as multiple modes of existence, and the spirit of the work concerns faith seeking understanding through a multitude of arguments – not a singular one. See Visser and Williams, *Anselm*, 73-75.

to the rational mind."¹⁰⁷ The remainder of the *Proslogion* is the process by which the fool should arrive at the stance of belief with the final and twenty-sixth chapter of the *Proslogion* having a devotional character much like the first. It is in this twenty-sixth chapter that Anselm claims through his process of discovery he has come to fuller faith:

> For I have discovered a joy that is complete and more than complete. Indeed, when the heart is filled with that joy, the mind is filled with it, the soul is filled with it, the whole man is filled with it, yet joy beyond measure will remain....I pray, O God, that I may know you and love you, so that I may rejoice in you.¹⁰⁸

Just as in the *Monologion,* Anselm breaks from Augustinian tradition in his *Proslogion*; the authority of the Augustinian presupposition while clear at the outset is seemingly discarded throughout the remainder of the argument by means of his methodology, giving the work a distinctly philosophical orientation.¹⁰⁹ In essence, there are three states of existence he delineates: "in the mind, in the mind and outside the mind, and in the mind and necessarily outside the mind."¹¹⁰ These three modes or states of existence correlate to a higher being, who is God, in which all things "find their highest degree of being,"¹¹¹ and these three modes also correlate to God, believers, and those whose understanding is darkened so they cannot see as anything existing outside of the mind (i.e. unbelievers). Notwithstanding the problematic nature of multiple modes of existence, while Anselm attempts to demonstrate why the fool is the fool, it is interesting his methodology quickly suspends Scripture and the materials of the Church. The development and structure of the *Proslogion* reveals how the application of the *credo ut intelligam* principle operates within the context of the *Proslogion*: (1) Anselm seems to have reoriented his writing perhaps because (a) the *Monologion* was met with less than enthusiastic acceptance and (b) because his desire is to reveal his belief and devotion to God by proving that there is a greater being existing outside the mind (i.e. thus proving the fool to be a fool); (2) the devotional quality in the *Proslogion*, is seemingly structured by a "devotional inclusio"¹¹² in which the belief expressed in the first chapter has grown in the last chapter because of the argument which proves the fool and has thus helped him, a believer, grow in his belief; (3) the thesis statement which Anselm makes about God as that which no greater can be thought of sets the methodologi-

---

¹⁰⁷ See P 3, 88.
¹⁰⁸ P 26, 103.
¹⁰⁹ Here the issue is not that Augustine did not write any philosophical treatises, but that Anselm was making a break from Augustinian tradition which pointed to the materials of the Church, most notably the authority of Scripture, tradition, and other materials of the Church.
¹¹⁰ Southern, *A Portrait*, 133.
¹¹¹ Southern, *A Portrait*, 133.
¹¹² An inclusio is a literary device often found in biblical literature in which the beginning and end of a certain boundary are marked by a similar phrase, word, or idea.

cal stage for the process Anselm utilizes throughout the remainder of his argument; and (4) there is a unique tension between (1) and (2) in that while Anselm first expresses his belief, it is the methodology that proves the fool wrong which leads him toward greater faith and more importantly, gives the fool a reason to believe.

Similar issues that surfaced in the *Monologion* are also present in the *Proslogion*. One must ask yet again if there remains a divide between the letter and spirit of the work, and while the first and last chapters are of intense devotional quality, pregnant with Scriptural usage and doctrinal language intending to show how the presuppositionary principle is in effect, there nonetheless remains a methodology which sets out to prove the fool incorrect by utilizing logic and not the Scriptures. This reality is the overwhelming purpose of the document, that is, an apologetic purpose to those who say there is no God. While the devotion Anselm expresses in the beginning as a presupposition of belief and in the conclusion an outcome of greater belief, the means by which Anselm arrives at such a juncture occurs by logic. One must ask if it is *credo* or *ratione* which drives the argument. Is the existence of God merely a logical proposition of mathematical certainty that needs no acceptance (which the *Proslogion* tends to suggest) or is it belief in the probability of such a proposition that assures people of the existence of God?[113] The manner in which one answers this question tends to push the argument and the presuppositionary principle toward either the pole of belief as primary or the pole of reason as primary.

Thirdly, *De Incarnatione Verbi*, generally dated as post 1090, provides a response to the heresy of Roscelin, and is an important evidentiary piece into the present inquiry.[114] While Roscelin may have been the primary target of this work, it is also an opportunity that Anselm creates to flesh out his *credo ut intelligam* principle. Anselm points to the inability of Roscelin to understand the Scriptures, the tradition and authority of the Roman Catholic Church, and his purpose of making a logical argument to expose the heretical views of Roscelin. The means by which he does this begins with the explanation of his presuppositionary principle, occurring from approximately the midpoint of the first chapter of the work:

> I do so to curb the presumption of those who, since they are unable to understand intellectually things the Christian faith professes, and with foolish pride think that there cannot in any way be things that they cannot understand, with unspeakable rashness dare to argue against such things rather than with humble wisdom admit their possibility. Indeed, no Christian ought to argue how things the Catholic Church sincerely believes and verbally professes are not so, but by always adhering to the same faith without hesitation, by loving it, and by humbly living according to it, a Chris-

---

[113] See Gilson, *A History of Philosophy*, 133-134.

[114] See Southern, *St. Anselm and His Biographer*, 77-82. Southern notes the challenge from Roscelin included the names of Anselm and his mentor Lanfranc. These materials included not only a challenge to his methodology and work, but also referenced the incarnation, perhaps an impetus for Anselm to write *Cur Deus Homo*.

tian ought to argue how they are, inasmuch as one can look for reasons. If one can understand, one should thank God; if one cannot, one should bow one's head in veneration rather than sound off trumpets. For human wisdom trusting in itself can more swiftly pluck out its trumpets by pressing against them than it can roll such a stone by leaning on it. For some beginners, in presuming to rise to the loftiest questions about faith, typically produce trumpets, as it were, of knowledge trusting itself. They do not know that if persons think they know something, they do not yet know, before they have spiritual wings through solidarity of faith, how they should know it. And so it happens that when beginners foolishly try to ascend intellectually to those things that first need the ladder of faith (as Scripture says: 'Unless you have believed you will not understand' [Isa. 7:9]), they sink into many kinds of errors by reason of the deficiency of their intellect.[115]

Anselm claims persons should not defend the faith until they have first believed and then lived the faith. It is clear Anselm thinks Roscelin has attempted to understand the faith without having believed it first. This is the primary error of Roscelin, and the reason why his heart "must be cleansed by faith."[116] It is only through faith and then the experience of living this faith that one begins to understand, and from belief, experience, and into understanding it becomes necessary for Christians to argue how faith is possible by utilizing logic and reason. He continues his delineation of the presuppositionary principle by reasoning that belief (the primary source) is the way to understanding, and that without belief understanding is not possible:

> For they evidently do not have the strength of faith, who since they cannot understand the things they believe, argue against the same faith's truth confirmed by the Holy Fathers. This is as if bats and owls, who see the heavens only at night, should argue about the midday rays of the sun with eagles, who gaze on the very sun with undeflected vision....This is surely the very thing that I am saying: those who have not believed will not understand. For those who have not believed will not find by experience, and those who have not found by experience will not know.[117]

The remainder of the first chapter is a continuation of what has been stated before and the necessity of belief in order for understanding to occur. There is a good deal of Scriptural support for his argument, a signal that this chapter is pointed more directly to those who already believe and may have familiarity with the previous works of Anselm. The concluding remarks of the chapter reveal Anselm saw this to be a necessary demonstration applicable to the argument directed toward Roscelin, and perhaps even more importantly to all who read his work. This principle he believes to be a basis for all his writings and after explaining it, Anselm is now ready to begin to address the matter that the letter is intended to address.

The deeper matter of *De Incarnatione Verbi* is that someone has tried to ascend to belief through understanding and their understanding was clouded

---

[115] See DIV 1, 235-236.
[116] See DIV 1, 235-236.
[117] DIV 1, 235-236.

because they had missed the necessary precondition of understanding: belief. Anselm thought it was right for unbelievers to raise questions against Christian belief, but it was a spiritual failure for Roscelin to go astray because he could not understand. McIntyre claims *De Incarnatione Verbi* is important for Anselm as it shows how faith and unfaith are held in dialectical tension and it is the process by which faith is built is through understanding. More importantly, the heretical view Roscelin held provided an opportunity to illumine the orthodoxy of Trinitarian thinking, and it is this dialectical conversation that enables greater faith.[118]

The very claim McIntyre makes concerning the potential divide between the letter and spirit of the work reveals itself in the *De Incarnatione Verbi*. Anselm makes an important claim concerning his previous work (the *Monologion* and *Proslogion*) in this document:

> They were written mainly so that what we hold by faith concerning the divine nature *and persons*, leaving aside the Incarnation, could be proved by necessary reasons, independently of the Scripture.[119]

Anselm writes not only for Roscelin but for those whom he desires to defend his own orthodoxy; he believes faith is primary although it seems there is some realization in his methodology that faith is garnered or perhaps even inaugurated through understanding. Moreover, why would Anselm write such a sentence if his orthodoxy was unchallenged, especially by Roscelin? Could it be that what surfaced were questions about his methodology and how that methodology may have contrasted or even contradicted his presupposition? Or perhaps other persons came to a place of understanding without a presupposition of belief? It seems the issue for Anselm was a tension created because of a milieu in which Anselm was entrenched: on the one hand he remains desirous to believe to understand maintaining continuity with past Augustinian propositions of the authority of the Scriptures and the Church, and yet on the other hand Anselm is pulled forward by the desires of his milieu and for proving unbelievers wrong by the use of logic and enabling the possibility for faith itself through an Aristotelian methodology. While his presupposition is noble, the methodology by which he chooses to argue his treatises are built upon a logical choice for the audience: he denies himself the luxuries of the authority and tradition of the Scriptures and the Church because unbelievers do not accept the truth or

---

[118] See Visser and Williams, *Anselm*, 19-20. While Anselm points to belief-understanding, here there is some level of development in the manner in which Anselm saw faith and unfaith working in a dialectical tension of sorts. See McIntyre, *St. Anselm and His Critics*, 12. It is possible to see how understanding gains a greater sense of prominence in the thought of Anselm by the time of the DIV when one considers while his presupposition contends belief is primary and then understanding the responsibility of the believer, for those who do not believe, understanding is a powerful combatant of unfaith.

[119] DIV 6, 245.

authority of either. This, of course, requires some further investigation, which shall be presented below.

Credo ut Intelligam Principle and *Cur Deus Homo*

While the words *credo ut intelligam* are not mentioned specifically within the context of the *Commendatio* or the *Praefatio* of the *Cur Deus Homo*, or at any other point in the work for that matter, this presupposition nonetheless governs his work and can be heard in terms of an echo:

> ...*nisi credideritis, non intelligetis*[120]
>
> *Hac igitur ego consideratione, licet sim homo parvae nimis scientiae, confortatus, ad eorum quae credimus rationem intuendam...*[121]
>
> *Ac tandem remoto Christo, quasi numquam aliquid fuerit de illo, probat rationibus necessariis esse impossibile ullum hominem salvari sine illo.*[122]
>
> *Quod petunt, non ut per rationem ad fidem accedant, sed ut eorum quae credunt intellectu et contemplatione delectentur, et ut sint, quantum possunt...*[123]

The scope of the Commendatio reveals the presuppositionary principle. Anselm claims understanding builds upon faith in his quotation of Isaiah 7:9 which is painted in the spirit of the Augustinian presupposition. He also describes his purpose as "to contemplate the logic of our beliefs,"[124] a further example of credo ut intelligam. The first chapter of the Cur Deus Homo reads that Anselm desires people to "first believe the 'deeper things' of the Christian faith as taught by the Scriptures and the Church, and then go on to understand them, if possible."[125] It is possible to see in the Commendatio and the first chapter of the work that Anselm longs to provide the understanding necessary for the comprehension of faith. This, he believes, is the necessary obligation for Christian believers. Jasper Hopkins points out that for this reason, he selects his pupil Boso for a dialogue partner as the tenets of faith do not have to be proven for Boso to accept them; rather, he is looking for reason to prove what he already believes.[126]

However, as McIntyre points out, Anselm states in the *Praefatio* a contradictory statement respective to the *Commendatio*, specifically his *remoto Christo* methodology:

> And eventually it proves, by unavoidable logical steps, that supposing Christ were left out of the case, as if there had never existed anything to do with him,

---

[120] CDH C, 40.
[121] CDH C, 40.
[122] CDH P, 42.
[123] CDH 1.1, 47.
[124] CDH P, 261.
[125] CDH 1.1, 39.
[126] See Hopkins, *A Companion to the Study of St. Anselm*, 40.

it is impossible that, without him, any member of the human race could be saved.[127]

This, McIntyre claims "is not a rhetorical boast or mere slip of the pen," as this methodology is employed throughout the book.[128] This makes for a more apologetic argument, and the *remoto Christo* methodology seemingly shifts the work from the presuppositionary principle and its desire for belief and then understanding to understanding and then belief. Hopkins attempts to sidestep the question McIntyre raises, namely whether or not the *remoto Christo* methodology Anselm utilizes conflicts with his presuppositionary principle of *credo ut intelligam*. He does so by appealing to Barth, who is very favorable to Anselm, and also by attempting to show that the *Cur Deus Homo* is a work that builds from the *Monologion* and *Proslogion* and that ultimately to suggest that the work involves an *intelligo ut credam* principle[129] involves a "discontinuity" in the work itself.[130] Hopkins also attempts to hold together the presuppositionary principle by offering a quote from within the *Cur Deus Homo*:

> We seem remiss if, having been established in faith, we do not strive to understand that which we believe.[131]

However, the quote he decides to use as a proof text to make his point is from the first chapter of the work, and this offers little proof that the presuppositionary principle is indeed carried forward through the whole of the work. Again, while McIntyre does not arrive at this conclusion (he only raises the question) his question is indeed the proper question.

Visser and Williams in their work entitled *Great Medieval Thinkers: Anselm*, carry forward the question that McIntyre raises. They contend while the unbeliever cannot discover the reason of faith, the believer can help the unbeliever by offering something they can understand and more importantly "unbelievers are brought into a state in which faithful inquiry is possible."[132] This is perhaps the middle ground between the question McIntyre raises on one side and Barth and Hopkins on the other. Visser and Williams raise a supposition in which reason leads persons toward belief and as such they are able to begin the possibility of believing in the Incarnate God in Jesus Christ, who according to Anselm came to satisfy the offended honor of God. In being led to this position by reason they understand that there is a response that is necessary, and it is faith that has led them to make that response. Yet,

---

[127] CDH P, 261-262.

[128] McIntyre, *St. Anselm and His Critics*, 4. Some recent scholarship has taken exception to this claiming that all the Scriptural tenets are upheld in the CDH. For example, Katherine Sonderegger. "Anselm, *Defensor Fidei*." *International Journal of Systematic Theology* Vol. 9, No 3. Oxford: Blackwell Publishing, 2007, 342-361.

[129] See McIntyre, *St. Anselm and His Critics*, 5.

[130] See Hopkins, *A Companion to the Study of St. Anselm*, 63-64.

[131] See Hopkins, *A Companion to the Study of St. Anselm*, 64. This is quoted from CDH 1.1.

[132] See Visser and Williams, *Anselm*, 24.

is this middle ground really necessary? Is the genius in the Anselmian Corpus the presuppositionary principle, or the methodology, which, although it compromises the presupposition, advanced the potentially underlying apologetic cause? Moreover, if one considers the challenges of the pre-scholastic currents and its use of logic and dialectic in the Anselmian era, and how that challenge most likely pushed the Roman Church toward utilizing logic while also struggling to maintain its delicate balance of power which was being brought into question by its challengers, Jewish or otherwise, is it surprising that there would be conflict between a presuppositionary principle from the previous era in Augustine and an Aristotelian methodology from the present era?

Conclusion: *Cur Deus Homo*—Presupposition

What is readily distinguishable at this juncture is the fact that Anselm sought to utilize the presuppositionary principle throughout his work. For him, belief was intended to be primary typical of the spirit of Augustinian theology that had governed the Roman Church for hundreds of years. This began in the *Monologion*, continued in the *Proslogion* with an even more intensely devotional and Scriptural first two chapters, and then by the time of the *De Incarnatione Verbi*, Anselm was required to defend his position. This was an important juncture for Anselm as it required him to more thoroughly think about his position and demonstrate it adequately from the challenge of heresy made by Roscelin. He elucidates that belief is the presupposition of understanding, and that while believers should seek to understand, understanding is not a prerequisite for belief. That he wrote the work in 1090 CE, three years before the *Cur Deus Homo*, is evidence of why this also operates within the corpus of the *Cur Deus Homo*, and this is why one can hear echoes of *credo ut intelligam* throughout the work.

And yet, at subtle work throughout all of this is an Aristotelian methodology that Anselm employed. Suspending Scripture, the doctrines and traditions of the Roman Church, and eventually knowledge of Jesus Christ himself, are all reasons why one can look to understanding as an important avenue to faith. The milieu which longed for Aristotelian logic as a means to understanding was also important, and it guided the way Anselm did theology. And finally, the challenges to the Roman Catholic Church, which Anselm came to lead necessitated a different approach as well – one that did not lean on the materials of the Church but the milieu.

1.1.3 Cur Deus Homo: **Methodology**

Given the above study in 1.1.2, this chapter now turns to 1.1.3, in part a continuation of what was revealed in embryonic form in 1.1.2, namely that the *remoto Christo* methodology of *Cur Deus Homo* compromises the presuppositionary principle of *credo ut intelligam*. This shall be demonstrated in two steps: (1) It shall first be argued that the *remoto Christo* methodology built upon logic and dialectic compromises the presupposition and it is the methodology which represents an *a priori* theology "from above," that is Aristotelian, and (2) that this methodology ultimately shapes the theological commitments and outcomes of the *Cur Deus Homo* thus juxtaposing the *credo ut intelligam* presupposition to *intelligo ut credam*.[133]

The Remoto Christo Methodology

The key text of the *remoto Christo* methodology Anselm utilizes is found in the *Praefatio* of the *Cur Deus Homo*:

> The first book contains the objections of unbelievers who reject the Christian faith because they think it militates against reason, and the answers given by the faithful. And eventually it proves by unavoidable logical steps, that, *supposing Christ were left out of the case*, as if there had never existed anything to do with him, it is impossible that, without him, any member of the human race could be saved. In the second book, similarly, the supposition is made that nothing were known about Christ, and it is demonstrated with no less clear logic and truth: that human nature was instituted with the specific aim that at some stage the whole human being should enjoy blessed immortality, 'whole' meaning with 'both body and soul'; that it was inevitable that the outcome concerning mankind which was the reason behind man's creation should become a reality, but that this could only happen through the agency of a God-Man; and that it is from necessity that all the things which we believe about Christ have come to pass.[134]

The distinctive sentence here is:

> Ac tandem remoto Christo, quasi numquam aliquid fuerit de illo, probat rationibus necessariis esse impossibile ullum hominem salvari sine illo.[135]

As already mentioned, the issue exists between the *credo ut intelligam* presupposition and the *remoto Christo* methodology. One sees this in the contrast between the *Commendatio* to Pope Urban II, and the *Praefatio*. Within the scope of the *Commendatio*, faith seeks understanding, a feature of *credo ut intelligam*; faith in Jesus Christ is followed by an obligatory response of seeking to understand what it is that is believed. The *Praefatio* emphasizes something entirely different. Here there is a desire to not only dispatch the challenges of the nonbelievers but also to prove by logically necessary steps that apart from Christ salvation is impossible, and all of this will be done as if Christ were set aside (*remoto Christo*).[136] Whereas the *Commendatio* emphasizes the *credo ut in-*

---

[133] Mentioned above, while McIntyre did not carry out his question to logical conclusion, it is possible to see how the Anselmian methodology compromises his presupposition. See McIntyre, *St. Anselm and His Critics*, 5.

[134] CDH P, 261-262. (Italics mine to indicate the *remoto Christo* key text).

[135] See CDH P, 42.

[136] See CDH P, 42. Colish shows how his methodology "while not claiming to be Aristotelian there are demonstrative syllogisms compelling consent to be necessarily true..." and "he means (these) are arguments based on reason alone, arguments making no appeal to authority." This is unique as Anselm attempts to address the issues by means of rational responses although there is potentiality for even better

telligam presupposition as the overarching desire for the argument, the *Praefatio* reveals a methodology suspending faith and knowledge, so that logic can lead toward belief.

In fact, this methodology becomes readily apparent in *Cur Deus Homo* as Anselm immediately notices this could become a possible outcome, and thus attempts to guard against it:

> For they say these explanations please them, and they think them satisfactory. They make this request, not with a view to arriving at faith through reason, but in order that they may take delight in the understanding and contemplation of the things which they believe, and may be, as far as they are able, 'ready to give satisfaction to all who ask the reason for the hope that is in us (1 Pet. 3:15).'[137]

One must also consider the purpose for why Anselm desires persons to give a satisfaction for the hope within them: the purpose is apologetic. This is illumined when one considers the Jewish challenges to Church doctrine, as well as the fading supernatural tendencies of the previous era and the monks desire to know what they believe through logic and dialectical thought. Whereas Anselm has claimed throughout many of his works that logic is to help those who believe understand, it seems from the outset of this argument that his audience is more likely to help those understand who do not believe. His purpose is to give an understanding of why one should believe from the perspective of why the incarnation is necessary so that humanity can be saved. The *remoto Christo* methodology employed to this end posits the Aristotelian methodology as operating primarily and the Augustinian presupposition as secondary.

The *remoto Christo* methodology mentioned at the outset of the work is maintained throughout the whole. For example Anselm writes in *Cur Deus Homo*:

> Let us posit, therefore, that the incarnation of God and the things which we say about him as man had never happened, and let it be agreed between us that man was created for a state of blessedness...[138]

---

rational responses. This is another example of how while tenets of scholasticism are apparent in his writing, there is still a level of the authority of the Roman Catholic Church present in his works that he finds necessary to maintain. See Colish, *Medieval Foundations*, 169. Williams also notes when Anselm utilized *necessitas* rather than the Augustinian *convenientia* there was a methodological change, as the concept of "necessary" forms from a more logically oriented position than "fitting." While Anselm takes an understanding of the fittingness of Christ to be the savior, he methodologically sets to the task of demonstrating why it is logically necessary for the God-Man (incarnation), and how the purpose of the God-Man is to provide a satisfaction for the sins of humanity. See Williams, *Anselm: Communion and Atonement*, 26-27.

[137] CDH 1.1, 265.
[138] CDH 1.10, 282.

There is also a continuation into the second book of *Cur Deus Homo* coming from Boso:

> Let us now revert to making investigations about Christ in the manner we adopted at the outset: as if there were no such person.[139]

These two direct instances of the *remoto Christo* methodology that Anselm employs are intended to govern the outline of the argument for the purpose of proving the God-Man. The manner in which this is advanced is through a conversation that does not assume knowledge of Jesus Christ, but rather the state of humanity, the state of the world, the need for salvation, and the God-Man who achieves it. Therefore, the *remoto Christo* methodology is not a feature Anselm utilized in the *Praefatio* to later break from; rather it is the overarching method by which Anselm achieves an answer to the overarching question of the work itself in the *Cur Deus Homo*.

The pre-scholastic utilization of logic and dialectical study arose from the contextual milieu. It is not surprising then that Anselm would utilize these monastic disciplines to uphold the faith in an apologetic and systematic form of doctrine. This *remoto Christo* methodology would carry substantial weight and be reason enough to convert persons to the faith or even to garner further faith for those who read the *Cur Deus Homo*. But, again, one must consider how this methodology fits with the presuppositionary principle – the Augustinian tradition which Anselm claimed to hold. Visser and Williams have argued although Anselm believes he maintains the Augustinian tradition, he nonetheless makes a break from it through his method. While he desires to maintain the authority of the Scriptures, the doctrines and traditions of the Church, keep in step with his teacher Lanfranc, and even does a good job of making this statement in the introductory chapters of the majority of his work including the *Cur Deus Homo*, he is charting newfound territory by breaking from them throughout the body of his argument. It is this methodology that inherently contains *a priori* "from above" assumptions which shape the argument and its outcomes.

An A Priori Argument

How is it possible then for Anselm to concede salvation history on the one hand because of methodological concerns, and on the other hand, not explicate the entirety of the Christ event: incarnation, crucifixion, and resurrection? First, consider the nature of an *a priori* argument. An *a priori* argument assumes that no prior experience of a certain principle exists and that principles can be derived from logic which reveals them to be eternally, universally, and necessarily true.[140] Truth is expressed more in terms of logical certainty, as principles are shown to be logically true and the given response is acceptance of such principles because they are eternally, universally, and nec-

---

[139] CDH 2.10, 326.
[140] See Edgar S. Brightman. *A Philosophy of Religion*, Englewood Cliffs: Prentice Hall, 1940, 1-7.

essarily true. One finds from the beginning *a priori* methodological language in the *Cur Deus Homo*:

> By what logic or necessity did God become man, and by his death, as we believe and profess, restore life to the world, when he could have done this through the agency of some other person, angelic or human by simply willing it?[141]

> Let us posit, therefore, that the incarnation of God and the things which we say about him as man had never happened, and let it be agreed between us that man was created for a state of blessedness...[142]

Anselm looks to logic for the necessarily and universally true reason God became human. The reason behind this is the reason for the very faith the Roman Church professes.

This not only dismissed the authority of the Roman Church and salvation history contained in the Scriptures which the unbeliever could take issue with, but also allowed Anselm to remove the supernatural battle between God and the devil that humanity was helplessly caught between from the previous era by removing the rights of the devil from the argument altogether. This gave a certain kind of status to humanity, making the issue at hand an issue of submission. Instead, Anselm turned to a logical question that presses upon the intentionality of creation. The issue is:

> Where there is only a debtor who cannot pay, and a creditor who cannot be paid, common sense and logic equally suggest that the creditor must forever forgo his payment. He may punish or he may forgive, but he cannot be paid; and there is an air of subterfuge and unreality in any attempt to show that he can.... He had destroyed a satisfying triangle of divine, demonic, and human rights, and had left man and God facing each other with no go-between to bridge the gap.[143]

Logically, Anselm wants to prove why God became human and how by the death of that God-Man life was given to the world. The manner in which he does so is to utilize a form of argumentation that demonstrates his argument is eternally, universally, and necessarily true. By not utilizing Scripture, doctrine, or the like – sources which have historical and religious bias – he is able to place persons within the scope of an argument that makes the incarnation eternally, universally, and necessarily true. This is similar to his argument in the *Proslogion* as showing something to be rationally true by persons who can conceive of a being outside of their mind as being the greatest being. In the same way, Anselm wants to show that principles operating as universally true draw all people into the need for an *a priori* principle known as the God-Man. Thus, Anselm builds his argument in such a way to offer an *a priori* principle that the God-Man is the logical outcome to satisfy the logical requirement of a payment that the debtor cannot pay and the creditor must receive. This is

---

[141] CDH 1.1, 48.
[142] CDH 1.10, 282.
[143] Southern, *A Portrait*, 211.

the means by which the intent of the Creator God before the act of creation (again an *a priori* convention) is fulfilled.

Given this *a priori* assumption, now it is possible to turn to the end of the *Cur Deus Homo* and see how Anselm claimed this very thought through his interlocutor Boso:

> Let us contemplate now, as far as we are able, with what very great logicality human salvation follows from his death....There can be nothing more logical, nothing sweeter, nothing more desirable that the world can hear. I indeed derive such confidence from this teaching that I cannot now express in words what joy my heart is rejoicing. For it seems to me that God rejects no member of the human race who approaches him on this authority.[144]

Inherent in the *remoto Christo* methodology is an *a priori* assumption: if nothing were known about Jesus Christ – if one had no knowledge of who Jesus Christ was, is, or what he has done – persons would still come to the juncture where they could logically see the need for the salvation he offers. From the beginning of the *remoto Christo* methodology, Anselm continues what he has done in previous works: he suspends the authority of the materials of the Church – Scripture, doctrines, and tradition, and describes the human need of salvation that comes through the God-Man. This need, as well as the purpose and act of the God-Man are described principally, not historically; they are spoken of as though they could be independent of existence and as principles satisfying a necessary condition. This *a priori* methodology creates outcomes that emphasize the satisfaction of this logical schism between God and humanity by means of a penalty of death that stems from his own milieu. The greatest struggle is how this penalty does not consider the need for resurrection, and how resurrection (with the exception of small inferences from Anselm) is relegated to the periphery. Ultimately, this methodological commitment shapes his soteriological commitments; instead of Christology shaping soteriology, it is soteriology providing shape and scope to Christology.

A Theology from Above

Secondly, let us consider how this theology is a "theology from above." Wolfhart Pannenberg argues in *Jesus – God and Man*, that most Christologies are constructed from a "theology from above" perspective. This, Pannenberg argues, began in "Ignatius of Antioch and the second-century Apologists."[145] The key distinction in the above/below theology which Pannenberg delineates is how the above position focuses on the divinity of Jesus that rises through the incarnation, and how the below position focuses on the historical man Jesus who arrives at the recognition of his divinity through the resurrection.[146] This is important, as Pannenberg argues a Christology from above presupposes the divinity of Jesus and never deals with the question of "why

---

[144] CDH 2.19, 352-353.
[145] Pannenberg, *JGM*, 33.
[146] See Pannenberg, *JGM*, 33.

must the man who is engaged by God also be subjected to the universal human fate of death?"[147]

The above question was answered by Anselm but from an *a priori* perspective that situated persons into a logically inescapable predicament. The death of Jesus was a satisfactory response to a debt which persons were logically unable to repay. The incarnation is the requirement to make this death efficacious. This is an interesting development as the *Cur Deus Homo* is first a question about incarnation, although the document is easily construed as a methodological explanation of Christology from the perspective of the cross. The atonement theology in most of the Early Fathers considered the history contained within the Scriptures (thus an *a posteriori* argument), rather than situating persons within an eternally and necessarily true argument first, and then providing an eternally and necessarily true answer to the human situation and need as in Anselm. Whereas theology had been constructed in light of the history of God in Jesus Christ as contained in the Holy Scriptures and as practiced in the Church, the preface of *Cur Deus Homo* reveals something different:

> Eventually it proves by unavoidable logical steps, that, supposing Christ were left out of the case...it is impossible that, without him, any member of the human race could be saved. In the second book, similarly, the supposition is made that if nothing were known about Christ, and it is demonstrated with no less clear logic and truth...from necessity all things we believe about Christ have come to pass.[148]

So, the suspension of Scriptural authority, the utilization of a universally applicable *a priori* condition, and the *a priori* requirement of satisfaction requires Anselm to rely upon logic to make his argument – this is the genesis of the *remoto Christo* methodology.[149]

Perhaps the most interesting development concerns the fact that while most Christologies have developed from a "theology from above" position because of the assumption of the divinity of Jesus in the incarnation, Anselm methodologically employs an ahistorical, *a priori*, theology from above which shaped the whole of his argument and created further questions. Anselm describes a need for the death of Jesus because of the human condition of sin, and then completes the circle by assuming the divinity of Jesus while eliminating the history of Jesus. It is merely assumed that Jesus is the person who fulfilled this divine destiny – not some other martyr during the Maccabaean period or otherwise. Thus many questions arise: how can one know the God-Man made a sacrifice that was acceptable at all? Is this simply a blind faith persons are to place in the satisfaction Jesus provided by means of his death? It is the development of these kinds of questions, and the Christological emphasis of crucifixion at the expense of the resurrection thus rele-

---

[147] Pannenberg, *JGM*, 35.
[148] CDH Preface, 261-262.
[149] Ted Peters. *God: the World's Future*. Minneapolis: Augsburg Fortress Press, 1992, 212-213.

gating resurrection to the periphery, which shall be illustrated in the next chapter.

Cur Deus Homo: Methodology

Some summary remarks can now be offered relative to the *credo ut intelligam* presuppositionary principle and the *remoto Christo* methodology. As to the presuppositionary principle: (1) There is little doubt Anselm longed to remain within the Augustinian tradition as he utilized the Augustinian proof texts; (2) he desired to help people understand their faith – even addressing the works as meant for believing Christians while recognizing that his work would help unbelievers as well; (3) he does point to the necessity of belief before understanding throughout his works; and (4) Anselm took an important step in describing his presuppositionary principle for fear that persons would try to understand before they could believe typical of Roscelin. However, as to the *remoto Christo* methodology, it remains Anselm was a theologian unafraid to push the boundaries to challenge his context with well-reasoned logical arguments which suspended the materials of the Church such as the Scriptures and/or its doctrines and traditions. The methodology Anselm utilizes to craft his arguments is the challenge to the presuppositionary principle, occurring through his utilization of the Aristotelian tools of his milieu.

Logic and dialectical thought present in monasticism were important, as well as how Anselm possessed the tenets of what was later called scholasticism in his thought and writings. It is not so much the use of logic that sets Anselm apart from others, but more importantly the use of logic without the authority of the Scriptures or the tradition of the Church – this sets Anselm apart from his contemporaries. Anselm answered a milieu which sought answers that were well-reasoned, and the *Monologion* and *Proslogion* readily reveal this as he states within the initial sentences of his work that he is undertaking a pattern (*exemplum*) to answer the questions of his monks. The same holds true for the *Cur Deus Homo*. The thrust of his argument is to confute the unbelievers of his day, and these unbelievers were most likely Jewish persons and others who did not believe the central tenets of Christianity. What sets the *Cur Deus Homo* apart from some of the earlier works of Anselm is the high regard for logic within the scope of his argument, and the way that well-reasoned arguments contrast the more typical and long-standing arguments for the incarnation:

> By the time he writes *Cur Deus Homo*, however, he unabashedly acknowledges that he is doing something altogether new…Anselm does not go so far as to say that it is permissible to contradict the fathers, as opposed to merely supplementing them; but he does in fact reject a venerable patristic view through the arguments against the ransom theory that he puts into the mouth of Boso.[150]

---

[150] Visser and Williams, *Anselm*, 22-23.

Thus within the *Monologion, Proslogion, De Incarnatione Verbi,* and most notably the *Cur Deus Homo* there is at work Aristotelian methodology that subtly compromises the Augustinian *credo ut intelligam* principle. While McIntyre attempts to thoughtfully and semantically alleviate this issue, the issue nonetheless remains: Anselm from the preface of his materials seeks to build his arguments from reason, and not from the Scriptures which form the narrative for belief. It also seems apparent that Anselm builds these arguments from the position of those who do not believe toward the goal that they will understand which enables the possibility of belief. Though Anselm thoughtfully crafts his work with a devotional character and quality, appeals to the authority of the papacy, and claims the need for belief before understanding so as to remain within the Augustinian tradition, it remains clear in the *Monologion, Proslogion, and De Incarnatione Verbi* that his work is to provide a reason for one to believe. By the time that the *Cur Deus Homo* is written, the primary intended audience may have ultimately been unbelievers more than believers. Indeed, the *Cur Deus Homo* was written at least partly for those who believe, but it is so that those who believe can advance the case for the God-Man to those who do not believe. The manner in which Anselm does this is through a methodology that suspends the materials and traditions of the Church. His method of proving what is believed without holding to the core source of belief (i.e. the Scriptures, traditions, doctrines of the Church) in the first three writings mentioned above begins to set a precedent that is more evident in the *Cur Deus Homo* – that Anselm seeks to prove what should be believed, or better yet, that Anselm helps people arrive at the juncture in which they can or must believe.

1.1.4 Cur Deus Homo: Intelligo ut Credam?

Finally, from context, to presuppositionary principle, to methodological commitment, what is ultimately revealed is how the Aristotelian methodology compromises the Augustinian presupposition, thus juxtaposing it from *credo ut intelligam* to *"intelligo ut credam."*[151] Consider first the primary purposes of the *Cur Deus Homo* was to provide a theology of the atonement that eradicated the power of the devil (which the schools raised as an issue) and also as a means of confuting the Jewish opposition to incarnation. These two factors reveal Anselm had an apologetic purpose of this writing, whether explicitly stated or implicitly intended. This, from the outset, would methodologically tend to compromise a *credo ut intelligam* proposition. While some might think the utilization Anselm makes of logic is in some manner of speaking a capitulation to the audience of his day and their quest and desire for logic and dialectical thought, it was nonetheless an important issue and the means by which arguments were advanced. This was the growing demand of a world that was learning and growing in so many different spheres of life, and this became the answer of the monastic educational system to the challenges of the milieu. Moreover, while Anselm is systematic and doctrinal in the ap-

---

[151] See McIntyre, *St. Anselm and His Critics,* 5.

proach to his writings, they are even more, apologetic in orientation. Apologetics is not a *credo ut intelligam* undertaking; rather it is an undertaking of *intelligo ut credam*. His methodological undertaking concerned helping people come to a place in which the barriers are removed and belief becomes possible, although it is true that this is also dialectically charged so that the one learning the argument grows in his or her own belief or faith.

The lack of Scriptural authority in his works was most likely met with resistance from Lanfranc, as Anselm appealed to Lanfranc that nothing in his works lay outside the bounds of Scripture, Augustine, or the Early Fathers.[152] Given this lack of Scriptural authority and the preference for a utilization of logic, some question if Anselm had a boldness that challenged the authority of the Roman Catholic Church in his writings. For example, in the *Cur Deus Homo*, Anselm refutes the ransom theory of the atonement within the first book, a rather bold statement that challenges a more dominant atonement theme that set a precedent for hundreds of years.[153] Beyond some of the obvious conclusions one might draw about challenging this authority, one might also wonder if there is a refutation of a more supernatural oriented theology that was prevalent in days past. The dominant teaching of the Church during the primitive Middle Ages was the supernatural battle between good and evil and how the monk was "at war" in this reality.[154] Anselm "smiles assent while he triumphantly dismisses that theory to the limbo of grotesque fictions."[155] Also important is the exaltation of humanity that comes by way of the incarnation, a reality that was very fitting for people living in a world rising to find their own greatness. There are places in the argument where Anselm attempts to show his affinity with the doctrines of the Church, such as in 1.25 when his interlocutor Boso desires that he be brought to a place of understanding by means of that which the Roman Catholic Church teaches to believe. However, there remains at the end of the day a lack of the narrative of Scripture to support such teaching, and the doctrinal support is not explicit – it is only logically deduced at best.

Secondly, considering all that has been gained in this study of the *credo ut intelligam* presupposition that is intended to undergird the majority of the work of Anselm creates, and the *remoto Christo* methodology which relied heavily upon logic and reason, what the outcome reveals is that Anselm did more to reveal faith than uphold faith. At the very least, Anselm brought into dialectical tension faith and unfaith, and at the most Anselm in a brilliant manner pushed the Roman Catholic Church forward by challenging

---

[152] See Monologion – Preface.

[153] See CDH 1.6-1.7. Peter Schemiechen recapitulates the argument of Aulén, who claims that the ransom theory is the longest standing. See Peter Schemiechen. *Saving Power: Theories of Atonement and Forms of the Church*. Grand Rapids: William B. Eerdmans Publishing Company, 2005. See also Gustaf Aulén. *Christus Victor*, trans. by A.G. Herbert. London: SPCK, 1931.

[154] See 1.1.2.

[155] Rigg, *St. Anselm of Canterbury*, 170.

the boundaries of understanding to garner belief. Anselm may have wanted to maintain the Augustinian tradition and write from the basis of faith seeking understanding, but in the end he compromised his presuppositionary principle by means of a methodology that suspended not only Scripture but also the knowledge of Christ himself. Some who have raised questions have tried to downplay this by stating:

> Anselm's unusually high estimate of the power of human reason ultimately derives not from his confidence in human beings, but from his confidence in God – his conviction that God, who is supreme wisdom and exercises supreme wisdom in everything he does, has made human beings rational by nature.[156]

The above being said, the audience to whom Anselm was writing was a Christian audience who could utilize these works in debate with believers and unbelievers alike, a beloved pastime of his milieu.

Finally, the methodology he utilized compromised and also juxtaposed his presupposition. This methodological move leads to a Christology that is shaped through the cross and subsequently the incarnation at the expense of the resurrection, and Christology easily becomes a rational inference or transaction to be cognitively affirmed rather than a revelation that comes from salvation history. Anselm has an *a posteriori* knowledge of the history of Jesus Christ, but it is this history that cannot be bifurcated from faith. This is the same flawed methodological presupposition as is in Kant and the modernist existentialist movement; attempts to bifurcate faith from history in the empiricist and rationalist movements eventuated into a supernaturalism that had a God who was unknowable, and then from this unknowable God, a "death of God" theology emerged in Feuerbach and Nietzsche.[157] While faith indeed is rational, it cannot be bifurcated from history as if the history of Jesus Christ was a non-essential matter.[158] Rational thought is meant to interpret the history of God, and help one toward faith, not to eliminate the history of God and become a replacement for faith. Given this outcome in chapter two (1.1), this unit now shall now turn to consider the soteriology of Anselm in chapter three (1.2) as the concluding piece of this first unit, and the means by which Anselm conceives of an *a priori* Christology from above via the cross and incarnation at the expense of the resurrection, relegating it to the periphery.

---

[156] Visser and Williams, *Anselm*, 17.
[157] See Laurence Wood. *God and History*. USA: Emeth Press, 2005, 252. See also Laurence Wood. *Theology as History and Hermeneutics: A Post-Critical Conversation with Contemporary Theology*. USA: Emeth Press, 2005, 133.
[158] This is a point that Wolfhart Pannenberg holds in Wolfhart Pannenberg. *Faith and Reality*. Philadelphia: Westminster Press, 1977, viii, 6-7.

Chapter Three

Cur Deus Homo and Soteriology

The primary soteriological question Anselm seeks to answer in *Cur Deus Homo* is this:

> *By what logic or necessity* did God become man, *and by his death*, as we believe and profess, restore life to the world, when he could have done this through the agency of some other person, angelic or human, or simply by willing it.[159]

This statement raises two important questions: (1) How does the *remoto Christo* methodology set forth in the *Praefatio* and the phrase "*qua scilicet ratione vel necessitate deus homo factus sit*"[160] from *Cur Deus Homo* 1.1 shape the inclusion or exclusion of salvation history into the response Anselm formulates to his question and more importantly, (2) why is the primary emphasis of restoring life to the world fixated upon death (*et morte sua*) rather than by some other method? Finally, how do these methodological emphases shape the soteriological outcomes, which form the central point of not only the *Cur Deus Homo* but also Anselmian Christology?

Recall that chapter one (1.0) presented specific features of the Anselmian milieu including monasticism, pre-scholasticism, feudalism, and medieval penance. These contextual features shaped the writings of Anselm including the *Cur Deus Homo*. This became identifiable in the opening section of the second chapter (1.1), as it was demonstrated how the *Cur Deus Homo* itself rose out of the theological debates from the secular schools and criticisms of Christian doctrine which stemmed from Jewish communities in Western Europe.[161] Anselm desired to respond to the challenge and attempted to balance an Augustinian presuppositionary principle of the pre-

---

[159] CDH 1.1, 265, (italics mine).

[160] CDH *Praefatio*, Schmitt, 48. "By what logic or necessity did God become man or human" is inherent of his *remoto Christo* methodology that is of a logic-oriented Aristotelian origin. Here Anselm is chiefly concerned not with the materials of salvation history but the reason it was necessary for God to become human because of a historical or even existential condition indicating human soteriological need. As shall be revealed momentarily, this is an important distinction for the manner in which Anselm crafts his answer to the question *Cur Deus Homo*.

[161] See Asiedu, *Theological Studies, Vol. 62*, 533-541. See also Southern, *A Portrait*, 197. This point is referenced in further detail in chapter two, (1.1.1, (20-23)).

vious era (*credo ut intelligam*) and an Aristotelian methodology (*remoto Christo*) of his current era. Thus, his response was fashioned in a manner in which Anselm had already proved himself capable of offering by means of his logically formulated answers which did not require utilization of Scripture or materials of the Church. It was the *remoto Christo* methodology that compromised this presuppositionary principle of *credo ut intelligam* juxtaposing it to *intelligo ut credam*. While Anselm desired to maintain his presupposition and may have even intended his works to be of an intensely devotional nature, the methodological commitments Anselm made stood in contrast to the Augustinian tradition which utilized the Scriptures and materials of the Church, and called for believing before understanding.[162] Ironically, this methodological commitment concurrently allowed Anselm to communicate new thought, meeting the demands of his era.

Ultimately, the Anselmian context, as well as the presupposition and methodology Anselm utilized, eventuated the outcome of the primary topic of this chapter – soteriology. The questions respective to why Anselm looked to logic and the death of Jesus referenced above can be answered three-fold: (1) Anselm exchanges salvation history for feudal history (2) through this soteriological approach, he methodologically expresses Christology through cross at the expense of the resurrection, relegating resurrection to the periphery, thus deriving salvation as a logical transaction by means of a satisfaction oriented understanding of crucifixion[163]; and (3) finally, the Anselmian Chris-

---

[162] While G.R. Evans claims Augustine raised questions for Anselm in his *De Trinitate*, it still remains Anselm did not follow his methodology. By suspending the materials of salvation history and doctrines of the church (even though there may be implicit use of them at points in the CDH corpus), Anselm attempts to demonstrate the reason or logic of faith rather than explain how by faith one can logically understand. See Evans, *Anselm and Talking About God*, 154-155. In this same regard, McIntyre is helpful as he raised the question of a challenge due to the methodology Anselm employs respective to this issue. See McIntyre, *St. Anselm and His Critics*, 1-7. Hogg disagrees with this as he contends that intellectual persuasion is not the same as faith. See Hogg, *St. Anselm of Canterbury*, 157-160. Hogg is correct to claim that intellectual persuasion is not the same as faith. However, one might challenge Hogg by pointing out that the argument suspends faith and the knowledge of Christ to demonstrate via logic and dialectic that the God-Man (who is consequently the Christ) is necessary.

[163] *Satisfactio* is often utilized for making amends or reparations, or a satisfaction of a certain kind of punishment. Satisfaction is a term used by Anselm that stems from the Latin Vulgate in Mark 15:15, Acts 17:9 and 1 Peter 3:15. One of the key texts in CDH is 2.6, as it is necessary for the God-Man to repay the sin debt of humanity and offended honor of God. Augustine and Tertullian have utilized this terminology in the payment of ransom for redemption in speaking of the death of Christ. See H.D. McDonald. *The Atonement of the Death of Christ: In Faith, Revelation and History*. Grand Rapids: Baker Bookhouse, 1985, 168. Satisfaction also concerns "divine action in setting right that which has been thrown out of kilter by human sin." Gunton argues that this is the manner in which Anselm describes the act of God within the Triune relation, offered on behalf of humanity. It is noteworthy to mention Gunton focuses on the death of Jesus as a free act given unto God the Father out of obedience. See

tology features a Christ whose primary work is to satisfy the dishonor done unto God by his death which lends important influence to future Christologies featuring satisfaction as a primary purpose of atonement and the incarnation of Jesus Christ.

Thus, the third chapter shall bring this first unit of work to its conclusions in chapter four, demonstrating the interrelatedness of milieu, presupposition and methodology, and soteriology, offering clarity concerning how the Anselmian Christology is shaped methodologically by the cross as the incarnational question Anselm asked was answered with a crucifixional theme. While Anselm certainly met the demands and answered the questions of his milieu, he did so with important Christological implications. These implications shall later be compared and contrasted with Pannenbergian Christology which is constructed through a methodology from below via the retroactive significance of the resurrection of Jesus Christ.

1.2.1 *Cur Deus Homo*: An Exchanged Salvation History

In beginning, the initial question raised above is of great importance: "By what *logic* or *necessity* did God become man [human]?"[164] As 1.1.2 revealed, the *remoto Christo* methodology raised in the *Praefatio* was employed to answer this question, and it is that methodology which shaped the suspension of salvation history into the response Anselm formulates. What shall be demonstrated throughout 1.2.1 concerns how the contextual and methodological commitments from chapters one and two eventuate an exchange of salvation history for feudal history. The means by which this occurs is two-fold: (1) *first* through an *intellectual milieu* that desires logic as its primary means of argumentation, and (2) *secondly* through a *cultural milieu* that features feudalism as its primary hermeneutic for understanding the hierarchy of social order and relationships. The intellectual milieu creates room for the Anselmian *remoto Christo* methodology which contains an *a priori* theology from above, in addi-

---

Colin E. Gunton. *The Actuality of Atonement: A Study of Metaphor, Rationality, and the Christian Tradition*. Grand Rapids: William B. Eerdmans Publishing, 1989, 91-92. McIntyre takes satisfaction to be a payment term that God not only demands, but also provides for. He describes this as being analogous to public and private law, although (as he suggests) Anselm shows that it is incomparable because it is in relationship to God. Moreover he views satisfaction as a means of satisfying the dishonor done to God by humanity and regards the payment of satisfaction in terms of degrees – and in this case the degree is of the highest possible degree. See McIntyre, *St. Anselm and His Critics*, 76-95. Hopkins argues that Anselm sought to reform the Augustinian theory of ransom because it failed to explain the need for the incarnation. This is important for how Anselm will use satisfaction, as it is a break from the tradition of ransom. Rather, Anselm pointed to the necessity of someone within the scope of humanity without sin to satisfy the condition of redemption for the human race. See Hopkins, *A Companion to the Study of St. Anselm*, 187-212.

[164] CDH 1.1, 265 (italics mine).

tion to the possibility of eradicating the devil from the atonement debate, and the cultural milieu creates room for understanding the person and work of Christ as a necessity to satisfy the offended honor of God providing salvation for humanity. Thus, the intellectual and cultural milieu shape the theological commitments of Anselm and provide for an exchange of salvation history for feudal history. This exchange posits salvation as a crucifixional transaction relegating resurrection to the periphery (1.2.2), and these Anselmian commitments shall lend important influence to future Christologies.

The Intellectual Milieu

Chapter one revealed that Anselm lived at the crossroads of change, and logic and dialectic drove the educational system. The Rule of St. Benedict provided a structure of obedience and permanence to once ordinary men, and now these once ordinary men were warriors in the War of ultimate significance. The growth of logic and dialectic became even more pronounced after 1050. The Norman Conquest created opportunities for those once considered intellectually underdeveloped to develop their cognitive capabilities. Investments in building the monastic system were made and libraries grew. History, philosophy, dialectical theology, and political theories were developed. Theological doctrines and common laws were codified. Education slowly overcame pervasive superstitions and supernaturalism, and human experience became the primary vehicle for knowing God. The growth of the monastic and secular schools began to rationally consider human life and came to the realization that humanity was able to understand the structure of reality through both special revelation and human effort in the mind. Further extension of this intelligibility was recognition that the mysteries God had used to redeem mankind by the incarnation and sacrifice of Christ on the cross were also capable of being understood. Dialectic and debate were important methods of learning in the monastic and secular schools, which raised an important question of how persons were able to know truth; was it by belief and the revelation of God, or by reason? These types of questions began to frame a developing struggle of how to be thoroughly Christian and not heretical, and the anti-dialecticians such as Lanfranc began their quest to keep the Scriptures, doctrines, and materials of the Roman Catholic Church as primary and authoritative.[165] Lanfranc, the teacher of Anselm, taught Anselm to stay within the Augustinian tradition of maintaining the authority of the Scriptures and doctrines of the Church. More specifically, when Lanfranc did not respond to the *Monologion*, it is possible to see that Lanfranc was making the same point he did to Berengar in an earlier debate concerning Scriptural authority and the utilization of logic. Accordingly, Anselm began a new work in

---

[165] This is a recapitulation of elements of chapter one. These elements which are important in the Anselmian context shall be illumined momentarily to demonstrate an exchange of salvation history for feudal history. The intellectual milieu was important for this exchange that occurs within the CDH.

the *Proslogion* with an intensely devotional introduction built from Scripture.[166]

Given these elements from the intellectual milieu, the very manner in which the primary question of the *Cur Deus Homo* is structured becomes lucid: why was it logically necessary for God to become human? Taking into consideration the intellectual milieu and its commitment to the utilization of logic, and considering the previous milieu and its emphasis upon the authority of Scripture and the materials of the Roman Church, the *remoto Christo* methodology which suspends the salvation history of Jesus Christ for an *a priori* theology from above is more easily understood.[167] The question raised and the methodology employed is first born out of the challenges of the monks who wanted explanations independent of Scriptural and doctrinal authority, secondly from the challenges of the schools, and thirdly from the challenges of Western European Jews against the incarnation and the degradation of God due to the death of Jesus Christ. Given these currents within the intellectual milieu, it is not surprising that from the outset of the *Cur Deus Homo* Anselm would utilize a methodology of logic and dialectic, and a disputation oriented dialogue as was common in monastic and secular schools. This would not only offer a well-delineated response, but concurrently dispute various anticipated objections. Accordingly, Anselm utilized this format in which he was the teacher and Boso the interlocutor, student, and mouthpiece for those who raise objections to the Christian faith.[168] While Boso was indeed a Christian, he is also portrayed as a conversation partner representing unbelievers. Boso presents objections that seem contrary to reason, and is led throughout the corpus to a position in which reason proves to him that even if nothing were known about Jesus Christ, it is impossible for humanity to be saved without him.[169] While *credo ut intelligam* is claimed as the outlying purpose, there is seemingly a greater force at work: to help those who do not believe come to understanding so that they may believe. Faith working in dialectical tension with unfaith is another evidence for the utilization of logic inherent in this argument.

Beyond the structure and form of the *Cur Deus Homo* which arose due to the intellectual milieu, the very phrase, "By what logic or necessity did God become man,"[170] is a rational undertaking, imbued with monastic underpin-

---

[166] For more explanation, see chapter two (1.1.1, (20-25)).

[167] Theology from above references a Christological methodology proceeding from the incarnation and the assumption that Jesus Christ was divine. See, for example, Pannenberg, *JGM*. This shall be an important distinction in chapters five and six (2.1 and 2.2). Later in this section (1.2.1), it shall be demonstrated that Anselm took a Chalcedonian ontological position which likely helped to accentuate the incarnation and cross to the expense of the resurrection, thus relegating it to the periphery of his Christology.

[168] See Asiedu, *Theological Studies, Vol. 62*, 530-547. See also Hopkins, *A Companion to the Study of St. Anselm*, 165-166. See also Southern, *A Portrait*, 203-205.

[169] See CDH 1.25.

[170] See CDH 1.1.

nings. In essence, Anselm utilized contemplative reason to gain understanding of the incarnation.[171] Anselm sees the incarnation as a necessity signaling an *a priori* precondition; the incarnation is necessary because of an existing condition of human sin that offends the honor of God, providing the reason for the incarnation of Jesus Christ.[172] Jesus Christ then actively and obediently offers himself as an act of penitential supererogation on behalf of humanity for their sins which offended the honor of God, and it is that offer which ultimately satisfies the offended honor of God. Anselm spends much time focusing upon this issue from CDH 1.11-1.25 and 2.2-2.6. In fact, twenty of the forty-seven chapters in the *Cur Deus Homo* contain some delineation of the precondition which made it rationally and logically necessary for God to become human so that the honor of God could be restored and humanity might be blessedly happy. Thus, Anselm spends a good deal of space to lead his interlocutor Boso in an argument in which Boso (and therefore all believers and unbelievers) will come to see the incarnation is logically necessary because humanity is incapable of repaying the offended honor of God:

> You have brought me by logical reasoning to this point, so that I might see that man owes to God for his sin something which he is incapable of paying back, and cannot be saved unless he repays it.[173]

In the form of a scholarly debate, and suspending the Scriptures containing the salvation history of Jesus Christ and materials of the Church, Anselm created a logical case for sin and the offense to the honor of God. While some claim the logical case of Anselm for the incarnation is not as important as the missional one presented in the *Cur Deus* Homo, they fail to realize that through his rational argument Anselm has situated his audience in a place of great need by helping them logically reason the magnanimous

---

[171] See Glenn Olsen. "Hans Urs Von Balthasar and the Rehabilitation of St. Anselm's Doctrine of the Atonement." *Scottish Journal of Theology* Vol. 34. Edinburg: Scottish Academic Press, 1981, 54. This is an important distinction as some have noted (most particularly Southern and Schufreider) that there is a contrast between the treatises of Anselm and the reflective or devotional material of Anselm. Whereas the treatises possess great faith and certainty in what is written, the devotional materials reveal much anxiety. Both Southern and Schufreider are helpful here in that they contend the faith-unfaith dialectic (similar to what Hopkins proposes) is the outworking of monastic life and is thus apropos to questions of the milieu and the specific question present in the CDH. See Southern, *A Portrait*, 103-105. See Gregory Schufreider. *Confessions of a Rational Mystic: Anselm's Early Writings*. West Lafayette: Purdue University Press, 1994, 12-13. See also Bestul, *Anselm and Abelard*, 57-60.

[172] Jasper Hopkins argues that this is the primary explanation of *Cur Deus Homo* and is thus his doctrine of the atonement. See Hopkins, *A Companion to the Study of St. Anselm*. Glenn Olsen also takes this position in his understanding of St. Anselm's doctrine of atonement through a trinitarian lens. See Olsen, *Scottish Academic Press, 1981*, 49-61. Visser and Williams are similar to this as they claim Anselm seeks to give the reason for "what Christ must do so then people will see who Christ must be." See Visser and Williams, *Anselm*, 213.

[173] CDH 1.25, 314.

consequences of sin, and how they as sinners are unable to repay such a debt.[174] This creates the logical precondition for the God-Man, and more importantly the way for a satisfaction of a magnanimous debt owed unto God through him. Most interesting about this *a priori* precondition is how it makes the focus of the argument the need of humanity rather than the revelation of God in history through the Son, Jesus Christ. While revelation is important to Anselm, this is of secondary importance to the human need for its magnanimous debt to be satisfied because of an inherent human precondition. This focus is a feature of the intellectual milieu as it places emphasis on logic, and more importantly begins placing humanity at the center of existence rather than God.[175]

Building from this *a priori* precondition for a need of the God-Man, is the working of an *a priori remoto Christo* methodology. Mentioned in chapter two (1.1.3), this methodological commitment does not explicitly utilize the Scriptures and the salvation history contained therein to make a case for the God-Man. Rather, it begins from a posture of unbelief and human need. This commitment relocates salvation history from the forefront, and while Anselm intends the salvation history contained in the Scriptures to be a confirmatory corpus to the logic in the argument, he nonetheless utilizes little of the Scriptures as the primary shaping narrative for belief within the corpus itself. To be sure, there are glimpses of Scripture throughout[176] but it is typically utilized to confirm what has already been rationally delineated:

> All the things which you say to me seem logical and incontrovertible. All my understanding is that, through the solution given to the single problem which we set ourselves, all that is contained in the New Testament and Old has been proved….The God-Man himself it is who established the New

---

[174] See Olsen who along with von Balthasar claims Anselm is more or less interested in the mission of Christ, not so much the rational grounds of the incarnation in the *Cur Deus Homo*. See Olsen, *Scottish Academic Press, 1981*, 52. Given the objections of communities in Western Europe, this is a plausible understanding, although there is some difficulty in claiming mission is somehow separate from the reason for the incarnation.

[175] See Southern who argues that reason takes precedence over historical events during this time period. Southern, *Medieval Humanism and Other Studies*, 10.

[176] For example, Anselm utilizes Scripture for his presuppositionary principle in CDH 1.1, posits the death of Christ "annuls" the "bond of the decree against us" (Col. 2:14) in 1.7, describes the obedience of Christ in 1.8 (Rom. 8:31, John 6:38, 14:31, 18:11) and furthers this with the teaching in 1.9 (Luke 10:22, John 16:15). The point to be made here is that Scripture takes a confirmatory (rather than guiding) position of this work. Moreover, while it would be impossible for Anselm to eradicate Scripture from his memory, it operates at best subtly and implicitly, especially given the fact that Anselm utilizes a methodology which suspends the explicit utilization of such materials, and more importantly attempts to demonstrate the logical human need for a God-Man. Daniel Deme is important here as he claims that while one should consider the CDH as one of his works among many (including his devotional works), Anselm does not include the historical acts of Jesus Christ in his treatises due to his context. See Deme, *The Christology of Anselm of Canterbury*, 185-186.

Testament and confirms the Old. Therefore, in the same way that it is a necessity to acknowledge that the God-Man is truthful, likewise no one can fail to acknowledge that all that is contained in those Testaments is true.[177]

These words from Boso at the end of the entire argument demonstrate how Scripture has taken primarily a confirmatory position. The *a priori, remoto Christo* methodology has been utilized as a feature of the milieu, suspending Scripture and the materials of the Church so as to not utilize authoritative traditions, opting for logic instead.

The final element to consider in the intellectual milieu is an underlying desire to eradicate the devil from the scope of atonement in the *Cur Deus Homo*.[178] It has been argued the ransom theory of atonement had the longest standing place in the understanding of atonement, although the question to whom the ransom was paid varies.[179] The place of the devil became a standing debate occurring in the schools, and the struggle concerned the tension between the older framework of war happening between God and the devil in which humanity believed it participated, and the newer intellectual milieu that desired logical reasons for belief. The debate concerned a ransom oriented theology of incarnation, atonement, and resurrection fixating upon a payment necessary to free persons from the grasp of the devil,[180] and the incarnational question asked by Western European Jews who claimed the incarnation (not to mention crucifixion) of Jesus Christ was a degradation of the honor of God.[181] The older ransom theology posited:

> The Deity was hidden under the veil of our nature, that so, as with ravenous fish, the hook of the Deity might be gulped down along with the bait of flesh, and thus, life being introduced into the house of death, and light shining in darkness, that which is diametrically opposed to light and life might vanish; for it is not in the nature of darkness to remain when light is present, or of death to exist when life is active.[182]

---

[177] CDH 2.22, 355-356.

[178] This is a generally accepted point given the argument from 1.6-1.7 and the debates in the schools. See a variety of sources with respect to the eradication of the devil from the atonement argument, most notably, Gwenfair W. Walters. "The Atonement in Medieval Theology." *The Glory of the Atonement* ed. by Charles E. Hill and Frank A. James III. Downers Grove: Intervarsity Press, 2004, 241-242. See also Southern, *A Portrait*, 207-211.

[179] Schemiechen recapitulates Aulén, who claims the ransom theory is the longest standing. See Peter Schemiechen. *Saving Power: Theories of Atonement and Forms of the Church*. Grand Rapids: William B. Eerdmans Publishing Company, 2005, 1995. See also Aulén, *Christus Victor*.

[180] The ransom theory espoused here better fits Gregory of Nyssa than Irenaeus, who originated the ransom theology.

[181] For a more complete explanation, refer to the previous chapter. See chapter two, (1.1.1).

[182] Gregory of Nyssa. "The Great Catechism." *Readings in the History of Christian Thought*, ed. Robert L. Ferm. New York: Holt, Rinehart, and Winston, 1964, 24.

This debate that arose in the schools concerning the older theology allowed opportunity for the work of the *Sententiae* to develop. The *Sententiae* took the work of previous persons concerning ransom atonement and recapitulated it into a more rationalistic exchange:

> God became man because man was delivered into the power of the devil, but the devil overstepped his power by subjecting a sinless man to punishment for sin, and it is this sinless man (Christ) who rescues man from the power of the devil.[183]

The *Sententiae* maintained the older paradigm, but utilized logical argumentation which posited that the consequences of sin are in turn applied to a sinless person who should not have been punished. Because this is the case, redemption is possible because the rights of the honorable have been unjustly offended.

When Anselm wrote *Cur Deus Homo*, one can readily see he objects to the rights of the devil altogether and lobbies for a different approach that looks to logic:

> By what logic or necessity did God become man, and by his death, as we believe and profess, restore life to the world, when he could have done this through the agency of some other person, angelic or human, or simply by willing it.[184]

While others looked to the battle between God and the devil as reason for the incarnation, Anselm eradicates it from the solution altogether. As CDH 1.7 unfolds, Anselm claims the devil has no jurisdiction over man and that God was not obliged to act against the devil by means of justice but rather by mighty power.[185] Anselm argues humanity and the devil both belong to God and both stand inside the realm of the all-reaching power of God. Accordingly, God acted in such a way that humanity, who deserved to be punished (although not by the devil because the devil had no merit to inflict the punishment), deserved the punishment from the one offended – God. Yet, the one who was offended became incarnate and died to satisfy the offended honor of God to free humanity altogether. Anselm concludes 1.7 by stating:

> There was nothing in the devil, therefore, which made God obliged not to use his mighty power against him for the purpose of liberating mankind.[186]

Therefore, the intellectual milieu shaped the argument by lobbying for the logic of the incarnation while also eradicating the tendencies of the

---

[183] Southern, *A Portrait*, 204. This was demonstrated in chapter one. See chapter one, (1.1.1, (13-15)).
[184] CDH 1.1, 265.
[185] See CDH 1.7. The chapter heading reads: "that the devil had no jurisdiction over man (humanity)," 272. (*Quod nullam diabolus habebat iustitiam adversus hominem*), 55. Visser and Williams note that one chapter later in 1.8, Anselm has quickly shown there is no obligation for God to repay the devil. See Visser, and Williams, *Anselm*, 214.
[186] CDH 1.7, 274.

previous era that placed the saints against the forces of evil in a spiritual war of sorts. The death of Jesus Christ satisfies the offended honor of God.

Ultimately, the intellectual milieu shaped the presentation of the *Cur Deus Homo* so that salvation history has been exchanged for the logic of an *a priori* need for a God-Man. The crucifixion provides a solution to satisfy the honor of God, and more importantly, these events satisfy an *a priori* precondition (e.g. sin and the offended honor of God) which prevents humanity from being blessedly happy.[187] This, in turn, provides the logical reason for the incarnation. However there is an issue. *A priori* Christologies assume the divinity of Jesus Christ which is problematic. One cannot assume the incarnation to be true on the basis of an *a priori* condition. True, while there are starting points to theology and unavoidable presuppositions, the resurrection serves as key confirmation of the crucifixion and incarnation, and more importantly the divinity of Jesus Christ altogether. Perhaps this is a key fault of the *Cur Deus Homo*; while a God-Man may be necessary to provide a satisfaction via the cross for a magnanimous debt for those who cannot pay such a debt, it does not take into account the resurrection which shows this sacrifice to be satisfactory and/or demonstrate whether or not Jesus Christ is the God-Man. Rather, the CDH demonstrates a God-Man is logically necessary, and argues the satisfaction from this God-Man provides salvation to those who have offended the honor of God. This posits salvation to be a transactional event by which persons trust in the satisfactory transaction of the God-Man (i.e. the crucifixion) for which the God-Man came to exist (i.e. the incarnation). While some have claimed Anselm provided a work justifying the indignities offered to God in Christ because they provided a "rectification" of the universe,[188] they make this claim from an *a posteriori* perspective that does not account for an *a priori* argument. Anselm in responding to the intellectual milieu utilized an Aristotelian methodology relegating the Augustinian presupposition and historicity of the incarnation, crucifixion, and resurrection to the periphery to emphasize the human precondition and need for salvation through the God who becomes human in Jesus Christ to satisfy this offended honor of God. Abelard later asked why punishment upon the Son when it can simply be forgiven?

The Cultural Milieu

Having demonstrated how the demands and emphases of the intellectual milieu favored the movement of salvation history to the periphery, what was the exchange? The previous section indicated how Anselm responded to the intellectual milieu by utilizing logic to make the case for the incarnation of the God-Man via a methodological commitment creating the potentiality for an exchange of salvation history for something else. This section therefore

---

[187] For example see CDH 1.3 and 2.1, 268, 315-316.

[188] Southern, *A Portrait*, 212. Similarly Peter Schmiechen calls the *Cur Deus Homo* a "restoration of creation." See Schemiechen, *Saving Power: Theories of Atonement*, 194-221.

shall demonstrate how the cultural milieu was the answer to such an exchange in the *Cur Deus Homo*. The hierarchy of the social and relational structures in the Anselmian milieu in terms of feudal lord and vassal, the outworking of such relationships through a process of reciprocity in honor and patronage exchanges, and the penance and justice systems that upheld the hierarchy and its processes are found in the *Cur Deus Homo*. Thus the cultural conventions of the Anselmian era became the exchanged choice in place of salvation history, which imbues the *Cur Deus Homo*.

In beginning, feudalism was a key way of understanding relationships and the cultural and societal structures, principles, and agreements that comprised life. At its heart was a society of vassals, feudal lords, and justice, upon which fiefs or estates were held contractually in exchange for military service. As the J.H. Round thesis has indicated, from the time of William the Conqueror onward, feudalism was key to understanding medieval social life in England.[189] The manner in which this system imposed upon the milieu is far too ranging to begin to explicate here. What can generally be said is that anyone other than a king was a vassal of differing levels, and this social structure dominated society. The feudal lord provided protection as well as land and economic benefits in exchange for honor from the vassals who appeared at court to pay homage to the feudal lord. The expectations and service required (both military and appearances at court for example) provided a means of security, salvation even, in a world of constant intellectual, social, and political change. Even the monastic system thrived on a derivative of this system as the abbot functioned as a feudal lord and a variety of vassals existed, ranging from novice to fully embraced monk. In exchange for the teaching and safety of the monastery, the monk was "at war" in devotion to God and busy within the monastery walls so that the monastic system could continue to perpetuate itself.

The first question stemming from this understanding of relationships in the cultural milieu in terms of its connection with the *Cur Deus Homo* is namely, "Does this, and if so, how does this conceptualization of relationships between feudal lord and vassal present itself in the *Cur Deus Homo?*" Key is the orientation of feudal lord and vassal when it comes to the Anselmian concept of the offended honor of God and the dishonor done unto God by humanity. Sin and the offended honor of God can be seen as a negation of the feudal contract. The idea of satisfaction as a payment of the highest degree to satisfy this offended honor demonstrates at least a partial feudal analogy to medieval systems of law in the public and private sector.[190] The feudal system of justice posited the feudal lord to sit in judgment over his subordinates as both protector and punisher, which determined the fate and destiny of the lives of subordinates. Even the Roman Catholic Church had its own courts that were structured from a feudal perspective as they exercised power over their subordinates.[191]

---

[189] See chapter one, (1.0, (15-17)). See Round, *The Introduction of Knight Service*.
[190] See McIntyre, *St. Anselm and His Critics*, 79-80.
[191] See Bloch, *Feudal Society*, 360-362.

Obedience was an important reality in the cultural milieu in terms of the relational hierarchy between the feudal lord who demanded obedience and the vassal who was required to give obedience. Legal contracts dating back to the eight century exist in which men said to their new lords:

> As long as I live I give you service and obedience, benefitting my free status, and will not have the power to withdraw from your authority and protection.[192]

This relational understanding between feudal lord and vassal was legally binding until death. Similarly, one can look to the feudal orientation of relationships in the monastic communities who claimed permanence and obedience, as foundational elements of Benedictine Rule. These elements within the cultural context of feudalism find their way into the heart of the *Cur Deus Homo* as Anselm speaks of dishonor done to God, satisfaction needing to be made as a payment to God, and the obedience of Jesus the God-Man to God.

Pertinent to the feudal nature of the *Cur Deus Homo* as it relates to God (feudal lord) and humanity (vassal),[193] is the relationship Anselm describes between Jesus and the God he called Father and the importance of the word *oboedientia* in this relationship. Perhaps one of the most important expressions of *oboedientia* is the manner in which Anselm deals with both the freedom of Jesus Christ in his acceptance of his own death (i.e. the death that is a penitential act of supererogation that satisfies the offenses done unto God) and the necessity of this death to forgive humanity of its sins.[194] The

---

[192] Hoyt and Chodorow. *Europe in the Middle Ages*, 213.

[193] See Southern, *A Portrait*, 222-227. Southern is in agreement with McIntyre who claims the argument is feudal. See McIntyre, *St. Anselm and His Critics*, 76-95. Southern will go farther than McIntyre in his approach claiming that Anselm utilized his milieu of feudalism and monasticism to draw imagery as connectives for readers. Moreover, in his milieu he saw structure, order, and similarity with the sense of order as created by God. Green and Baker also claim that the feudal imagery is unmistakable in the *Cur Deus Homo*. See Green and Baker, *Recovering the Scandal of the Cross*. Colin Gunton also claims that the justice dimension within the Anselmian idea of satisfaction posits God as a "rather testy monarch punishing offenses against his personal honor." See Gunton, *The Actuality of Atonement*, 95. Hogg is silent on the issue of feudalism in his work, giving no space to its treatment. See Hogg, *Anselm of Canterbury*. Visser and Williams are similar in this regard, giving no treatment to feudalism. See Visser and Williams, *Anselm*. Deme is also mostly silent, claiming the imagery is Pauline. See Deme, *The Christology of Anselm of Canterbury*. One can observe how a disregard for context provides an incomplete understanding into the CDH, and how then, some authors take a purely textual approach without consideration for the sources from which Anselm built his treatises.

[194] Gunton demonstrates the Trinitarian language in Anselm and his theology of satisfaction, obedience is not a legal reality in which a penalty is taken out upon Jesus as a human being. Rather, the obedience is found in Jesus as God-Man who is obedient to the will of the Father. See Gunton, *The Actuality of Atonement*, 91-93. Deme looks to how Anselm understood obedience as a willful attitude that is important for the collective character of Christ, and is likely reflected from his participation in the

expression of *oboedientia* through acceptance, willingness, and necessity is found in 1.8-1.10, 2.11, and most notably 2.16-2.19. Anselm understood the relationship between Jesus and the God whom he called Father through the word *oboedientia*. *Oboedientia* carries these lexical senses:

> Listening or paying attention to; obeying, submitting to; and acting in accordance with the demands of a particular situation of, being a slave to a specific vice, or being responsive to.[195]

While the lexical senses of listening or acting in accordance with the demands of a particular situation imply some level of freedom, one must immediately ask who is setting the stage for the necessity of *oboedientia* in the first place? If it is God the Father, it seems there is great potentiality in a feudal lord/vassal type relationship within the Triune relation. In this regard, Boso pushes Anselm in his understanding of the Scriptures and the *oboedientia* of Jesus Christ to God the Father in his death, and Anselm summarizes 1.8 by stating:

> Everywhere here it is apparent that Christ endured death under the compulsion of obedience, rather than through the intention of his own free will.[196]

Dániel Deme argues Anselm builds his theology of obedience around the "two wills in Christ," which is a Chalcedonian Christological position.[197] Jesus Christ in his divinity has perfect obedience, and it is the obedience in his divinity that is upheld in his humanity. This creates an elimination of human obedience so that the divine obedience becomes the one will of Jesus Christ. This, in turn, facilitates the restoration of humanity which Jesus Christ began.[198] Essentially, this calls for the elimination of human will

---

Benedictine community. As such, his obedience as a monk is typical of the obedience of Christ to his Father. This obedience, as Deme claims, Anselm believes is due God from every human being. See Deme, *The Christology of Anselm of Canterbury*, 191-197.

[195] *Oxford Latin Dictionary*. Oxford: The Clarendon Press, 1968, 1217.

[196] CDH 1.8, 276.

[197] Deme, *The Christology of Anselm of Canterbury*, 164. Similarly, McIntyre agrees with this as he claims that his theology of satisfaction is an ontological enterprise directly linked to the ontology of Jesus Christ who is able to make such satisfaction. See McIntyre, *St. Anselm and His Critics*, 114-116. Michael Deem is similar in this regard as he goes so far as to say that Anselm represents a new direction in Christology as he utilizes the Chalcedonian definition of two natures in one person. As such, he demonstrates the new direction is to "provide a rational defense of the incarnation" and claims the "value of satisfaction is inseparable from the holistic reality of the incarnation." See Michael J. Deem. "A Christological Renaissance: The Chalcedonian Turn of St. Anselm of Canterbury." *St. Anselm Journal 2.1*. Manchester: The St. Anselm Journal, 2004, 49-50. This is evidentiary of the from above Christology which Anselm utilizes and as such in presupposing the divinity of Jesus Christ in the incarnation, Anselm creates the potentiality for the relegation of the resurrection to the periphery of his Christology.

[198] This is a position that I have recapitulated from Deme: "We can speak about genuine obedience when one person, from his own free initiative, internalises about someone else's will, in which case the plurality of wills will be eliminated in their

to participate in the divine will, thus allowing humanity to become willfully subordinated to God, so that it is not what humanity wills but rather what God wills. If this is true, Anselm believes this level of *oboedientia* has happened in Jesus Christ, as the first man who was not made to die, but freely willing to die. It is this same reality of eliminating human will through permanence and obedience that finds locus in the monastic order Anselm has given his life to. This is similar to the same service and obedience the vassal owes to the feudal lord because of the benefit of land and safety he has received, so freedom of will is exchanged for the will of the feudal lord. While Anselm may have built his theology of obedience from Chalcedonian Christology, one could at the very most question if there is a hierarchical relational understanding in his Trinitarian thought, and one could at the very least question the manner in which feudalism has colored his understanding of obedience and disobedience to God. More importantly is the challenge eventuated from his position in that his Christology is built from an *a priori* from above assumption that (ontologically speaking) Jesus Christ is the one who is divine and thus the payment made to God is satisfactory.

Secondly, the manner in which this feudal understanding of relationship between humanity and God, as well as the Father and Son, is expressed in terms of a relational outworking that becomes readily apparent as a feudal construct of honor and patronage between feudal lord and vassal imbues the *Cur Deus Homo*. Feudalism was a complex system of vassals that ultimately had one feudal lord – the king of a given land – with other feudal lords who had land to disperse to their vassals in exchange for loyalty and service. In the case of the *Cur Deus Homo*, Anselm likely sees the king or feudal lord as God, the being to which all vassals are subjected. The feudal lord demanded honor, homage, and loyalty due to all of the benefits which were given the vassals such as protection from enemies, freedom, land, food, and other resources. The manner in which vassals showed this honor was to be present at court to show such honor, homage, and loyalty. If such honor, homage, and loyalty went unpaid to the sovereign or feudal lord then the benefits for the vassal were revoked, the grant of land reclaimed by the feudal lord, and in some cases even death resulted. Similarly, in the *Cur Deus Homo*, Anselm constructs a theology of sin and redemption through an understanding of offending the honor of God by means of disobedience or sin, and as such this is a dishonoring of God which shows a break in the patronage between feudal lord and vassal:

---

identity." See Deme, *The Christology of Anselm*, 164. Sonderegger agrees with the language of obedience position, claiming obedience is important to the whole of the CDH demonstrating the proper response of humanity to God. She also illustrates this drives a theology of satisfaction. See Sonderegger, *International Journal of Systematic Theology* Vol. 9, No 3, 352-354.

The stability of this social world rested on slavish fidelity and allegiance. In this context, Anselm's understanding of the atonement reads as a kind of allegory, with the lord as the Lord and the serfs as the human family.[199]

The theology of redemption comes through Jesus Christ as the obedient one who rightly honors God in and through his penitential death to free the disobedient from their sins and repay the offended honor of God. It is quite easy to make the comparison if one takes into account the Anselmian cultural milieu, as the exchanges between culture and *Cur Deus Homo* reveal feudal and monastic images which Anselm has created. These images deal with the necessary requirement of obedience in honoring of God and the necessary consequences which must result from not honoring God.

While obedience was part of the argument above in reference to language concerning the social relational structures of feudal lord and vassal, the inner workings of this language in reference to the reciprocity of honor and patronage now become more important. Anselm claims in 1.9, "...every creature owes this (truth/righteousness) as a matter of *oboedientiam*."[200] Anselm furthers this argument claiming that while Jesus Christ was not forced to die, he underwent death out of "*oboedientiam* consisting in upholding of righteousness, so bravely and pertinaciously that as a result he incurred death,"[201] and goes on to say that Jesus Christ "was made obedient to the Father 'even to death'," and "learnt obedience from his sufferings."[202] While this level of obedience might raise questions about God the Father, Anselm concludes 1.9 by summarizing:

> The Father wished the death of the Son in the sense that it was not his will that the world should be saved by any means, as I have said, other than that a man should perform an action of this magnitude.[203]

Anselm then spends an entire chapter (1.10) toward a theology of obedience as being voluntary, trying to prevent coercion on the part of the Father toward the Son regarding his death. Ironically, Anselm states the "Son could not avoid death if he wished to,"[204] because the world could not be saved by any other than him, and then attempts to hold this in tension with the Father agreeing with the Son that the Son desired to praise God and be obedient even unto death. Similarly, in 2.11 Anselm devotes a chapter to the claim that Jesus Christ dies of his own power, and that it was in his power to die and rise again if he so wished.[205] The reason, Anselm claims, is that Jesus

---

[199] Green and Baker, *Recovering the Scandal of the Cross*, 22. See also Southern, *A Portrait*, 221-227.

[200] CDH 1.9, 276. Here the use of the Latin has been inserted in the English translation so as to demonstrate the word usage consistently in the CDH.

[201] CDH 1.9, 277.

[202] See CDH 1.9, 277.

[203] CDH 1.9, 279.

[204] CDH 1.10, 281.

[205] See CDH 2.11, 329.

Christ dies for the "honor of God,"[206] and does so to pay "recompense" for the sin of mankind, "of his own free will, because this will be necessary."[207] Within the framework of these two chapters is the relational outworking of feudal honor and patronage. God the Father, as feudal lord, is worthy of honor for all the benefits that humanity, the vassals, receives. Unfortunately, the precondition of humanity is sin, and as such, humanity is unable to repay or be rightful patrons who show God the honor that is rightly due unto God. Jesus Christ is then, the first patron of humanity who shows God the Father the honor due him by being obedient as a good vassal would, and fulfills the will of God necessarily by his death. It is this death which enables humanity to become patrons of God once again.

Now it is possible to consider how the hierarchy of feudal relationships, the outworking of those relationships in terms of honor and patronage, eventuate the understanding medieval penance and justice in the *Cur Deus Homo*. The example above concerning the obedience of the Son to the Father is a prime instance of how medieval penance finds its way into the *Cur Deus Homo*. The obedience of the Son through his suffering and death reveals how medieval penance was meant to be public, occuring under a well codified system in *contritio cordis, confessio oris,* and *satisfactio operis* (all terms used by Anselm). Key to this was "the importance of contrition to the making of satisfaction of sins," language in the *Cur Deus Homo* from its outset. The obedience, sufferings, and death of Jesus Christ provide a satisfaction for the offended honor of God and also the human need for salvation.[208] More importantly, Anselm understood sin and the need for penance based on the understanding of beauty and how beauty fit into the order and will of God for all things. The view of Anselm is that sin created a disrupted order and marred the beauty which God intended.[209] As such, contrition enables forgiveness of sin, which is considered a penitential act. Penance brings about the restoration of beauty and order through the forgiveness of sin, a point raised in CDH 1.20. This is the manner Anselm begins bringing Book One to its climax, namely that humanity is in need of the salvation Jesus Christ offers. The question Abelard later raised against the *Cur Deus Homo* – "why not simply forgive humanity?" – is answered through the Anselmian understanding of penance; one cannot forgive sin without recompense from the offender.[210] Thus, Anselm neatly ties medieval penance, satisfaction, and the act of

---

[206] CDH 2.11, 330.
[207] CDH 2.11, 331.
[208] See Hamilton, *The Practice of Penance*, 15.
[209] See for example CDH 1.11, 1.22.
[210] See CDH 1.11-1.15, 1.19-21. See Katherin A. Rogers. "Anselm on Forgiveness, Patience, and Free Will." *Anselm Journal 6.2.* Manchester: The St. Anselm Journal, 2009, 1-7. The Latin word here is *satisfactio* and is the crux of the Anselmian doctrine of satisfaction concerning how it is necessary to provide a satisfaction to the offended honor of God. It is noteworthy to mention how this fits within the doctrine of penance as the offender is seeking to make a satisfaction for their sin through an act

Jesus Christ and his death on the cross (the penitential act of supererogation) as a recompense for the debt that humanity owes unto God for offending the honor of God. This in turn provides the restoration of beauty and order, and offers humanity the gift of redemption and salvation in Jesus Christ.

Concurrently, feudalism also maintained in proximity with law and politics, and while the feudalism of the tenth through twelfth centuries is difficult to reconstruct, what is readily recognizable is the nature in which legal acts created new relationships.[211] As seen earlier, homage or honor and patronage created relationships in which the feudal lord received the benefits of vassals to work the lands and provide an army for himself, and the vassals received the fief or land grant for the blessing of raising a family and being self-supportive. The *Cur Deus Homo* demonstrates Anselm believes God has created humanity for the purpose of bliss and that humanity has sinned and offended the honor of God.[212] This disobedience of sin is a break in the system of honor, homage, and loyalty God demands, and the punishment due to humanity because of this sin is that humans may not be taken up into the heavenly city, the place of angels, because they have not paid their recompense for violating the honor due to God.[213] Jesus Christ is the one who handles the justice element of this transaction by repaying the offended honor of God because humanity is unable to pay such a heavy penalty for offending this honor. Yet, the very definition Anselm creates for sin is a dishonoring of God or failure to pay a debt (*debitum*) owed to God. Consequently, while the punishment required for sin has continuity with the medieval penance system, it is also typical of a penal code, and this is critical to seeing the feudal nature inherent within his argument. The last of these (punishment of sin as a penal code) has been the argument of other scholars, as they have stated Anselm focuses on a legal metaphor for the satisfaction of a penal code.[214]

---

that has dishonored God and brought disharmony to the intentions for humanity and the created order which was meant to be of a beautiful harmony.

[211] See Hoyt and Chodorow, *Europe in the Middle Ages*, 229-230.

[212] See CDH 1.25, 314-315.

[213] See CDH 1.19, 300-301.

[214] See Green and Baker, *Recovering the Scandal of the Cross*, 129-130. See also F.W. Dillistone. *The Christian Understanding of Atonement*. Philadelphia: Westminster Press, 1968, 190-195. See also Stephen Finlan. *Problems with Atonement*. Collegeville: Liturgical Press, 2005, 71-74. David Neelands has shown that Anselm conceives of original sin as "original guilt" following from Augustine. This is interesting as it fits the "penal code" metaphor that Anselm creates given guilt is a legal term for sin - proof that one has offended the honor of God. See David Neelands. "Crime, Guilt, and the Punishment of Christ: Traveling Another Way With Anselm of Canterbury and Richard Hooker." *Anglican Theological Review* Vol. 88 No. 2., 2006. McIntyre notes the Anselmian view of sin is that God holds humanity in obligation to pay a "just debt" of what God desires, and the failure to make satisfaction for sin is punishment. This is a reality seen in the fact that humanity has a death of spiritual, physical, and eternal dimensions. See McIntyre, *St. Anselm and His Critics*, 68-76. Southern also refers to this terminology as feudal. See Southern, *A Portrait*, 221-227.

Anselm holds human sin as a breech of rightly honoring God which is worthy of severe punishment and need for justice or recompense:

> A: *There is nothing more intolerable in the universal order than that a creature should take away honor from the creator and not repay what he takes away.*
>
> B: *Nothing is more self-evident than this...*[215]
>
> A: *If the divine Wisdom did not impose these forms of recompense in cases where wrongdoing is endeavoring to upset the right order of things, there would be in the universe, which God ought to be regulating, a certain ugliness, resulting from the violation of the beauty of the order, and God would appear to be failing in his governance. Since these two consequences are as impossible as they are unfitting, it is inevitable that recompense or punishment follows upon every sin.*
>
> B: *You have given a satisfactory answer to my objection*
>
> A: *It is plain, therefore, that no one can honor or dishonor God, so far as God himself is concerned, but, in so far as the other party is concerned, a person appears to do this when he subjects himself to God's will, or does not subject himself...*[216]
>
> A: *Consider it, then, an absolute certainty, that God cannot remit a sin unpunished, without recompense, that is, without the voluntary paying off of a debt, and that a sinner cannot, without this, attain to a state of blessedness, not even the state which was his before he sinned. For in this case, the person would not be restored, even to being the kind of person he was before his sin.*[217]

This becomes apparent as Anselm later describes the debt owed is only capable of being repaid by a God-Man.[218] The logic inherent within his argument invariably leads to a theology combating the error of human sin with a payment for that sin, all of which fits within not only the religious structure but also the social structure of his day. For Anselm, it is more a question of what is necessary to pay the debt to restore honor to God and satisfy the provisions of justice that have been offended; thus justice satisfies offended honor, and offended honor is a feudal feature of the cultural milieu and the *Cur Deus Homo*.

Anselm then considers a feudal argument in the possibility of God not upholding his honor, or not punishing sin because God, in his freedom, could decide not to do so:

> Some scholars have noted it is an eleventh century feudal concern for honor, including the restitution owed the noble lord when he has not been duly honored.[219]

The conclusions Anselm draws are that it is not fitting for God to not punish sin because God cannot do anything in an unjust or unfitting manner violat-

---

[215] CDH 1.13, 286.
[216] CDH 1.15, 289.
[217] CDH 1.19, 302.
[218] See CDH 2.18, 348.
[219] McMahon, *Saint Anselm – His Origins and Influence* ed. by J. Fortin, 58.

ing the honor of God.[220] Green and Baker argue these feudalistic concepts have the following tendencies:

> To make forgiveness something earned by Jesus from God...(and) a distorted concept of God is promoted because the linking of God with a feudal lord diminishes God's active role in reconciliation and because many readers may too easily associate God's character and practice with those of feudal lords.[221]

Even more, having heard the feudal understanding of relationship present in the *Cur Deus Homo* between God the Father and God the Son, seeing how the dimensions of that relationship are feudal in terms of honor and patronage, and hearing of the feudal images of justice imbued in the argument, it is possible to consider the most poignant of feudal images in the *Cur Deus Homo*. This feudal image is painted beginning in 2.16, and it is this image which describes and casts understanding back upon the whole of the argument. This image is key to understanding the Anselmian relational hierarchy between Father and Son, the relational outworking of Father in Son in terms of honor and patronage, and the means of feudal justice:

> Let us imagine that there is a king and that the entire populace of his cities has sinned against him with the exception of one man, who is nonetheless of the same race...Now the man who is the only innocent party enjoys such favor with the king that he has it in his power to bring about the reconciliation of all those who believe in his advice, and he has such love towards the guilty that he wishes to do this. This reconciliation will be brought about by means of some service which will be very pleasing to the king, and which he will perform on a stated day in accordance with the king's desire. And since not all who are in need of reconciliation are to assemble on that day, the king makes the concession, in view of the magnitude of service, that any people who acknowledge before or after that day that they wish to receive pardon through the act that is to be performed on that day, and that they accede to the agreement concluded on that occasion, will be absolved from all their past guilt...[222]

There is undoubtedly some semantic freedom to make the argument that the innocent man possesses the same bloodline or characteristics of the king. However, there remains a large chasm between the king and innocent subject. The language of how reconciliation occurs, namely by the means of a service that is pleasing (i.e. satisfying) to the king, suggests not only a medieval penitential understanding (in that there is public confession and a "service" or penance), but also a feudal order of relationship. The distribution of justice for the guilty suggests a feudal system of justice that is handled through service of punishment and act of pardon by means of agreement and absolution.

---

[220] See CDH 1.12, 1.15, and 1.19.

[221] Green and Baker, *Recovering the Scandal of the Cross*, 132. While this point is contestable, it is nonetheless a potential point of illumination of the feudal imagery involved, and has found support of other scholars as noted in the preceding pages. In this corpus, God is seemingly more concerned with maintaining honor and minimally involved with his vassals, except from a distance.

[222] CDH 2.16, 338.

Anselm will continue the chapter by making the case for how it was necessary for Jesus Christ to die. Moreover, although it was the will of God for Jesus Christ to die, he (Jesus) willingly did so.[223]

Anselm then moves forward in 2.17 delineating how the will of God is not contingent upon capabilities or impossibilities, or even necessities; rather, it is the "existence of actuality that makes it a necessary fact."[224] Anselm in effect reasons that the prophecies concerning the Christ who would die voluntarily and not out of necessity were true, and that it was necessary for such things to come to pass.[225] Accordingly, while it was willed by God (a point made above), it was also a free act which Jesus Christ necessarily willed to be so. So then, Anselm is able to finish his argument that leads to the salvation of humanity by claiming God became man, and through his death, brought salvation. Jesus Christ did this freely and necessarily to honor God for the sake of truth and righteousness, although God willed it to be so. In giving something he did not owe, providing a satisfaction unto God (and himself in being one with God Anselm argues), Jesus Christ "offered up to humanity his divinity."[226]

Ultimately, Anselm constructs an argument from an *a priori* perspective for the intellectual milieu, yet exchanges it with the feudal cultural milieu. It has been argued Anselm utilizes feudal imagery alongside logic, and whereas Anselm cannot explain the logical requirement of the mercy of God, the fulfillment of justice through the God-Man, and the inability for all persons to receive the benefits of this fulfillment even though it is indeed extended to all, Anselm relies on a metaphor of an innocent man who fulfills the offended honor of a king on behalf of all the guilty subjects. The king wishes to extend the benefit of pardon to all so long as all subjects present themselves in court on a given day in which the service was performed. However, not all subjects attend.[227] The logic of why some do not respond to the salvation Jesus Christ attains is disregarded because it is already inherent with the cultural milieu and cultural narrative. The beauty of this cultural narrative is that the benefits of salvation are more readily accessible to all who read it from the perspective of being immersed in that culture; the disadvantage is that salvation quickly becomes transactional and salvation history as being of lesser importance, if any importance at all.

Conclusion: *Cur Deus Homo*—
An Exchanged Salvation History

The end result is that by means of an intellectual milieu that longs for logic and a cultural milieu that utilizes feudalism, Anselm exchanges salvation

---

[223] See CDH 2.16, 342.
[224] CDH 2.17, 346.
[225] See CDH 2.17, 347.
[226] CDH 2.18, 351.
[227] See CDH 2.16. See Southern, *A Portrait*, 214-215.

history for feudal history. Whereas previous theologies often looked to the salvation history of the Scriptures, Anselm looks to his intellectual and cultural milieu. Whereas previous theologies considered the incarnation, death, and resurrection of Jesus Christ as the salvific work of God and the culmination of salvation history, here the death of Jesus Christ is given primary authority as the transactional act of salvation which satisfies the honor of God and ascribes the atoning benefits therein to humanity. The key emphases in his work are placed upon the honor of God which has been offended, the blissful state intended for humanity that has been thwarted, and the satisfaction made by the death of Jesus Christ to restore the honor of God and the benefits of salvation to humanity.

Even more, the soteriological question Anselm asks does not consider the resurrection of Jesus Christ within the scope of his *Cur Deus Homo*:

> *By what logic or necessity* did God become man, *and by his death*, as we believe and profess, restore life to the world, when he could have done this through the agency of some other person, angelic or human, or simply by willing it.[228]

Death is the mechanism of restoring life to the world, and the purpose of the incarnation is for the God-Man to restore honor to God through obedience and the satisfaction founded in his penitential death, making Jesus "the originator of justification."[229] This seems inconsistent or at least incomplete compared with previous theologies, as a legal transaction of death somehow restores life to the world, the universe, humanity, rather than how Jesus of Nazareth, the incarnate Christ, overcame the power of sin, death, and evil in his resurrection from the crucifixion of the cross.

Jürgen Moltmann said, "In the New Testament there is no faith that does not start *a priori* with the resurrection of Jesus."[230] One must therefore ask a few questions of Anselm beginning with why does his argument commence *a priori* with a precondition of humanity? Why does the death of Jesus Christ restore life to the world, and what of the resurrection in the work of Jesus Christ? These questions have been partly answered as the history of salvation has been exchanged for feudal history. Feudalism looked to the honor and patronage relationship between lord and vassal as a key concept in the social structure, and it was this relationship that governed the whole of society. The vassal had benefits and was required to be obedient in the showing of honor to the lord. The lord provided these benefits to the vassal allowing the vassal to be kept safe from invaders and receive the provisions necessary to live. Satisfying the legal code and arrangements of feudalism contained therein were paramount to this system and to negate this when the lord had acted rightly on the behalf of his vassals was a serious breach of honor which would be defended in the court system. The defense of this honor required satisfaction. This was also true of the medieval penance system that similarly required a recompense for sin.

---

[228] CDH 1.1, 265, (italics mine).
[229] CDH 1.3, 268-269.
[230] Jürgen Moltmann. *Theology of Hope*. Minneapolis: Fortress Press, 1993, 161.

If the hope of the work was to make Christian faith intelligible and reasonable to the people of his day, the utilization of socio-religious structures and logic was brilliant. To the aim of providing a logical apologetic that was situated in a contemporary setting and intellectually reflective as an illumined answer was offered to the previous era and its ransom theories and superstitious tendencies, Anselm succeeded. He constructed a theology containing a worldview of a legal socio-religious structure that his contemporaries understood. However, while this might have helped persons make sense of faith, or even lead them to a place of understanding so as to garner greater faith, he has seemingly broken with Augustinian tradition and the salvation history of the Scriptures by means of an Aristotelian methodology that looks to logic and the transactional death of Jesus Christ with little if any consideration for the resurrection of Jesus Christ. Moreover, the argument is deeply colored by the milieu as the primary means of illustration.[231]

The key nuance here is not that Anselm completely ignored the Scriptures, or the Augustinian tradition. Rather, Anselm made his cultural milieu the key text and utilized a *remoto Christo* methodology to demonstrate the need for the God-Man. It was not so much faith seeking understanding but understanding making the way for faith as biblical materials were exchanged for cultural ones. Rather than explicating the context in which salvation oc-

---

[231] Richard Campbell is important here as he is dismissive of feudal and societal conceptions in Anselm claiming they are superficial. Based upon the Anselmian language in *Cur Deus Homo*, one can see cultural concepts and inquisitions from the milieu, especially in the case of Anselm who is addressing particular communities that have raised these important doctrinal questions and challenges. That Anselm addressed these communities is further indicative of the exchange proposed in the preceding work of 1.2.1. See Richard Campbell. "The Conceptual Roots of Anselm's Soteriology." *Anselm, Aosta, Bec, and Canterbury: Papers in Commemoration of the Nine-Hundredth Anniversary of Anselm's Enthronement as Archbishop, 25 September, 1093*, ed. by D.E. Luscombe and G.R. Evans. Sheffield: Sheffield Academic Press, 1996, 256-258. Conversely, Southern claims the argument is feudal and is colored by feudal language. See Southern, *A Portrait*, 221-227. McIntyre has also made a successful case of this in McIntyre, *St. Anselm and His Critics*. Sonderegger claims that the issue with the challenges to CDH began at Adolf Harnack and continue today because of the modern assumption of theologians to eliminate the supernatural due to our own human intelligences. Moreover she claims that the paradox of death restoring the human race is replaced by our own modern anthropologies. See Sonderegger, *International Journal of Systematic Theology Vol. 9, No 3*, 342-361. Nicholas Cohen challenges those who have raised the feudal suspicions or are dismissive of the work in CDH, claiming that it is not feudal but patristic in orientation. In this regard, his claim is that Aulèn is responsible for creating this shift in critical thought as he claimed the Anselmian approach to atonement deals with Latin medieval theology. Cohen instead attempts to bridge Anselm with Athanasius in the spirit of the work of Gasper. See Nicholas Cohen. "Feudal Imagery or Christian Tradition? A Defense of the Rationale for Anselm's *Cur Deus Homo*." *St. Anselm Journal 2.1*. Manchester: St. Anselm Journal, 2004, 22-30. Where Cohen succeeds is to say that the argument is not fallen entirely to feudalism. Where his argument fails is the disregard for the apparent feudal influences and key distinctives in which the CDH is constructed.

curs, the explication of the necessity of salvation in cultural metaphor is offered. This in turn, created a Christology shaped by the necessary presupposition of the deity of Jesus Christ in the incarnation because of the offended honor of God by means of the sins of humanity. Moreover, it featured death as the means of satisfying the offended honor of God, which in turn extended salvation to all offenders. Thus, methodologically speaking, crucifixion and incarnation become primary, at the expense of the resurrection that has been relegated to the periphery of his Christology. And now it is toward this issue, to which this present chapter turns.

1.2.2 Cur Deus Homo: A Logical Crucifixional Transaction by Satisfaction

To this point, this chapter has demonstrated how Anselm exchanged salvation history for feudal history. It is this exchange that shapes the soteriology of the *Cur Deus Homo*, which in turn answers the incarnational question Anselm asked. That question (*Cur Deus Homo*) is echoed within the statement Anselm makes in CDH 1.1, as he asks by what necessity God became human and restored life to humanity and the universe by way of death (*et morte sua*). This is significant, for the death of Jesus Christ forms a satisfaction for the offended honor of God and the penitential act of supererogation for the salvation of humanity. The death of Jesus restores humanity and the created order to its intended beauty, and restores humanity to its intended happiness and relationship with the Creator God.[232] While some have tried to claim that a title concerning the restoration of humanity by way of the death of the God-Man is reason enough to believe that Anselm took into consideration the whole of the life of Jesus Christ in the incarnation, death, and resurrection,[233] it remains that the primary feature of the work *Cur Deus Homo* is from the perspective of the cross and death – Jesus became human, to die, to satisfy the offended honor of God, and restore humanity and the created order to its intended beauty. Therefore, the second portion of this chapter (1.2.2) will consider how the Christology of Anselm methodologically emphasizes the cross and incarnation. These elements of his Christology thus feature incar-

---

[232] See Southern, *A Portrait*, 226-227.

[233] See especially Daniel Deme who attempts to show in God's becoming man that the whole of the Christ event is taken into consideration within the *Cur Deus Homo* question. Deme, *The Christology of Anselm of Canterbury*, 175-183. It is noteworthy to mention that elsewhere in the very same work, Deme readily admits the minimal treatment that Anselm gives to the resurrection, even calling it problematic to one degree or another. See Deme, *The Christology of Anselm of Canterbury*, 227-235. Again, it is important to note that Anselm clearly believed in the resurrection. Moreover, his devotional works (a point Deme is quick to point out) offer reflection upon the resurrection. However, what remains is the methodological expression of his Christology that is from the cross and incarnation, a point that Anselm makes at the beginning of the *Cur Deus Homo* when he considers how Jesus Christ restores life to the world *et morte sua*.

nation and crucifixion as central, which relegates resurrection to the periphery in the *Cur Deus Homo*.

Christology by Cross & Incarnation

The strong sense in which logic and dialectic were prominent features in the schools and monasteries predating the writing of *Cur Deus Homo* is significant, especially when the tension between an Augustinian presupposition and Aristotelian methodology Anselm attempted to hold together in dialectical tension, even if unsuccessfully, is considered. Surprisingly, given the logical and dialectical presentation of the *Cur Deus Homo*, it is curious that Anselm would say little of resurrection in the work. By doing so, a stronger dialectical tension between cross, resurrection, and incarnation would have been maintained. If one were to reflect upon the earliest days after the death and resurrection of Jesus Christ, the reason for "good news" was that the crucified Jesus of Friday was established as Lord and Messiah in the empty tomb of Sunday.[234] Anselm vaguely references the resurrection as he describes the restoration of humanity via the death of the God-Man in 1.1, and then again in 2.3, but this functions secondarily on the basis of the concern Anselm has for the order of beauty which God intended for humanity and the universe which has fallen due to humanity offending the honor of God.[235] Accordingly, this first unit turns to its most important claim: Anselm of Canterbury by means of his presupposition, methodology, and exchange of salvation history, methodologically emphasized the cross and incarnation by means of an *a priori* Christology featuring the death of Jesus as the satisfaction of the honor of God and the restoration of the bliss humanity was created for, thus relegating resurrection to the periphery.

---

[234] See for example, Wright, N.T. *The Resurrection of the Son of God*. Minneapolis: Fortress Press, 2003. While there are a variety of schools of thought with respect to the nature of the resurrection – bodily, spiritual, the rise of faith, or the like – key here is the possibility for the dialectical tension between crucifixion and resurrection. Regardless of the mode of resurrection, it is that tension between resurrection and crucifixion that provided the message of good news which the apostles and early Church sought to convey from Jerusalem to the ends of the earth.

[235] The key text referenced in CDH 1.1 is, "By what logic or necessity did God become man, and by his death, as we believe and profess, restore life to the world when he could have done this through the agency of some other person, angelic or human, or simply by willing it." CDH 1.1, 265. The key text referenced in 2.3 is, "Here is the proof that there is to be at some time a resurrection of the dead. For if man is to be restored in perfection, he ought to be reconstituted as the sort of being he would have been if he had not sinned." CDH 2.3, 316. As mentioned in the outset of this thesis, the issue is not whether or not Anselm believed in the resurrection. Given the nature of his devotional work, he clearly did. The issue is the methodological expression of cross and incarnation in his theological corpora, most notably the *Cur Deus Homo*. Anselm in 2.4 moves from a proof for the resurrection of the dead to the necessity of "God finishing what he had begun." The only way he sees this as happening is through the "complete recompense for sin, something which no sinner can bring about." CDH 2.4, 317.

The previous section in this chapter (1.2.1) demonstrated how Anselm exchanged salvation history for feudal history. Whereas previous atonement metaphors for understanding the work of Jesus Christ captured both death and resurrection because of their primary utilization of salvation history, Anselm utilized a feudal history instead. For example, a Christus Victor understanding of the death and resurrection of Jesus are not based upon a socially situated presupposition – the presupposition is based upon salvation history and an understanding of defeat, victory, and the overcoming of death itself via resurrection. A ransom understanding (having its most foundational origins in Irenaeus), while problematic in wondering who the ransom was paid to (especially if the devil), is nonetheless situated in the cosmic battle between the God of Abraham, Isaac, and Jacob, the evil slanderer the devil, and humanity who through sin, sold themselves into slavery to the power of evil and the devil. While slavery was indeed a social structure during the lifetime of Irenaeus and later theologians as well, it was also a social structure throughout the biblical narrative. Moreover, slavery is a legitimate biblical issue since the Exodus event and has a typology from the Exodus event that sees redemption and "buying back" those who have sold themselves or have been forced into slavery that is found throughout the Old Testament and is fulfilled in the death and resurrection of Jesus Christ.[236] Ellen Charry reports in her work *By the Renewing of Your Minds*, Anselm will cite Scripture only 69 times in the whole of his work *Cur Deus Homo*.[237] More importantly, Scripture more often functions in a confirmatory role to the overarching argument of *Cur Deus Homo*. The treatise is not an explication of the incarnation and/or crucifixion according to Scripture, but one according to the logical need that humanity has for salvation. Accordingly, whether or not one chooses to agree with Charry about Scriptural usage, it is unique Anselm makes an important methodological move from the outset of the work by methodologically employing *remoto Christo* to suspend salvation history and instead look to the social order of his era to do theology. This decision eventuates from the outset of his work in *Cur Deus Homo* the potentiality for a different understanding of the work of Jesus Christ and salvation for humanity.

Whereas the early church transmitted its tradition via an updated understanding of messiahship as was found to be the case in the death and resurrection of Jesus, something changes in and through the theology of the

---

[236] A classical work on differing theories of the atonement can be found in Aulén, *Christus Victor*. His work is not without contestation. See also H. Rashdall. *The Idea of Atonement in Christian Theology*. London, MacMillan Publishers, 1919. See also Exodus 6:6, Leviticus 25, Deuteronomy 25:5-10, Ruth, Hosea 13:14, Luke 24:21.

[237] One point of contestation with Charry is the notion that Anselm makes parallel arguments throughout CDH that are rooted in Scriptures. While he may not have explicitly quoted Scripture, one can find Scriptural arguments in the CDH. Cited from Green and Baker, *Recovering the Scandal of the Cross*, 22. Original work Ellen Charry. *By the Renewing of Your Minds: The Pastoral Function of Christian Doctrine*. New York: Oxford, 1997, 169.

Church. In time, it finds the incarnation and proving Jesus to be of the same substance as God through philosophical argumentation. This shall be revisited later, but Ignatius is a prime candidate for the answer. Wolfhart Pannenberg claims Ignatius began to alter the center point of Christology and he (Pannenberg) demonstrates this contrast in terms of Christologies constructed from above and from below. He does so by stating three primary reasons a theology from above is not feasible in his own Christological methodology:

> (1) A Christology from above presupposes the divinity of Jesus...instead of presupposing it, we must inquire how Jesus' appearance in history led to the recognition of his divinity; (2) A Christology that takes the divinity of the Logos as its point of departure and finds its problems only in the union of God and man in Jesus recognizes only with difficulty the determinative significance inherent in the distinctive features of the real, historical man, Jesus of Nazareth...which leads to the question of why the man who is engaged by God also be subjected to the universal human fate of death; (3) One would have to stand in the position of God himself in order to follow the way of God's Son into the world...as a matter of fact, however, we always think from the context of a historically determined human situation. We can never leap over this limitation.[238]

Pannenberg raises some extraordinary implications for this present work. If the witness of Scripture points to the death and resurrection of Jesus Christ as being the fulfillment of salvation history, and if this in turn points to an intended dialectical tension between the death and resurrection of Jesus Christ, why has theology gravitated toward one of the two extremes (cross or resurrection) as Barth claimed?[239] To answer this question, one may look to the first criticism Pannenberg offers to a Christology from above proposal: the issue stems from Christologies that have methodological presuppositions and assumptions of the divinity of Jesus Christ that the New Testament seeks to resolve through the three day historical narrative of death and resurrection. When theologians have constructed their Christologies with this *a priori* assumption (that is of the divinity of Jesus Christ), they have started in a place that lends itself toward identifying crucifixion as central, because of the second criticism Pannenberg offers, namely that when the divinity of Jesus Christ is assumed, God and humanity in Jesus are united in the real historical person Jesus of Nazareth so that he may be subjected to the fate of humanity in death.[240] So then, from the very beginning, a Christology constructed from above gravitates toward incarnation and crucifixion. Similarly, Ted Peters argues *Cur Deus Homo* occurs from an *a priori* position as Anselm constructs a Christology that was intended for incarnation, but becomes primarily an understanding of atonement.[241]

---

[238] Pannenberg, *JGM*, 34-35.

[239] Karl Barth. *Dogmatics in Outline.* New York: Harper and Row Publishers, 1959, 114.

[240] See Pannenberg, *JGM*, 34-35.

[241] See Peters, *God the World's Future*, 212-213.

This Christological emphasis on cross as the reason for the incarnation occurs at the expense of the resurrection, thus moving resurrection toward the periphery of Christology. Moreover, through this emphasis Christology is nuanced differently as the victory of God over suffering and death and the central message of the New Testament that the Crucified One is the Risen One are diminished, if not mislocated. If such a methodological decision is made, it is then plausible to see how then Christology becomes founded in a cultural narrative of medieval feudal lords and vassals as opposed to salvation history. It becomes readily apparent that with the exception of CDH 2.3,[242] Anselm relegates resurrection to the periphery in the argument, as it is satisfaction of the offended honor of God that is central not only to salvation but also as the reason for a God-Man.[243] Perhaps this was not the original intention of Anselm, but it is nonetheless the outcome that flows from his presupposition and methodology. Anselm asked "Why the God-Man?" but in the exchange of salvation history for a feudal one, and the undermining of the *credo ut intelligam* presupposition through his *remoto Christo* methodology, he presupposes the divinity of Jesus. This, in turn, makes the satisfaction of a debt which humanity could not repay possible without the resurrection. If one presupposes Jesus is God from the beginning, the necessity of resurrection to establish the divinity of Jesus becomes superfluous, for the presupposition is the unity of Jesus and God. And yet people living during the crucifixion of Jesus of Nazareth would have raised questions to this, exemplified by Luke in the story of the road to Emmaus.[244] For them, without resurrection there could be no confirmation of the divinity of Jesus, especially given the reality of his shameful death which was contrary to the heart of the meaning of messiahship. This, ironically, is part of the challenge of the Western Jews during the writing of *Cur Deus Homo* – a point Anselm was contesting. This assumption of the divinity of Jesus reveals a Christology from above positing *a priori* the divinity of Jesus and thus the assumption of his unity with God, and eventuates the potentiality for emphasis upon the cross as the means to satisfy a God who has been dishonored through human sin.[245]

Mentioned throughout these first three chapters, this word "satisfaction" is such an important expression of the debt that humanity owes to God, and

---

[242] Mentioned above, the thrust of 2.3 concerns the restoration of humanity to perfection through the resurrection of the dead, a state of "reconstitution...as the sort of being he would have been if he had not sinned." CDH 2.3, 316.

[243] McMahon, *Saint Anselm – His Origins and Influence* ed. by J. Fortin, 58.

[244] The point here is not to unpack the entire New Testament, but to demonstrate one example of the theological contradiction that is inherent in a crucified messiah without a resurrection to claim the authentication of this sacrifice, even if it was considered satisfactory by God. That Cleopas and his traveling companion in Luke 24 were hopeful that Jesus was the long promised messiah and had their hopes shattered at the death of Jesus is theologically indicative of the importance for dialectical tension between cross and resurrection.

[245] Pannenberg, *JGM*, 33-35.

the reason humanity needs the God-Man. Humanity needs a God-Man to satisfy their debt via a penitential act. Peters argues:

> He also had in mind an apologetic mission: to demonstrate convincingly to nonbelievers that the doctrine of the atonement makes sense. So he set out to prove the necessity of the incarnation by the use of reasoning alone apart from any prior historical knowledge regarding the work of Christ (*remoto Christo*).[246]

The answer Anselm provided to incarnation is crucifixion. To satisfy the possibility of salvation, God is made incarnate into the God-Man, and in becoming incarnate, it is possible for the one who is fully God and fully human to satisfy the necessary requirements for salvation. Thus, satisfying the offenses of humanity toward God by providing a remedy for this dishonor to God is paramount in his theology. His work represents a Christology constructed soteriologically with emphasis upon the presupposition of the divinity of Jesus of Nazareth as the Christ, and the necessity of the incarnation by means of the crucifixion to satisfy the debt of the offended honor of God via the God-Man. Satisfaction concerns the recompense or reparations required in a certain kind of punishment, and as indicated earlier, Anselm takes his cue from a few key texts in the Latin Vulgate of the New Testament, and especially from Augustine and Tertullian who have utilized *satisfactio* for their ransom understanding of the atonement.[247] For Anselm, satisfaction is the manner in which he can show some level of continuity with past Christologies as in Augustine and yet methodologically move into newer ground by applying logic to answer the questions of his milieu regarding the incarnation without involving implications of the devil. Humanity has offended the honor of God requiring payment of a magnanimous debt – a debt which they cannot repay, thus requiring a God-Man to pay such a debt. Anselm answered the incarnational question (albeit by a different methodology which relegated resurrection toward the periphery of Christology), and did so in a way that the milieu would have difficulty logically refuting. In the end, the God-Man provides a transaction that pays the debt humanity owed unto God and satisfies this debt through his obedience and death on the cross. This transaction restores the bliss humanity has lost, and is appropriated by faith which brings persons back into the state of bliss for which they were created and intended to live.

Ultimately, why God and humanity are united in one person is the issue Anselm seeks to resolve, but he does so through a methodology that presses upon crucifixion as its central Christological theme. Why the God-Man? Because humanity had offended the honor of God and stood in a place of magnanimous debt – a debt which they could not repay – which in turn required a God-Man to satisfy such a debt. This is the presupposition of the divinity Anselm held respective to the divinity of Jesus Christ that necessarily occurs from the outset of the work. For Anselm, a God-man was necessary to satisfy the offended honor of God, a satisfaction which no other could pro-

---

[246] Peters, *God the World's Future*, 212-213.
[247] See p. 46 ff.

vide.[248] Moreover, rather than look to the salvation history of the Scriptures as being primary, Anselm methodologically suspends Scripture to be relevant to the apologetic cause in the work, but such a move posits logic as well as an understanding of the social hierarchy of feudalism, for people to recognize the need for the satisfaction of a debt they owe which they cannot repay. Coupled with an understanding of medieval penance and the death of Jesus Christ as being a penitential act of supererogation which he offers on behalf of humanity to satisfy the offended honor of God, the cultural narrative is common understanding to his readers. This in turn does not require the entirety of the context of salvation history upon which the death of Jesus Christ emerges, nor does it necessarily require the resurrection, because according to Anselm, the key is in the satisfaction that Jesus Christ provides by means of his death, the death that was due humanity for its sins against God which offended the honor of God.[249] Thus, while Anselm constructed the argument within the Augustinian tradition of *fides quaerens intellectum*, his Aristotelian methodology that sought to answer the incarnational question was ultimately answered through the cross because of the need of humanity to satisfy a debt and the need of God to satisfy the honor of God. Therefore, the Christological outcome is from the cross which necessarily drives the need for incarnation. There is little need for the resurrection in the scope of the argument as death is the means of restoring life. This has been a presupposition of his from 1.1 forward as he asked the question:

> By *what logic or necessity* did God become man, *and by his death*, as we believe and profess, restore life to the world, when he could have done this through the agency of some other person, angelic or human, or simply by willing it.[250]

So then, the genius of Anselm also presents his greatest challenge: the methodology which made for an argument relevant to the milieu, is also the methodology that presents Christological challenges as the cross becomes the ultimate Christological expression, and along with it the incarnation. These methodological decisions came at the expense of the resurrection, a central element of Christology that is glaringly absent in the *Cur Deus Homo*.

Cur Deus Homo: Satisfaction and the Future

The series of transitions begun in Anselm seemingly anticipate what will later come in Kantian modernity. Essentially, his presupposition of faith and revelation existing at two opposite ends of the spectrum is a modernistic one. This is pre-Kantian, a divorce between revelation as the activity of God in history and faith as the activity of humanity. This continuum suggests revelation is almost an unattainable from above oriented activity, and faith is the

---

[248] See especially CDH 1.25 as the outcome of the argument in CDH 1 comes to a conclusion. See also CDH 2.6 concerning the God-Man being necessary, and the God-Man being the only possibility for satisfying the offended honor of God.

[249] See especially CDH 2.18-2.19.

[250] CDH 1.1, 265, (italics mine).

activity of humanity happening within the naturally created order below. Rationalism or knowledge becomes a human oriented activity as persons attempt to bridge the gap from revelation toward faith. This is an Aristotelian notion, as Aristotle held, "that the defining characteristic of human life is one's true self in relation to divine truth."[251] But this is flawed: faith arises from the activity of God in history, not out of rationalistic, human cognition. Later, the existentialist movement attempted to jump from the "throwness" of humanity into the world toward the courage to be and attain authentic human existence. Faith is not the activity of humanity apart from revelation; faith is the gift of God, which is a divine activity in response to ivine revelation as faith arises from the revelation of the acts of God in space-time.

To be sure, Anselm sought to bring understanding to *what* was believed, but what he succeeded in doing was giving a logical reason *why one should believe*. The reason? The satisfaction of a debt one cannot pay via the cross of Jesus Christ. This is a marked difference from previous theologies and one might question if the Kantian split between noumena and phenomena may have found a bit of its genesis in Anselm. Coupled with an impossibility of miracles (i.e. the resurrection) in the work of David Hume in *An Enquiry Concerning Human Understanding*, Immanuel Kant will also appeal to Abelard in describing Jesus Christ as being the "moral ideal,"[252] and it will be the deistic conceptualization of God (noumena) and the reality of the empirical world of five senses below (phenomena) that bifurcates God and the world in the culmination of modern thought. The dialectical tension between cross and resurrection at that point is dissolved as two entirely different non-symbiotic entities. Pannenberg argues in his systematic theology that Anselm "demanded in the field of rational argumentation that theology should examine what it believes by reason alone (*sola ratione*)."[253] This is a curious reflection of Anselm, as Anselm himself claimed to hold to the Augustinian presupposition of believing first in order to understand. Pannenberg illumines the notion that the *remoto Christo* methodology Anselm utilized looked to reason to prove the incarnation by way of the cross.

Accordingly, while his theology was dominant and in many ways unsurpassed in his time, his method may have anticipated the divorce of faith and revelation, between appearance and reality. One can see this especially by viewing the work of Peter Abelard (1079-1142). Abelard challenges the work of Anselm with his moral influence theory of atonement, relegating the doctrine of resurrection as an almost non-essential matter; what mattered most in his theology of atonement was the sacrificial example of Christ. It is from this sacrificial example which Christ offers, that humanity is meant to engage in a new behavior by repenting of their selfishness and responding to the love

---

[251] See Wood, *God and History*, 13. Original source: Gilson, *God and Philosophy*, 33.

[252] Peters, *God the World's Future*, 209. Original source: Immanuel Kant. *Religion Within the Limits of Reason Alone*. New York: Harper and Row, 1960, 54-55.

[253] Pannenberg, *ST I*, 51.

God has shown them.²⁵⁴ Jarislov Pelikan is quick to point out that Abelard had a purpose to help Christians think, not to make philosophers or Jews accept Christianity.²⁵⁵ The progressive connection between Anselm and Abelard becomes apparent: whereas Anselm presents a logical, feudal, metaphor for understanding the reason God became human (to repay the offended honor of God which humanity owed God through the satisfaction by death via the cross), Abelard takes the next step in claiming the work of Christ is relegated to an existential level. The suffering of Jesus Christ evokes an internal change in humanity and allows them to respond to the love of God shown them. Later in the period of the Protestant Reformation, Luther will move toward a substitutionary view of atonement similar to Anselm, Calvin will take a predominantly Anselmian view of substitutionary atonement,²⁵⁶ and then Charles Hodge will make the transition to full penal substitutionary atonement. Clearly, there are differences in the notion of satisfaction and substitution, but it is possible to see how the newer methodology of Anselm in his understanding of satisfaction that claimed a Christology from the cross could potentially lead toward the notion of substitution and then later penal substitutionary atonement. The importance of Jesus Christ being risen from the dead to vindicate the suffering of his cross is further relegated to the periphery in Anselm, and from this point forward, resurrection begins making a greater movement toward the periphery of systematic theology as each epoch passes.

What then are the implications of these findings? The first implication is that Anselm provides a Christology from the cross. Given the Scriptural account of the work of Jesus Christ in the crucifixion and resurrection event, Anselm suspends the utilization of Scripture as well as the materials of the Church. This is recognizable from the tradition of the Early Church Fathers. Irenaeus, for example, offered this relational understanding of the work of Christ, rooted in the two Adam theology of Paul:

> [Christ came down from heaven] that he might destroy sin, overcome death, and give life to man...Man had been created by God that he might have life...through the Second Man he bourne the strong one, and spoiled his goods, and annihilated death, bringing life to man who had become subject to death.²⁵⁷

It is the restoration of humanity that is important for Irenaeus, the overcoming of death, the restoration of life and relationship. A commonality shared by Eastern Theologians is, namely, that salvation is a "bestowal of life rather than forgiveness."²⁵⁸ Certainly, this is not the case in Anselm, as satisfying an

---

²⁵⁴ See Peters, *God the World's Future*, 208. See also, Green and Baker, *Recovering the Scandal of the Cross*, 137.
²⁵⁵ Pelikan, *The Christian Tradition Volume 1*, 16.
²⁵⁶ See John Calvin. *Institutes of the Christian Religion*. Peabody: Hendrickson Publishers, 2009, 2.16.3-6, 3.11.2.
²⁵⁷ Aulén, *Christus Victor*, 19. Original source: Irenaeus. *Adversus Haereses, III.18.7*.
²⁵⁸ Aulén, *Christus Victor*, 22.

offense through a legal transaction is key. Moreover, whereas biblical redemption stems from a change in masters, Anselm is not interested in a change in masters but in a redemption from indebtedness.[259] Jesus Christ becomes reduced more or less to a transaction for freedom that brings persons from a state of guilt and offending the honor of God, to a transactional state of pardon. God is seemingly less than relational in this model and is more or less a feudal lord concerned about maintaining honor and upholding law and justice rather than overcoming sin and death which alienates potentiality for relationship. This crucifixion-as-salvation theology points to death, not the reversal of it, as the key ingredient, and resurrection is relegated to a peripheral importance. Unfortunately, as has been stated earlier, this precedent sets forth a new means to think about the work of Christ well into the future. Many Protestant Reformers will utilize an Anselmian motif, and when coupled with a distance of faith and reality, the feudal lord who seemingly stands so far above "his" vassals it is possible to see how Feuerbach and Nietzsche would later raise questions about the existence of God altogether due to the defunct supernaturalistic tendencies in theological modernity.

The use of an Aristotelian methodology also set a precedent toward the period of modernity. Anselm looks not to the Scriptures or tradition of the Church (which would have taken greater precedence in years past); rather, he places persons into a logical and moral dilemma. Persons are brought to faith in Christ by placing them in a logically inescapable situation of sin, with the solution being the atoning work of Christ who satisfies the conditions of penance for humanity from this great and inescapable debt.[260] Logic will continue to play an important role not only in the work of Anselm, but in theological development moving forward. While the effects of this work will lead others who seek to bring coherence and a greater degree of plausibility to the Church, it will nonetheless shape the life of the Church from the scholastic period forward into the period of modernity, eventuating two branches of Protestant theology: rationalists and pietists. From such a juncture, faith and reason which were meant to be mutually supporting will be further divorced in modern criticism so that rationalism or empiricism become decisive methodologies for doing theology.

Tillich contended the rise of rational theology beginning early in the scholastic writings of Anselm and his contemporaries was the final step in a divorce between the authority of the Church and reason by the end of the Middle Ages, setting the stage for the Renaissance.[261] While reason was intended to synthesize the authority of tradition, helping interpret the authority of the Church in a non-combative manner, ultimately reason became the tool of enlightenment modernity. Because of this, what might be

---

[259] See Green and Baker, *Recovering the Scandal of the Cross*, 132.

[260] CDH 1.19-1.25. Here Anselm takes great care to illumine the inescapable nature of sin: humanity owes God a debt for offending the honor of God, but cannot repay God because of its fallen nature. Anselm did not disagree with the Early Fathers or doctrines of the Church. Rather, he methodologically suspended them.

[261] Tillich, *A History of Christian Thought*, 139-140.

said is that modernity existed in embryonic form in the scholastics, and given that Anselm and his work existed at the impetus of the scholastic period, one finds at the very least is an embryonic, pre-modernistic theology in Anselm. While Anselm did not divorce the experience of God and the rational underpinnings to interpret this experience, there was at the heart of his methodology and the juxtaposition of his presupposition, a theological precedent. This allowed for the satisfaction of individual guilt through a logical and feudalistic metaphor in which the transaction of the cross is central to Christology with little, if any, implication of victory and the promise of new life via the resurrection as contained in the Scriptures.

Chapter 4

Conclusion of Part One

This first unit concerning Anselmian Christology now draws to a close. The context of Anselm involving monasticism, pre-scholasticism, feudalism, and penance were important shaping narratives for his theology and provide much insight to the crossroads in which Anselm lived and did theology. The Norman Conquest was important for changing the landscape of church and education. Monastic life, feudal life, and medieval penance were dominant social arrangements that shaped the way Anselm understood the hierarchy, beauty of the world, and God. He was at the crossroads of the Roman Church utilizing an Augustinian presupposition of *credo ut intelligam* from the previous era, and the Aristotelian methodology that utilized logic and dialectic of the present era and the one to come. While he sought to utilize both the presupposition of the previous era and the methodology of his present era, his presupposition was compromised by his methodology, which shaped the outcome of his proposal. The *Cur Deus Homo* featured a an exchange of salvation history for feudal history. This was an important outcome as he methodologically suspended salvation history and the knowledge of Jesus Christ from the *Cur Deus Homo*. At the heart of his Christology is a logical soteriology that methodologically posits the crucifixion and death of Jesus as satisfaction for the offended honor of God. This transaction is the reason for the incarnation, for the sake of humanity.

It has further been demonstrated that his methodological commitments (*remoto Christo*) necessarily led to a desire to prove Christianity true by means of logic, and this situated persons within the scope of a need for salvation that could only come by the satisfaction made by the God-Man in his penitential act of supererogation on the cross. The death of Jesus was the transaction which restored life, and it becomes the necessity for humanity to respond by looking to Jesus as the object of faith. By featuring death as the mechanism for restoring life and the necessary reason for the incarnation, the resurrection was relegated to the periphery of his Christology. The reason? Anselm viewed the payment of a debt as the key transactional element of salvation in his argument. Moreover, Anselm assumed Jesus is the Christ of God *a priori* and thus the resurrection as offering a confirmatory response of satisfaction is of secondary importance, if any at all. In essence, there is no confirmation necessary of his messianic status as it is assumed *a priori* that because a debt has to be paid to satisfy the offended honor of God and restore humanity, that Christ is Jesus of Nazareth. Anselmian Christology is thus constructed from the cross and then the incarnation, and Anselm brings humanity to the logical conclusion that to regain the state of bliss they were intended to possess, they need the God-Man to satisfy their debt. Satisfaction in this sense has a medieval penitential nuance.

It cannot be overstated that Anselm was in his milieu, and remains in the present milieu, a genius. His work far surpassed his time. He succeeded in creating a logical apologetic to answer the critics of his day about one view of the reason God became human. His *remoto Christo* methodology pushed the envelope much like how the Early Church Fathers utilized philosophical thought to add rational categories to revelational content. Perhaps the reason for his *credo ut intelligam* presupposition was due to the crossroads in which he lived. He utilized the presupposition because it was a product of his schooling, his mentor was zealous for it, and the acceptance of the Roman Catholic Church was of paramount importance, especially given the communal nature of his existence as a monk. And yet, his work was very much for the people of the Roman Catholic Church so that they might be unafraid in giving a reason for the hope within them toward those who would challenge their faith. The ability to live and do theology in a world of great change is a powerful testimony to Anselm.

However, his argument came with certain costs as it traded salvation history for feudal history and relegated resurrection to the periphery. The resurrection is central to establishing and interpreting the person and work of Jesus Christ, and enhances the meaning of the cross. Moreover, his work opened the way for Abelard to challenge the manner in which he understood the cross and introduce a new nuance to the cross that is based upon moral influence. Later, in Luther and Hodge, penal substitutionary atonement became the key nuance of the cross, and at first glance, one might question if their understanding of atonement even more so emphasized the cross and relegated resurrection to the periphery. This penal substitutionary understanding of atonement while different in some regard than the Anselmian satisfactionary understanding of atonement, has been challenged in recent years in terms of whether or not this understanding of atonement is abusive, a product of cultural conventions, overly violent, or even helpful at all. And so, as this first unit has looked at Anselmian Christology which is constructed from the cross and incarnation at the expense of the resurrection which has been thus relegated to the periphery, so now this work turns to unit two and Pannenberg whose Christology is constructed from the retroactive significance of the resurrection.

Part Two

The Christology of Wolhart Pannenberg via the Retroactive Significance of the Resurrection

Chapter 5

Introduction to the Pannenbergian Milieu—A Survey of the Context

2.0 A Survey of the Pannenbergian Context

The first unit demonstrated that Anselm constructed a Christology flowing from his milieu, presupposition, methodology, and soteriological commitments. More importantly, his Christology was developed from an *a priori* from above methodology via the cross and incarnation, which relegated the resurrection to the periphery of his Christology. Anselm followed Ignatius and other second century apologists of the Church, keeping in step with a Christological scheme from above that looks to the incarnation as being central to Christology.[262] It is this move demonstrated by means of logical steps, in which Anselm posits incarnation as a necessary presupposition of the satisfaction needed by God in the cross of Jesus Christ. And, while the end of chapter two and the first unit did not conclude with an exhaustive history of theology that demonstrated how the Anselmian Christology of the cross was decisively influential for the years following his legacy, it is at least possible to see how Abelard, Luther, Schleiermacher, and Hodge likely built upon the centrality of the cross for Christology. This emphasis on cross with the resurrection relegated to the periphery is an interesting challenge for Christology. This challenge manifests itself beyond the time of Anselm in theological modernity and the insistence by some, like David Hume, who argued that the resurrection of Jesus Christ was a miracle and should therefore be denied of its historicity. This historical criticism becomes even more pronounced later as some will claim that historical-critical methodologies do not support the resurrection of Jesus Christ.[263] These methods will shape theology for years to come.

---

[262] This is a point made by Pannenberg in *ST I* among other places. See Pannenberg, *ST I*, 278.

[263] See David Hume. *An Enquiry Concerning Human Understanding*, ed. by Tom Beauchamp. Oxford: Oxford University Press, 1999, 169-186. See also, for example, the quest for the historical Jesus that began in Albert Schweitzer and was later revived by Ernst Käseman. Barth and Bultmann who had their own theological agendas that will be delineated momentarily, denounced Schweitzer, even though their Christologies also posited challenges to the historicity of the resurrection. See Albert Schweitzer. *Von Reimarus zu Wrede*. 1906.

Similar to Anselm, Pannenberg does theology in a milieu of great change, featuring a multitude of theological viewpoints ranging from the death-of-God theology to the present contemporary atonement conversation. Accordingly, this study turns to Wolfhart Pannenberg, arguably one of the key theologians of the twentieth century.[264] Pannenberg is part of a milieu of many theological vignettes: quests for the historical Jesus, Barthianism, Bultmannianism, the "death-of-God-theology," liberation theologies, and other theologies which have all found influences from the milieu of modernity and the divide between the "historical Jesus" and the "Christ of faith."[265] For example, Barth and his theology of the Word continued forth the tradition of Kähler, shielding the Christ of faith from the so-called historical Jesus. His Christology, based largely upon the incarnation of the pre-existent logos, concerned a self-revealing Word in which God is only made knowable in the moment of revelation through this Word.[266] Bultmann developed a theology that posited the death of Jesus as a historical event and dismissed the resurrection as a non-historical and mythic element contained in the Scriptures giving people a metaphor for authentic human existence.[267] Much like the Anselmian exchange of salvation history for feudal history, Bultmann exchanged salvation history for mythical history and existentialist philosophy. Nietzsche claimed before Bultmann "God is dead," and not long before Feuerbach claimed, "God is little more than a projection of

---

[264] Again, for the sake of clarity, this is not to say that Anselm did not believe in the resurrection, but rather his methodological commitments relegated resurrection from the center of his Christology to the periphery. Raised throughout chapters two and three (1.1 and 1.2), it is notable that Anselm did not include the resurrection in the *Cur Deus Homo* with the exception of CDH 2.3. Barring his devotional material, Anselm takes little time throughout his corpus to integrate the resurrection into his theology or Christology. This is a point that is upheld by Deme, *The Christology of Anselm of Canterbury*, 227-235, Southern, and others. What shall be of contrast now in this second unit of 2.1, 2.2, and 2.3 (chapters five through seven), is how Pannenberg constructs his Christology from a from below *a posteriori* methodology that begins with the resurrection.

[265] This distinction was first made by Martin Kähler in his attempt to shield the "Christ of Faith" from the "Historical Jesus," and the historical-critical methodologies that were present in which had tendencies to undermine the historicity of the Gospel narratives. This theology became important in some modern theologians, especially Bultmann. See Martin Kähler. *Der sogenannte historische Jesus und der geschichtliche, biblische Christus*. For a modern English translation see especially Martin Kähler. *So-Called Historical Jesus and the Historic-Biblical Christ*, ed. by Carl E. Braaten. Minneapolis: Fortress Press, 1988. For a helpful delineation of Kähler and its subsequent impact on theology in later years, see Wood, *God and History*.

[266] See Karl Barth. *Church Dogmatics IV, I*. London: T and T Clark, 1936-1969, 123-126.

[267] For example see Rudolf K. Bultmann. *History and Eschatology: The Gifford Lectures, 1955*. Edinburgh: The University Press, 1957. See also Rudolf K. Bultmann. *Theology of the New Testament Vol. I and II*. New York: Charles Scribner and Sons Publishing, 1951, 1955. See Charles W. Kegley. *The Theology of Rudolph Bultmann*. New York: Harper and Row Publishers, 1966, for a helpful synopsis of much of the theology of Bultmann.

ourselves onto the screen of reality."[268] From Kähler to Barth, Bultmann, Feuerbach, and Nietzsche, modern theologies presented challenges requiring a response.[269] In addition, a variety of quests for the historical Jesus occurred prior to the writings of Pannenberg, and all along, a ditch Lessing said was "uncrossable" became a force Pannenberg sought to overcome.[270] This wide chasm in modern theological thought was challenged by a growing stream of new theologians, which Pannenberg was linked to – theologians that fashioned a "theology of hope."[271]

Perhaps then, the challenge of the Pannenbergian milieu was similar to that of Anselm – he was a man who stood at the crossroads of theology. Analogous to Anselm, he faced the product of what could be understood as the remnant of Enlightenment modernity which divorced fact and value as in Kant, accidental proofs of history and necessary proofs of reason as in Lessing, and the God is dead theology which leveled a serious claim altogether. These theologies and the quests for the historical Jesus posed serious challenges for orthodox Christianity and the responses to these challenges prior to Pannenberg turned to neo-orthodoxy, existentialism, and Barthianism which claimed that the Word was a self-revealing one not subject to historical-critical methodologies. Much like the changing social and intellectual milieu of Anselm and the challenges of persons from outside Christendom regarding the incarnation, Pannenberg lived at the crossroads between the death of God theology and the theology of hope. He sought to respond to his milieu accordingly with a fresh approach to the challenges of the day by looking back to the core content of Christian faith.

Pannenberg was born October 2, 1928 in Stettin, Germany, a town now located in present-day Poland. His early years are best described as a young man with an incredibly gifted mind, a love and devotion for history, philosophy, and music held in tension with the perils of World War II and its resultative family relocations and military service. After being spared from death by sickness, Pannenberg was relocated as a prisoner-of-war to Northern Germany and shortly thereafter begin to study at the university. His studies included philosophy and theology, and Pannenberg at first grew fond of Marxism. Later he was liberated from Marxist philosophy, especially through the work of his mentor Gerhard von Rad and Hans von Campenhausen.[272] By 1958, Pannenberg became a professor of systematic theology and began to

---

[268] See Ludwig Feuerbach. *The Essence of Christianity, trans. by George* Eliot. Amherst: Prometheus Books, 1989.

[269] See Friedrich Nietzsche. *Die fröhliche Wissenschaft.* 1882. See also Feuerbach, *Das Wesen des Christentums*, 141.

[270] "Lessing's Ditch" was that the accidental truths of history can never become the necessary truths of reason. Lessing argued for a separation between truth and history. For a helpful delineation of "Lessing's Ditch," see Wood, *God and History*, 77-85.

[271] See Stanley J. Grenz. *Reason for Hope: The Systematic Theology of Wolfhart Pannenberg, 2nd Ed.* Grand Rapids: Eerdmans Publishing, 2005, 3.

[272] See Don H. Olive. *Makers of the Modern Theological Mind: Wolfhart Pannenberg.* Waco: Word Books, 1973, 19.

develop his theology with even greater fervor.[273] His essay, *Redemptive Event and History* was a "bold new eschatological theology"[274] which revealed that history was the most important framework for theology. The work concerned how history defends against existentialism (see for example Bultmann and his contemporaries) on one side, and on the other, the suprahistorical theology of Martin Kähler.[275] Furthermore, Pannenberg emphasized the importance of the resurrection and how the resurrection is a historical event that establishes the identity of Jesus Christ.[276] He has been an important theologian who has been quoted throughout the works of other theologians throughout the last fifty years.[277] Pannenberg does not fit neatly into any one theological camp, as his theology places great emphasis on history and yet it is that emphasis which also leads him to not give carte blanche historical authority to every event contained in the Scriptures. Braaten noted that it is this reality which makes Pannenberg unique; Pannenberg does not fit into one theological school, schema, or position, but rather seems to offer elements which everyone on one hand could agree with and on the other hand elements which they completely reject.[278]

More specifically, the Pannenbergian systematic theology features a number of key elements: God as the unity of all reality, an anthropological theology, the proleptic nature of Jesus of Nazareth who is established as the Christ by means of his resurrection from the dead, the importance of revelation as a historical process, and his eschatological theology that is indicative of his affinity for a theology of hope. One element that might receive more treatment by critics and aficionados alike concerns his utilization of modern science, an element that flows from his desire to do theology in his milieu. In this regard, Pannenberg is similar to Anselm in that he sought to answer the questions driven prior to and from within his milieu with the tools, language,

---

[273] The biographical information is drawn from a number of sources here. See Frank E. Tupper. *The Theology of Wolfhart Pannenberg*. Philadelphia: The Westminster Press, 1973, 13-27. See also Carl E. Braaten, and Philip Clayton. *The Theology of Wolfhart Pannenberg: Twelve American Critiques with an Autobiographical Essay and Response*. Minneapolis: Augsburg Publishing House, 1988, 9-18. See also Grenz, *Reason for Hope*, 1-2.

[274] Tupper, *The Theology of Wolfhart Pannenberg*, 19.

[275] See Pannenberg, *BQT I*, 15-80.

[276] See Pannenberg, *JGM*.

[277] See Grenz, *Reason for Hope*, 2. Grenz notes that almost every theologian of significance since 1970 references some aspect of the Pannenbergian corpus in their work. That Pannenberg appears in so many works for almost the last 50 years regardless of the given area of theology or the theological commitments of the authors, is of significant importance.

[278] For example, Pannenberg makes his argument on the resurrection of Jesus as a historical event yet denies the historicity of the virgin birth. See Pannenberg, *ST II*, 317-319. Similarly, Carl Braaten argues that "Pannenberg's theology obviously escapes ready-made labels." See Carl E. Braaten. "The Current Controversy on Revelation: Pannenberg and His Critics." *Journal of Religion Vol. 45.* 1965, 233-34. This is also noted in Grenz, *Reason for Hope*, 3.

and elements from within that milieu. Pannenberg has spent time and energy on works incorporating science and theology, particularly concerning space-time and how space-time is influential in theology. His understanding grows out of an Einsteinian view of space-time based upon the formula for the theory of relativity, $E = mc^2$. This is an important realization for his theology, as Pannenberg contends that the future creates the present to transform the past. His understanding of time is influential in his from below methodology, as well as the proleptic and eschatological theology he espouses. If God is the unity of all reality and the unbound power of the future; if the unity of Jesus with God is established by means of the resurrection as a powerful reversal of his rejection on Friday at the cross, and if the resurrection of Jesus Christ from the dead is proleptic in character, then the future creates the present to transform the past.[279]

This is a critical piece of information for his theology, one in which he has been criticized for as it can easily lead to theological determinism.[280] Pannenberg has responded to many of these questions regarding the charges of theological determinism by claiming that the future creating the present does not necessarily preclude the element of freedom, although he readily admits that there are weaknesses with the argument. More importantly, this establishes Pannenberg as having an eschatological systematic theology – he contends that the God of the Future is the one creating the present to transform the past. This understanding will be important as shall be argued in chapter seven (2.2): his retroactive theology of the resurrection has the resurrection retroactively establishing the incarnation. Whereas a Newtonian view of physics looks to a causal chain of past – present – future, Pannenberg looks to an Einstenian view of reality, claiming space-time stems from the future – present – past, and thus since the resurrection is the future event that has proleptically occurred, it is the resurrection which establishes the cross and incarnation, not vice versa. Hence, this is not just an epistemological reality in terms of what humanity knows about Jesus Christ in light of his resurrection, but an ontological one as well that claims the ontology of Jesus of Nazareth is established as the Christ by means of his resurrection from the dead. For obvious reasons, this is a significant claim. Pannenberg is not claiming that the ontology of Jesus changed because of the resurrection, but rather, that it was established.

---

[279] A number of sources are helpful here from both within the Pannenbergian corpus and outside it. For the most recent update regarding his thought on eschatological ontology and/or time, see Pannenberg, *ST II*, 84-102. See also, Pannenberg, *Theology and The Kingdom of God*, 127-143. See also Wolfhart Pannenberg. *What is Man?* Philadelphia: Fortress Press, 1970, 68-81.

[280] See for example Christiaan Mostert. *God and The Future: Wolfhart Pannenberg's Eschatological Doctrine of God.* London: T and T Clark, 2002, 89-126. Within chapter four, Mostert considers the eschatological ontology and the priority of the future and its impact upon the present. Lewis Ford questions the potentialities of this in Lewis S. Ford. "The Nature of the Power of the Future." *The Theology of Wolfhart Pannenberg*, ed. by Carl E. Braaten and Philip Clayton. Minneapolis: Augsburg Press, 1988.

There has been a good deal of material written about Pannenberg and his theology, much like Anselm of Canterbury. For the purposes of this study, there is however a singular emphasis: while Anselm constructed his Christology *a priori* from above, answering the incarnational question soteriologically via the cross, Pannenberg conversely does Christology *a posteriori* from below via the resurrection. Whereas unit one revealed how Anselm compromised his *credo ut intelligam* presuppositionary principle by means of his *remoto Christo* methodology, Pannenberg finds the locus for his Christological corpus in the narrative of salvation history. This is to say, it is because of the historical events occurring in Jesus of Nazareth who is established as Christ in his resurrection from the dead, Christology comes to expression and exist. Pannenberg claims:

> Therefore, Christology, the question about Jesus himself, about his person, as he lived on earth in the time of Emperor Tiberius, must remain prior to all questions about his significance, to all soteriology. Soteriology must follow from Christology, not vice versa. Otherwise, faith in salvation itself loses any real foundation...Christology must start from Jesus of Nazareth, not from his significance for us as, for instance, the proclamation directly offers it.[281]

The impetus of this second unit concerns the above quotation and how it is a key distinction in the manner in which Pannenberg crafts his Christology from below: whereas Christology was the product of soteriology in Anselm, Pannenberg will construct a Christology from the resurrection and the history of Jesus Christ. This is why Anselmian Christology is constructed from an *a priori* theology from above to tell humanity how to regain its intended state of bliss through the cross at the expense of relegating resurrection to the periphery, and why the Pannenbergian Christology utilizes an *a posteriori* theology from below which begins with the resurrection as the means to establish the cross and subsequently the incarnation.

---

[281] Pannenberg, *JGM*, 48.

Chapter 6

The Pannenbergian Christological Methodology: A Theology from Below

Wolfhart Pannenberg utilizes a theological methodology "from below," the product of his own milieu and also a product of the challenges he sought to answer. Anselmian Christology featured an *a priori* "from above" methodology that posited the divinity of Jesus Christ on the basis of the necessity of satisfaction that happened through the cross. Post-Anselmian Christology later took this type of methodology and when coupled with theological modernity, historical challenges developed regarding the resurrection of Jesus Christ. Questions were asked regarding the nature of miracles, the legendary status of the resurrection, the inability to historically verify the resurrection event itself, and unsurprisingly these questions and their subsequent answers further drove Christological methods and therefore the outcomes of Christology. Eventually, historical-critical methodologies developed, which further relegated resurrection to the periphery, and it was these primary voices with whom Pannenberg engaged.

Methodologically speaking, Pannenberg forms his Christology by means of three key theological presuppositions that are formative for the "from below" methodology. Just as the integration of presupposition and methodology was important for Anselm, so too Pannenberg proctors methodological commitments based upon his presuppositions. Thus, to begin understanding the manner in which Pannenberg shall methodologically emphasize resurrection as being central for his Christology, it is necessary to understand these key elements. Therefore chapter six, (2.1) shall be comprised of two parts that provide an understanding of presupposition and methodology: (1) the three key presuppositions that Pannenberg espouses regarding indirect revelation, truth as a historical process, and truth as it reveals the eschatological destiny of humanity in Jesus Christ, and (2) secondly, the "from below" methodology Pannenberg employs for his Christology.

2.1.1 The Pannenbergian Christological Methodology: Three Key Presuppositions

In beginning, in order to understand the crux of the Pannenbergian Christological Methodology of a "theology from below," there is need to perceive what elements and presuppositions are formative. Pannenberg begins his systematic theology from a different position than many systematic theologies, as he does not presuppose "a specifically Christian understanding of God because such a formulation must be won."[282] His intentions here are to demonstrate that a Christian understanding of God is formed on the basis of the relations between God and humanity in the world happening in real time – in history – and as such, it is the outworking of such relations in history and the general religious nature of humanity (and their search for God) which is representative of the process of God revealing universal truth.[283] This position reveals that the manner in which Pannenberg constructs his "from below" methodology will stem from three key presuppositions: (1) first, his understanding of the relations between God and humanity in the world as the process of indirect revelation which is being relationally worked out in real history; (2) secondly, Pannenberg contends that truth is a process, formulated through relations between God and the world, and is being confirmed or disproven by a process of historical debate which must be subjected to historical-critical methodologies; (3) and thirdly, truth is found in the narrative of salvation history that reveals the eschatological destiny of humanity in the resurrection of Jesus Christ. These three key pieces are paramount to understanding how the "theology from below" methodology is formulated in part two (2.1.2) of this chapter.

---

[282] Grenz, *Reason for Hope*, 12. See also Pannenberg, *ST I*, 63-107.

[283] See Pannenberg, *ST I*, 189-258. Much of this can be gleaned from the earlier work of Pannenberg in what came to be *Basic Questions in Theology*. See Pannenberg, *BQT II*, 1-27. An additional earlier source that is influential here comes from his proposal in *Revelation as History* in which he demonstrates the indirect self-revelation of God in salvation history and how the revelation of God is not only a series of ongoing occurrences but more notably the direct self-revelation of God at the end of history to give validity and full disclosure to the earlier indirect events. See Wolfhart Pannenberg. *Revelation as History*. New York: The Macmillan Company, 1968, 123-158. This, of course, has not been without contestation, especially from some who claim that Pannenberg gleans his theology of revelation from either a Hegelian influence or from his anthropological underpinnings. See for example Alan D. Galloway. *Wolfhart Pannenberg*. London: Allen and Unwin, 1973. See also Christoph Shwoebel. "Wolfhart Pannenberg." *The Modern Theologians*, ed. by D.F. Ford. New York: Basil Blackwell Publishers, 1989, 257-293. See also Pailin who challenges the notion of universal history given it is incomplete at present. David Pailin. "Lessing's Ditch Revisited: The Problem of Faith and History." *Theology and Change*, ed. by Ronald H. Preston. London: Student Christian Movement, 1975, 98. See also, Grenz, *Reason for Hope*, 46.

Presupposition Number One: God, Humanity, and Historical Relationship

The first key presupposition in understanding the theology from below methodology Pannenberg utilizes in creating his Christology stems from his theology of God, humanity, and the process of indirect revelation through historical relationship. This key presupposition emerges from the confrontation Pannenberg has with the milieu of his day, especially those who have drawn their theological and philosophical cues from Kant, Lessing, Nietzsche, Feuerbach, and the loss of historicity in the Scriptures.[284] Pannenberg claims the undermining of Scriptural historicity began during the Enlightenment. This posited the concurrent development of some who claimed the unquestionable authoritarian revelatory nature of the Scriptures. He then contends that this was also the very principle to begin the claim that the Scriptures lacked historicity.

What is important, Pannenberg claims, is the historical divine manifestation to Israel and the divine unfolding of history proving to be the impetus for Israel as a people and the reality upon which the Scriptures are derived.[285] The approach Pannenberg utilizes attacks the methodologies of such Enlightenment authoritarian views that weakened the historicity of the Scriptures and offered a new alternative: not to presume God, but to see God as the power of the unbound future who works in history by being in relationship with humanity. Moreover, whereas there is dispute about the existence of God, Pannenberg demonstrates how this dispute is adjudicated in the historical self-revelation of God whose divinity is directly revealed in the end event and in Scripture as the sole "God and God of the whole world."[286] Therefore, what Pannenberg attempts to do from the outset is answer the questions of the milieu by illustrating how the history of the religion of the

---

[284] The specific challenges here stem from the issues presented above dealing with the fact-value dichotomy and the challenges posed by the historical-critical methodologies that had tendencies to leave the Scriptures void of their historicity. For helpful background here, see Wood, *God and History*. See also Tupper, *The Theology of Wolfhart Pannenberg*, 28-44. See also Pannenberg, *ST I*, 63-73.

[285] See Pannenberg, *BQT I*, 1-14. See also Pannenberg, *BQT I*, 15-80. This has not been without challenge from the theological community. For example, see Braaten, Klooster, Galloway and Barr who is especially critical of Pannenberg in this regard. See James Barr. "Revelation Through History in the Old Testament and in Modern Theology." *Interpretation 17*. 1963, 193-205. See also James Barr. "Old and New in Interpretation." *Scottish Journal of Theology No. 19*. London: SPC Publishers, 1966, 82-90. Pannenberg delineates his position in chapter four of *ST I* against Barr who criticizes the idea of revelation in history on the one hand, and yet is accepting of it (as Pannenberg notes) in a similar fashion to Barth and Bultmann. Pannenberg demonstrates how Barr has sought to replace revelation as history for "revelation as word." See Pannenberg, *ST I*, 230-257.

[286] Grenz, *Reason for Hope*, 32. See also Pannenberg, *ST I*, 249-257. It is important to note that Pannenberg denotes revelation as being self-revelation. This concept is Hegelian and Barthian in nature. See Pannenberg, *JGM*, 127-130.

God of Israel is the expression of the truth of God and the meaning of history for the whole world. The essence of this revelation of history is that there will be in the future an end of history in which God will reveal a univocal meaning, purpose, and goal of history for the whole world. Whereas others, such as Barth and Kähler, have claimed the revelation of God is not subject to historical-critical methodologies and the like, Pannenberg utilizes these methodologies, even being faulted by some for not giving enough primacy to the Scriptures, as he sees them as the "sourcebook" for the historical acts of God with Israel and in Christianity.[287]

The manner in which Pannenberg sees the relations between God and humanity is through the lens of his theology of revelation as history. An understanding of the nuance of what he means by revelation is critical for understanding how then Pannenberg does theology. He contends revelation is an indirect self-revelation; acts in which God is revealing the very self of God. As such, direct revelation is a singular and ultimately a one-time event happening at the end of human history in which God directly and fully self-discloses to humanity. The events along the spectrum of history leading to this event are indirect revelation or partial and anticipatory events of that one final act of self-disclosure. Thus, for Pannenberg, historical revelation is the foundation of Christian faith, and must therefore be confirmed through historical investigation.[288] The confirmation of this shall be examined in our second key presupposition, but for now, it shall suffice to say that this is the importance of historical revelation as the unfolding of faith by means of relations between God and humanity in space-time. Pannenberg forms his theological premise of revelation as history from the perspective of bridging interpreter and text because of the great chasm of time between event and interpretation.[289] Pannenberg claims:

---

[287] This is a point well developed by Grenz and Tupper. Pannenberg has been faulted for a "lower" view of Scripture, even though his theology of Scripture is central to his systematic theology. Barthian scholars typically take issue with his view given the high view that "Word of God" theology plays in his systematic theology. This is unsurprising given the notion of Word is disclosed to whom God chooses in the moment of Revelation in Barth. See Grenz, *Reason for Hope*, 47-49. See also Tupper, *The Theology of Wolfhart Pannenberg*, 81-86.

[288] There are a number of sources helpful in making this distinction, most notably Pannenberg, *Revelation as History*, 1-21. See also Pannenberg, *BQT II*, 15-80. See also Pannenberg, *ST I*, 63-73, 189-257. See also Tupper, *The Theology of Wolfhart Pannenberg*, 79-89 for a helpful synopsis.

[289] See Don H. Olive. *Makers of the Modern Theological Mind: Wolfhart Pannenberg*. Waco: Word Books, 1973, 41. The challenge here concerns the question of who is the proper person to interpret the events. This has been raised by a number of scholars from Carl F.H. Henry to Braaten and Bloesch. These are noted in Grenz, *Reason for Hope*, 50. The main point of contention is that Pannenberg leaves too much power in the hands of historical investigation and in that of the historian. This is a similar point to Barth who rejected Pannenberg near the outset of his work. Pannenberg answers this challenge by pointing to the need to recognize the historical nature of revelation and how without a faith that is historically situated, the tenets proposed by

The Pannenbergian Christological Methodology: A Theology from Below 99

All theological questions and answers are meaningful only within the framework of the history which God has with humanity and through humanity with his whole creation – the history moving toward a future still hidden from the world but already revealed in Jesus Christ.[290]

His theology of revelation as history is founded in the experience of Israel and her God, a relationship expressed through an unparalleled historical consciousness that was realized in historical events bringing about historical changes, and it is this revelation of history that expresses the whole of reality which remains incomplete and open to the future in which the final act of direct self-disclosure shall be made by God to humanity.[291] Whereas the Greeks experienced history in a cyclical course of repeating events, Israel had an experience of her God in new and unexpected acts, and it was in those acts in which Israel came to understand that history was not a cycle, but rather had a unified tangential goal toward which all of history was moving.[292] To this end, the theology of history Pannenberg espouses is that of a universal history, and it is this universal history that shall be completely comprehended at the end of all history.[293] These actions God performed are the revelation to humanity of the very selfhood of God. The backdrop of this claim is that through this singular religious history, all of the truth claims for the world are made. Pannenberg claims that the scrutiny of these truth claims made by the history of world religions is necessary, and he argues that these truth claims must ultimately be either accepted or rejected.[294] This will be an im-

---

modern atheism and other historical-critical methodologies quickly gain acceptance. See also Galloway, *Wolfhart Pannenberg*, 42-45.

[290] Pannenberg, *BQT I*, 15.

[291] See Pannenberg, *BQT I*, 17. See also Tupper, *The Theology of Wolfhart Pannenberg*, 79-81. It is important to recognize that this does not mean Pannenberg is espousing open theism, but rather contends it is in the future of the resurrection which has already been proleptically revealed in Jesus Christ in his resurrection from the dead that the final and direct self-disclosure shall then be made. In this moment, humanity will then understand the meaning of history. This is also the juncture in which his understanding of the future eventuating the present to transform the past is derived. See Pannenberg, *Theology and The Kingdom of God*, 127-143. See also Pannenberg, *ST I*, 247-250 among a variety of other sources.

[292] See Pannenberg, *BQT I*, 18-19. As Grenz notes, Murdock has challenged Pannenberg on this point claiming that apocalypticism does not necessarily entail the goal of history. See Grenz, *Reason for Hope*, 47. See W.R. Murdock. "History and Revelation in Jewish Apocalypticism." *Interpretation 21*. 1967, 167-187.

[293] It is important to differentiate Pannenberg and his history as revelation from Hegelianism and its philosophy of the Spirit. Don Olive is helpful in this regard as he demonstrates that Pannenberg agrees with Hegel about world history as being the revelation of God, and yet is quick to claim the finite nature of humanity. This maintains the subject-object distinction and maintains a more orthodox view against pantheism, a point in which Hegel was challenged by others. See Olive, *Makers of the Modern Theological Mind: Wolfhart Pannenberg*, 43-44.

[294] This is a point Pannenberg makes in *BQT II*, 65-118. See also chapter three of his systematic theology for a developed version of this argument. See Pannenberg, *ST I*, 119-188.

portant part of the second key presupposition offered below, namely, the process and scrutiny of truth.

Presently, it is critical to perceive how Pannenberg takes great care to illustrate how Israel came to understand that its history was the very meaning and goal of all history. This is the purpose of the fourth chapter of his systematic theology, and one of the landmark works Pannenberg offers in *Revelation as History*. The basis for his understanding is that revelation is not a new concept but a concept found within the scope of all world religions. In fact, Pannenberg shows how the God who self-revealed to Abram was not unknown but known to others.[295] What was unique, concerned the special revelation God made to Israel and how that special revelation was specific in that it contained specific claims unlike other world religions. For example, the Decalogue and the first commandment is an exclusive and special revelation just as the Exodus event and the remembrance of that event is also a special revelation. Pannenberg offers examples of special revelation that correspond to the acts of Yahweh in history, and it is these acts in which God is revealing the self of God to Israel often through acts of promise and fulfillment.[296] Pannenberg realizes there is discrepancy between the reality of the deity and the experience of revelation, and this is why the revelation of the God of Israel was unique: "it was from the awareness of history by which Israel became the people of God."[297]

These early events within the scope of the history of Israel were connected by later events, most notably, the prophets and apocalyptic predictions which promised that after the covenant-making God was rejected by a covenant-breaking people and after an exile occurred, there would be a future and final direct self-revelation by the God of Israel who would reveal that the "God of Israel is the one true God, the Creator of the world."[298] Again, the expression of this self-disclosure of God is by means of apocalyptic revelation:

> There developed the eschatological expectation of a final actualizing of the Kingdom of God at the end of the series of earthly kingdoms. Linked to this was the expectation of God's righteousness for individuals beyond this earthly life with the resurrection of the just and judgment for sinners.[299]

---

[295] Pannenberg demonstrates while special revelation was made to Abram, others such as Cain, Noah, and the table of nations were not specially addressed and yet knew God. Thus, there was an awareness or some kind of revelation (perhaps a generalized one) in which humanity was then, and remains now, aware of God. This is also evidenced by the utilization of *Elohim* a plural term meaning "gods" Israel used of her God, *Yahweh*. See Pannenberg, *ST I*, 190.

[296] See Pannenberg, *ST*, 191. See also Pannenberg, *BQT I*, 15-38.

[297] Pannenberg, *ST I*, 192.

[298] Pannenberg, *ST I*, 193. This is an important understanding in his theology of revelation as Pannenberg notes that the events throughout the history of Israel are indirect and thus have some level of interpretation but in the eschaton God will through a final and direct act of self-disclosure make all things fully known. See also Gallaway, *Wolfhart Pannenberg*, 60-69.

[299] Pannenberg, *ST I*, 207.

The Pannenbergian Christological Methodology: A Theology from Below 101

This is why Pannenberg offers a unique proposal in his theology of revelation as history; he demonstrates how historical relationship is not only being worked out between God and a specific people whom God elects, but also how history is the very self-revelation of God which is not a foreign concept but a commonality to all humanity. More importantly, Pannenberg moves the connection from revelation as a concept of world religion to the claims of historical revelation from Israel, to the apocalyptic promises which have been fulfilled through the prolepsis of Jesus Christ who embodied and enacted the eschatological revelation of God that is significant for all humanity. Jesus Christ is therefore held in connection with Israel and the God of Israel on the basis of prophecy and the fulfillment of such prophetic announcements. While the fulfillment of these promises and prophetic announcements was not met in the manner in which they were first understood, they were nonetheless fulfilled in history and in the context of the relationship between Israel and her God. Whereas some have tried to claim the historicity of Jesus in the incarnation, Pannenberg grounds the historicity of Jesus on the basis of the history of Israel, and holds (as did von Rad) the meaning of Jesus to be dependent upon, and incomplete without the witness of the Old Testament Scriptures.[300]

Pannenberg then builds upon this history to note that Jesus Christ is the revelation of God by the means of fulfillment of the promises in the history of Israel contained in the Old Testament Scripture, and it is only upon this – that is, the fulfillment of these promises as contained in the history of Israel – which the incarnation of Jesus Christ must be judged.[301] In his estimation this is why the Christian Community utilized the Old Testament promises as the proof of Jesus Christ being the very self-revelation of God. Jesus Christ claimed that the Kingdom had come in him, that he was the self-revelation of God, and that the confirmation of this message was founded in the Christ-event.[302] It is in Jesus Christ and the Christ-event, that is the death and resurrection of Jesus Christ which is part of this history between God and humanity, that the end of history is proleptically revealed in the middle of history, which in turn begins offering the meaning of history itself. The end of history is the resurrection of humanity, and it is Jesus Christ who reveals this presently to humanity. Therefore it is the future and the revelation of God in its entirety that is found in the Christ-event. And yet, even as humanity participates and longs to participate in the hope of the resurrection, "it is still hidden under the experience of the cross... (as) everything earthly must pass

---

[300] The mentor to Pannenberg, von Rad believes the knowledge of Christ is incomplete without the witness of the Old Testament. Pannenberg quotes him in his own explanation. See Pannenberg, *BQT I*, 27-31. See also Gerhard von Rad. "Typological Interpretation of the Old Testament." *Essays on Old Testament Hermeneutics, ed. by Claus Westermann*. Philadelphia: John Knox Press, 1963, 17-39.

[301] See Pannenberg, *BQT I*, 26-27. See also Pannenberg, *ST I*, 247-257.

[302] See Olive, *Makers of the Modern Theological Mind: Wolfhart Pannenberg*, 50. See Pannenberg, *ST I*, 209-215.

through the cross."[303] This, Pannenberg claims, is why the nature of salvation is a universal reality as the God of Israel reveals the very self of God to be the God of the whole world. This is also the stumbling block which others have fallen upon, as it is incredulous for humanity to be bound to a historical origin and for reality to be a historical process of revelation which God is co-authoring.[304]

Finally, directly related to his theology of revelation as history is his theology concerning the "Word of God," and how this is related to his theology of revelation as history. This position has not been without criticism as Grenz notes, "Evangelical scholars have repeatedly faulted him for minimizing the Bible as divine revelation."[305] For Pannenberg, the term "word of God" is related to the historical and divine acts of God, as opposed to Barth who is often found to have three meanings inherent in his theology of the Word of God:

> The three forms of the Word in Barth are presented in such a way that the claim to communicate God's Word refers back from Christian proclamation to scripture and from scripture to Jesus Christ as the Word of God revealed. Christ alone as the revelation of God is directly God's Word. The Bible and church proclamation are God's Word indirectly and derivatively. They have to become God's Word in specific occasions as witness is borne to Jesus Christ.[306]

Whereas Barth sought to maintain the authoritarian and modernistic principle of self-disclosure in his theology of the Word of God, Pannenberg derives his theology of revelation as being indirect and open to interpretation until the direct revelation of God at the end of history in the eschaton.[307] Essentially, he sees the historical process as divine action followed by divine knowledge that offers meaning of this divine action. Only in the eschaton will the nature and meaning of what has been indirectly revealed throughout history be direct and complete. Then the God of Israel will give a direct and divine revelation which conveys the meaning of history altogether.[308] This is

---

[303] Pannenberg, *BQT I*, 37. Here there is also an important reality for his Christology, namely the manner in which Pannenberg seeks to hold the dialectical tension of cross and resurrection.

[304] Pannenberg critiques among others Dilthey, Heidegger, Barth, and Bultmann and their longing to "liberate man from historicity." See Pannenberg, *BQT I*, 34-35.

[305] Grenz is speaking in particular of Fred Klooster. See Fred H. Klooster. "Aspects of Historical Method in Pannenberg's Theology." *Septuagesimo Anno: Festschrift for G.C.. Berkouwer, ed. by J.T. Bakker*. Kampen: Kok Publishers, 1973, 116. Quoted in Grenz, *Reason for Hope*, 47. There are, of course, others who have disagreed with Pannenberg on this point on the basis of minimizing the Scriptures and taking an unorthodox position.

[306] Pannenberg paraphrases Barth and his theology of revelation here. See Karl Barth. *Church Dogmatics Vol. I.*, ed. by G.W. Bromiley and T.F. Torrance. Edinburgh: T and T Clark Publishers, 1936-1969, 117. Quoted from Pannenberg, *ST I*, 235.

[307] See Pannenberg, *Revelation as History*, 131-135.

[308] See Pannenberg, *Revelation as History*, 123-158. See also Pannenberg, *ST I*, 198-214. Noted above, there are a number of theologians who take exception to Pannenberg on his theology of history as revelation, even some of his greatest

why the Bible is not direct revelation, but indirect; there is a shaping of history and the meaning of the historical acts of God which reveal the very self of God to the world. God leaves the interpretation of history that is being debated and scrutinized for its veracity until the eschaton.[309]

It cannot be stressed enough that history – the historical self-revelation of God to people in space-time – is the primary Pannenbergian presuppositionary concern rather than the bible being the Word of God as the kerygma in which the Christ of faith is encountered. In so doing, what Pannenberg attempts to avoid is the position which Barth, Kähler, and others lobbied for: the Scriptures being of an authoritarian, self-authenticating, and exclusive regard, without potentiality for critical interaction. Instead, Pannenberg contends through the very historical-critical methodologies that have tended to undermine the historicity of Scripture, the revelation of God in Jesus Christ is maintained. This, of course, is not without fault, as the Scriptures in this manner might quickly devolve into any other challengeable text and give too much credit to the historian to debate and decide their veracity. However, Pannenberg by addressing his milieu and its questions contends that in the end whereas the Scriptures might have a point of historical contestability, there will be a final act of self-disclosure to settle the matter eternally. Given the explanation of the revelation of God as the working of God in history for the people of God, now this study moves toward what has been raised at the end of this section, namely how truth has a process and is being scrutinized among the world religions.

---

supporters. For example, Braaten is critical of part of his proposal (although affirming of it for the most part) as he methodologically suspends the *sola Scriptura* principle and questions whether or not this is necessary given that religious experience is being interpreted and one cannot fully eliminate religious experience as if it did not exist. In this regard, Braaten claimed that Pannenberg sought to guard against fideism. In this regard, Braaten has warrant to make such a claim, although one might question if Pannenberg would not recognize religious experience as a presupposition even though he methodologically sought to work from objectivity rather than the subjective as in Schleiermacher. See Carl E. Braaten. "The Place of Christianity Among the World Religions: Wolfhart Pannenberg's Theology of Religions and the History of Religions." *The Theology of Wolfhart Pannenberg: Twelve American Critiques*. Minneapolis: Augsburg Publishing House, 1988, 287-312. Jüngel said the Pannenbergian methodology was to "think of God with God having been removed (*remoto deo*) was a challenge to Barth whose theology of revelation was a capitulation in some regard to the historical-critical methodologies of the milieu. See Eberhard Jüngel. *God as the Mystery of the World*, trans. by Darrell L. Guder. Grand Rapids: Eerdmans Publishing, 1983. See also Klooster who is helpful in describing how Pannenberg saw theology as being grounded in history, although Klooster claims that Pannenberg did not fully solve the methodological problem of a positivistic view of history. See Klooster, *Septuagesimo Anno: Festschrift for C.G. Berkouwer*.

[309] See Pannenberg, *ST I*, 230-257. See also Grenz, *Reason for Hope*, 47-55.

Presupposition Number Two:
The Process of Truth and the Scrutiny of Truth

The second key presupposition in understanding the theology from below method Pannenberg utilizes in creating his Christology is founded in his understanding of truth as a process of the relations between God and the world (which has been delineated above), but even more, of truth as a process of historical debate subject to historical-critical methodologies. Noted above, Pannenberg sees revelation as an indirect rather than direct mediation, which is universally accessible and open to interpretation throughout history by means of a process of scrutiny and debate. Direct communication intends to communicate its content with immediacy and a sense of complete meaning, whereas indirect communication has some other initial information that is expounded upon or updated at a later time. Accordingly, Pannenberg opts for a God who discloses selfhood in terms of indirect events, and it is the outcome of the events that provides outcomes of the actions of God.[310] This is a unique feature, as it is through historical events God is made manifest and while those events are interpretable, God has not revealed univocal meaning of those events presently – only anticipatorily. Moreover, Pannenberg claims it is due to the indirect nature of revelation that "the revelation of God is open to everyone who has eyes to see, requiring no additional inspiration."[311] To this end, Pannenberg sees indirect communication to be on a "higher level: it always has direct communication as its basis, but takes this into a new perspective.[312] The primary reason that Pannenberg lobbies for revelation as being indirect rather than direct, is the desire for the only direct revelation to occur at the end of history in the eschaton.[313] Thus he presupposes revelation is a historical reality in his theology, and it is through the passing of time that the knowledge and understanding of those events come to be mediated to humanity. The final understanding of the events of God in

---

[310] See Gallaway, *Wolfhart Pannenberg*, 49. See also Pannenberg, *Revelation as History*, 13-19.

[311] Grenz, *Reason for Hope*, 36. This differs from Barth who contended that the Word of God was revealed only to those whom God chose and was thus void of natural reason, and also Bultmann who contended that there was an existential moment of revelation independent of reason. See Pannenberg, *Revelation as History*, 1-21. See also Bradshaw who gives a good synopsis of revelation as history in Timothy Bradshaw. *Pannenberg: A Guide for the Perplexed*. London: T and T Clark Publishers, 2009, 30-34.

[312] Pannenberg, *Revelation as History*, 14. The point to be made here is that indirect communication has a sense of interruption or broken transmission and the reason Pannenberg points to it being on a higher level is the importance of consideration of perspectives and connection with the intent of meaning. Indirect communication therefore reveals something indirectly about God because the content is not God himself. Only in the end – the direct self-disclosure of God will there be a full disclosure of God himself to humanity and the world.

[313] See Pannenberg, *Revelation as History*, 6-8. See also Tupper, *The Theology of Wolfhart Pannenberg*, 80.

history shall be fully and directly disclosed in a final and direct act of self-disclosure in which the God of Israel will be fully known as the God of the whole world and all that is in it.

Having delineated the Pannenbergian understanding of indirect revelation, it is now important to see that the question of truth is an important one for Pannenberg, and he notes that since the Enlightenment this has been an important question for Christianity especially the truth of the Christian message as it relates to reality itself.[314] The importance of this dovetails with his theology of indirect self-revelation and how at the end of history there will be a final act of direct revelation and full disclosure so that truth shall be fully known. In this manner, his understanding of how truth has progressed is founded in a transition from passive to active principle, namely that truth was once passively received and is now actively created by humanity. Specifically, Pannenberg claims modern culture has severed humanity from religion, so the understanding of truth has come to be not so much truth "as it is," but the truth "for me."[315] This is the place in which the historical acts of God confront a subjective role of truth, especially in the Pannenbergian revelation as history model, for truth in his theology is not active but a passively received truth – it is the truth of God which is personal and unifies all truth.[316] Thus, truth in his estimation is relational and revelational, ultimately having occurred in the resurrection of Jesus Christ which is proleptically the revelation of the end of history. Truth, then, is located in the future by means of trust in the God who comes from the future to reveal the future, thus binding truth to the future and the time in which the process of conceptualizing truth ends.[317]

So for Pannenberg, truth has been revealed proleptically in Jesus Christ, but the meaning of truth and the final confirmation of truth shall be established in the eschaton.

---

[314] An important essay of Pannenberg relative to his theology of truth is found in "What is Truth?" In it, he sets some of the basic tenets for his understanding and theology of truth and paves the way for his later well-delineated argument concerning truth as a process of scrutiny among the world religions in Systematic Theology Vol. I, Chapter Three. See Pannenberg, *BQT II*, 1-2. See also Galloway, *Wolfhart Pannenberg*. 46-59.

[315] Pannenberg, *BQT II*, 12-13. See also Pannenberg, *ST I*, 150-151.

[316] See Pannenberg, *BQT II*, 17-19.

[317] See Pannenberg, *BQT II*, 24-25. This move binds the future and truth together and more readily identifies his systematic theology as being eschatological in form. Mentioned at the outset of unit two, this manifests itself in the future shaping the present to transform the past. Given that the final self-revelation of God is at the end of history and given that God has indirectly manifested and been revealed in history, the process of history is being shaped from the future in this methodology which shapes the present understanding of history, thus transforming the past of history. For a deeper view of the Pannenbergian eschatological understanding of time see chapter five (2.0, (94-96)). See also Pannenberg, *ST II*, 84-102. See also, Pannenberg, *Theology and The Kingdom of God*, 127-143. See Pannenberg, *What is Man?*, 68-81.

His initial premise of truth is an important one as it is now possible to see that truth is a historical process of scrutiny being worked out among the world religions. Pannenberg contends humanity is at its core religious; what is unique is how the truth of Christianity is expressed as universally true for the world. The means by which he sees this expression is through a process of reconciling the competing truth claims of the religions, and the manner in which the gods of the religions show in our experience of the world that they are the powers they claim to be. This process is at its heart revelation – a process by which the God of the universe is competing with other rival claims to express the true reality of who God is, and the nature of truth and reality itself.[318] Pannenberg offers a lucid example when he demonstrates how Yahweh, the God of Israel, accompanied the Israelites to the Land of Canaan, when the god Baal was well known there. The competing claims of both religions led to clashes between these rival deities and over time, the monotheism of the Israelites which demanded complete loyalty to Yahweh founded in the Decalogue, emerged as the unifying reality of humanity.[319] Pannenberg offers a specific understanding of the truthfulness of religion through three litmus tests:

1. The confirmation or non-confirmation of religious assertions and especially of belief in the existence and work of the deity is experienced and established in the first instance by the adherents of the relevant religious fellowship, by the worshippers of the deity....The tension which is required for interpretation of both the tradition and the common experience of the world also arises when belief in the deity is brought to those who thus far have not belonged to the circle of worshippers of this deity.

2. The question of the confirmation or non-confirmation of belief in a deity, and therefore of the truth or untruth of the deity itself, often stands under the competitive pressure of the truth claims of other deities which claim the same sphere of experience of the world as proof....The challenging of the competence of a deity by another deity and its alternative interpretive potential is not everywhere, perhaps, an everyday problem of religious life and religious tradition.

3. The demand of faith that a deity should prove its power in relation to changed experience of the world leads in the positive instances of confirmation to a change in the understanding of the nature and working of the deity....For Israel, the experience of historical change itself became a medium of awareness of God in the patriarchal traditions, the exodus tradition, recollection of the election of David and his house, and also of Jerusalem as the place in which to worship

---

[318] See Pannenberg, *ST I*, 167-171.
[319] See Pannenberg, *ST I*, 147-150.

Yahweh, and finally in the message of the prophets....For Israel, the history which it experienced, along with its unfinished future, which included the future of the world and humanity, was seen as the history of the manifestation of God. Interpretations of historical experience of the world as an expression of the power and activity of God had an impact on the actual understanding of God, so that in the medium of history the deity and attributes of God were increasingly manifested not in steady advances – for there were also times of obscurity in the march of events – but in progression toward the future in which the glory of the God of Israel would be definitively manifesto to all people in his historical acts.[320]

Finally, Pannenberg asserts revelation must be subjected to historical-critical methodologies and historical research. While there are issues of validity with this which have been noted above in the first presupposition, there remains the possibility for a further investigation of revelation when compared to the historical background that lends greater meaning and understanding. Pannenberg illustrates his longing for the truth to be proved through these methodologies rather than disputed by them:

> The reference of the Christian faith to history unavoidably carries with it the demand that the believer must not try to save himself from historical-critical questions by means of some "invulnerable area" – otherwise it will lose its historical basis.[321]

Within the scope of historical method, Pannenberg holds redemptive and ordinary history are not unrelated but interrelated, and it is in the interrelatedness of these histories that one finds a principle of universal correlation.[322] The antithetical issue is founded in anthropocentrism of the very methodological concerns of historical-critical methodologies to begin with, namely the exclusion of transcendence and the elevation of humanity to the active author of history rather than passive receiver of history.[323] Accordingly, the truth of the Christian faith is based upon "the historical figure of Jesus and his message, and then on the position of the Christian message among

---

[320] Pannenberg, *ST I*, 168-169.
[321] Pannenberg, *BQT I*, 56. Tupper argues that Herrmann and Kähler attempted "to establish the basis of faith independent of the shifting currents of historical research and thereby fell victim to the fatal consequence of actually building faith upon faith itself." Tupper, *The Theology of Wolfhart Pannenberg*, 110. See also Pannenberg, *BQT I*, 38. This is also similar to Barth and Bultmann, noted at the beginning of this second presupposition. Both attempted to deny the historical question for alternative methodologies. Pannenberg conversely utilizes historical-critical method to support his process.
[322] See Pannenberg, *BQT I*, 39-50. See also Pannenberg, *ST I*, 142-143.
[323] The passive/active author of history has been explained above, and the importance of this is now revealed in how the anthropocentric tendencies of historical-critical method undermine a theology of revelation as history. See Pannenberg, *BQT I*, 39-42.

the other religions of humanity."³²⁴ What Pannenberg offers overcomes Kähler in his division between the historical Jesus and the historic biblical Christ and even Barthianism and its *Heilsgeschichte*. Pannenberg does not sidestep the issue by claiming revelation occurs in the Scriptures through the preached kerygma as the divine revelation of God, but rather claims that the utilization of historical-critical methodologies and research techniques which are universally accessible are important for upholding the universal history contained in the Scriptures. Whereas universal correlation tends to eliminate revelatory history from universal history, Pannenberg offers a proposal for revelatory history to be understood within the context of the background of history itself. Thus the historical background in which revelation occurred is the rightful place for such revelation to be investigated utilizing this method. Moreover, whereas analogy is contingent upon correlation, it does not mean that it must be restricted as such. The key of analogy is the potentiality of commonality and transcendence.³²⁵

Ultimately, Pannenberg contends truth is a historical enterprise being identified, tested, re-shaped, and directly revealed in the eschaton. The history of the religions of the world is the stage upon which truth is debated, and even atheism has rightly entered into the debate by asserting the claims of religion are merely anthropocentric realities. History itself has led to the development of truth claims being passively received through the gods and God of Israel until at some point history was believed to be actively created by humanity. Whereas some claim direct manifestation and communication of the revelation of God, Pannenberg contends indirect revelation is the manner in which God reveals the self of God to humanity, allowing for an event(s) to continually unfold and grow in meaning. This, of course, makes revelation a future event, and it is the future of humanity revealed proleptically in the death and resurrection of Jesus that opens up future possibilities for humanity and the final direct self-disclosure of God to humanity. Whereas Barth and Kähler sidestepped historical method and historical-critical methodologies, Pannenberg claims they help establish the veracity of Christianity among competing claims.³²⁶

---

³²⁴ Pannenberg, *ST I*, 131.

³²⁵ Tupper offers illumination on Pannenberg here. See Tupper, *The Theology of Wolfhart Pannenberg*, 111-113. Tupper argues that the genius of analogy is the illumination of "what is obscure to what is plain," and in this regard historical method demonstrates mutuality between items.

³²⁶ See Olive, *Makers of the Modern Theological Mind: Wolfhart Pannenberg*, 43-45. Essentially Pannenberg utilizes universally accessible principles to objectively establish the truth of the Christian religion by pointing to the resurrection of Jesus Christ as a prolepsis of what the end of history will be in the direct self-revelation of God. Bradshaw is helpful here by pointing out how Pannenberg "spread out the hermeneutical content whereas Barth personalizes it, and Bultmann makes it an intense event of the individual subjectivity." Bradshaw goes on to describe how this move is Hegelian in blending revelation, biblical narrative, and reality. See Bradshaw, *Pannenberg*, 36.

Now that two presuppositions of Pannenbergian theological methodology have been explored, namely, historical relationship as revelation and the process of truth as confirmation or non-confirmation of that revelation, this chapter turns to the third presupposition: the truth of revelation in Jesus Christ who reveals the eschatological destiny of humanity.

Presupposition Number Three: Salvation History and the Resurrection of Jesus Christ

This third key presupposition is simply a conclusion of the first two: whereas truth is being revealed in the historical relationship between God and humanity which is the indirect revelation of God; and whereas that truth is being tested, scrutinized, confirmed throughout time, and shall be directly revealed and established at the end of time in the eschaton; then it is that future truth proleptically revealed in the resurrection of Jesus Christ which reveals the impending eschaton and thus the eschatological destiny of humanity. It has been said above that the resurrection of Jesus Christ is the future revelation of God. It is that revelation that opens the future for humanity by revealing at least a glimpse of the future now in the present. More importantly, it is that revelation which Pannenberg contends is the final direct self-disclosure of God in which the God of Israel will be proven as the God of the world and of history.

Pannenberg argues Jesus Christ connects the final direct self-disclosure of God in the future with the history of God and Israel of the past, and the prophetic promises which foretold of a coming Messiah.[327] Utilizing a typological interpretation of the Old Testament set forth by his mentor von Rad, Pannenberg finds the "Christ-event of the New Testament is prefigured."[328] Accordingly, whereas some might say it is difficult to find relevance in the Old Testament because of the manner in which the Christ-event seemingly surpasses these events, Pannenberg guards against this. He contends it is the whole of the history of God and humanity that comes to its penultimate fulfillment in the proleptic Christ-event which prefigures the eschaton. He trusts much of his systematic theology to the Christ-event, for Pannenberg believes Christology has to do with not only the confession of Christ, but with the grounding of Christ in the historical activity of Jesus, and most particularly in the cross and resurrection:

---

[327] See Pannenberg, *BQT I*, 26-27. This is contested by Bultmann who claims that the connection between Old Testament and New Testament is in a "history of failure," in which fulfillment is based on the failure of hopes of covenant and relationship between God and humanity, arises the justified man. See Rudolf K. Bultmann. "Prophecy and Fulfillment." *Essays, ed. by Westermann*. 50-75.

[328] See Von Rad, Gerhard. "Typological Interpretation of the Old Testament." *Essays, ed. by Westermann*. 17-39. Quotation cited from Pannenberg, *BQT I*, 29.

Only in trust in the reliability of the report of Jesus' resurrection and exaltation are we able to turn in prayer to the one who is exalted and now lives, and thus to associate with him in the present.[329]

Thus, without the whole of the history of the indirect self-disclosure of God, the meaning of Christ is incomplete. Whereas some have lobbied for the historicity of man as the means to the freedom of humanity,[330] Pannenberg grounds the freedom of humanity solely in the history of God which comes to fulfillment in the resurrection of Jesus Christ:

> This happens first of all through the unexpected way in which God fulfills his promise, but then through the fact that this fulfillment, the end of history in Jesus Christ, had provisionally already come – and yet precisely thereby is deprived of all comprehension. We can say what such an outbreak of the incomprehensibility of the eschaton in history means only in the framework of a universal historical understanding of the reality in which this outbreak occurs, just because through it the universal historical scheme is itself forced open.[331]

Finally, while this is simple enough logic to follow, there is a methodological question Pannenberg asks which features an answer marking the bridge between his presuppositions having to do with the historical acts of indirect self-revelation between God and Israel which culminated in the death and resurrection of Jesus Christ, the scrutiny of such events throughout time, the final and direct self-revelation in the eschaton, and his "from below" methodology. It is precisely this methodological question which is featured in *Jesus – God and Man*:

> Must Christology begin with Jesus himself or with the kerygma of his community?[332]

The answer to this presuppositional question forms the impetus to his methodology. Pannenberg contends Kähler and subsequent theologies began at the place of the kerygma of Jesus, which did not concern the revelation of God in history, but merely the faith of the apostles concerning Jesus the Christ.[333] In other words, revelational content was not the issue for Kähler as much as belief in the person and faith-propositions about Jesus the Christ. This is an important issue, which seemingly has some continuity with the Anselmian *credo ut intelligam* presupposition. For Anselm, the issue was belief, and understanding was meant to follow this belief. However, as argued earlier, Anselm utilized a "from above" methodology which sought understanding for the purposes of responding to the unbelief of his milieu, which compromised his presuppositionary principle. Perhaps Anselm and Pannenberg hold a point of continuity in this regard, as Pannenberg will uti-

---

[329] Pannenberg, *JGM*, 28.
[330] For example, see Bultmann, Tillich, and many modern theologians whose focus is existentialism.
[331] Pannenberg, *BQT I*, 37-38.
[332] Pannenberg, *JGM*, 22.
[333] Pannenberg, *JGM*, 22.

lize historical-critical methodologies to help one understand what one should believe. Anselm and his *remoto Christo* methodology had concern for the acts of God through Jesus Christ but only insofar as a faith-proposition in which Jesus Christ freed humanity from its offenses that required a magnanimous payment to God which only Jesus Christ can pay. Both in Kähler and in Anselm is the "from above" methodology that posits great value upon the incarnation and the subsequent value Jesus Christ has for humanity. The results of this methodology concern the lesser value given to how the historical acts of God that culminate in the resurrection of Jesus Christ have been used by God to open the future and presently reveal what has not yet come to pass. Whereas Anselm assumed the incarnation as the basis for the divinity of Jesus Christ which enabled him to satisfy the offended honor of God, Kähler similarly presupposed key meaning in the Christological confessions concerning the Christ of faith in the kerygma which delivers these confessions. Thus meaning and truth are not derived from their historical perspective in Anselm or Kähler but from logic, as well as confessional doctrines, and kerygma.[334] Given the authority of the Church and the desire for the utilization of logic, this is unsurprising.

When one considers the Pannenbergian presuppositions of revelation as history, utilizing historical-critical methodologies and the like, Pannenberg refutes these "from above" methodologies. He contends that one must ask, "Is one is able to ground any hope for the future if it cannot be determined what happened historically to Jesus of Nazareth?" This is why Pannenberg states:

> Christology is concerned, therefore, not only with unfolding the Christian community's confession of Christ, but above all with grounding it in the activity and fate of Jesus in the past. The confession of Christ cannot be presupposed already and simply interpreted. Christology cannot take its point of departure from the confessions of the Reformation, for example, from the Christological statements of the Formula of Concord, or from the Christological formula of the council of Chalcedon, nor can it simply develop the oldest primitive Christian confession, the sentence Iesous (Christos) Kyrios ("Jesus is Lord," Rom. 1:4; 10:9; I Cor. 12:3). The confession itself must be grounded by Christology.[335]

So, then, his Christological method seeks to fulfill what the previous two presuppositions have stated: (1) to look at the content of revelation as the relations between God and humanity in history as the product of indirect self-disclosure, and (2) to demonstrate against the backdrop of historical in-

---

[334] Careful nuance must be made here. This is not to say that Anselm and Kähler did not believe in the resurrection or the historical acts of God in Jesus Christ. Rather, they methodologically suspend the historical materials, logically deduce the incarnation and the divinity of Jesus Christ, and the salvation which Jesus offers as a logical conclusion of the incarnation. The confessions and kerygma are a derivation of a methodological assumption similar to Anselm; rather than the history of Jesus Christ, the confessional statements and kerygmatic acts convey the content of faith.

[335] Pannenberg, *JGM*, 28-29.

vestigations and the history of other religions, that the history of Jesus Christ substantiates faith, especially through the Christ-event.

2.1.2 The Pannenbergian Christological Methodology: A Theology from Below

Given the above three key presuppositions, what then of the Pannenbergian Christological methodology? Pannenberg espouses the meaning of history is founded in the completion of history, and how reality is determined by its completion in the future. This completion has been revealed proleptically in the resurrection of Jesus, and therefore the meaning of history has been at least partially established before it has been completed. Inherent in the Christ-event is the meaning and understanding of Jesus Christ and his universal significance, which is the reason Pannenberg utilizes a methodology featuring a "Christology from below;" that is, a methodology grounded in the historical acts of Jesus of Nazareth who is revealed to be the Christ of God. Whereas much of theological modernity excised the resurrection of its historicity, he posits the death and resurrection of Jesus Christ as the central focal point of his theology, claiming that it is in this event that the divinity of Jesus of Nazareth as the Christ is revealed.

Key to his proposal is the recognition that rather than assuming the divinity of Jesus, the divinity of Jesus Christ must be understood from the historical acts of Jesus Christ to warrant the possibility or probability for such a claim. Accordingly, the remainder of chapter six (2.1.2) shall deal with two important issues in the Pannenbergian Christological Methodology: (1) first a delineation of the "from above" methodology with, (2) a delineation of the "from below" methodology with emphasis on the contrast between the two, and (3) thirdly, the seemingly contrasting Logos Christology versus Historical Christology which Pannenberg creatively resolves through his "from below" methodological proposal. This methodology shall then be pressed forward in chapter seven to illustrate how the retroactive significance of the resurrection featured in this methodology "from below" is the means by which Pannenberg constructs his Christology, and is also the very means by which he maintains the dialectical tension between the cross and resurrection.

Christology from Above

The present study now turns to what has already been introduced in 1.1.3, namely the from above versus from below Christological methodologies. This consideration is essential, as it is the Christological undertaking which is central to Christian doctrine.[336] The study of chapter two (1.1.3) demonstrated

---

[336] This point is argued by Grenz. He claims Christology is central to Christian doctrine. He utilizes not only Pannenberg and also offers Karl Barth as an example of

that Anselm utilized an *a priori* theology from above methodology which assumed the divinity of Jesus in the incarnation on the basis of the need of his crucifixion to provide a satisfaction unto God for the sins of humanity.[337] Set in contrast is a theology from below methodology Pannenberg utilizes.[338] Whereas a theology from above *a priori* assumes the divinity of Jesus in the incarnation with the incarnation being central to this Christology, a theology from below begins with history and "arrives only at the end at the concept of the incarnation."[339] This is an important distinction readily setting Pannenberg apart from not only Anselm but also many modern theologians, especially Karl Barth.[340] Given these generalizations, the first section of 2.1.2 shall deal with the specificities of a theology from above and from below, which shall illumine the remainder of 2.1.2.

Outlined briefly in chapters one and two, one must ask what can be said of a theology from above, and more specifically, what are the issues inherent within this theological methodology? Citing Ignatius of Antioch and the second-century Apologists, the Alexandrian Christology of Athanasius and Cyril, as well as the modern theologian Karl Barth, Pannenberg readily admits some Scriptural precedent supports a theology from above.[341] Within this tradition, Barthian Christology utilizes the from above methodology, placing emphasis on the divinity of Jesus with the incarnation of the preexistent Son at the center. Thus, the history of the Son becoming human is the concern for Barth and showing "how Christ is Jesus of Nazareth."[342] Notwithstanding these Scriptural evidences, Pannenberg claims dissonance is found in the transmission of the tradition of Christianity with this methodology of Christology. This dissonance is founded through an understanding of how history revealed (i.e. a theology from below) Jesus of Nazareth to be the Christ of God which stands in contradiction with a theology from above. Even more, one

---

this. See below as Pannenberg describes Barth as utilizing a methodology that deals with ascent and descent. See Grenz, *Reason for Hope*, 147-148.

[337] See chapter two (1.1.3, (40-48)). See also chapter three (1.2.2 (74-81)).

[338] See Pannenberg, *JGM*, 33-37. See also, Pannenberg, *ST I*, 277-297.

[339] Pannenberg, *JGM*, 33. Pannenberg debates his proposal in the footnotes of *Jesus – God and Man* with Otto Weber who believes that the "encounter with Jesus Christ" is the proper starting places for Christological method. See Otto Weber. *Grundlagen der Dogmatik*, Vol. II. Neukirchen Kreis Moers: Verlag der Buchhandlung des Erziehungsvereins, 1955.

[340] Pannenberg describes the differences in his methodology versus Barth who utilizes a from above methodology featuring ascent and descent. See Pannenberg, *JGM*, 33-37.

[341] He contends the kenotic passage of Philippians 2:5 is a good example. See Pannenberg, *JGM*, 33.

[342] This point made by Don Olive, is namely that Barthian Christology focuses on the incarnation and how the history of the Son is derived by the Son becoming man, and by uniting divinity with humanity. This unification of the Divine Son with humanity is what is historical in the opinion of Barth. See Olive, *Wolfhart Pannenberg*, 55. See also Pannenberg, *JGM*, 33-34. See Karl Barth. *Church Dogmatics*, IV/2. London: T and T Clark, 1932-1968.

cannot simply claim the confessional statements of Jesus Christ are enough for faith; rather, it is because God has acted through Jesus Christ in history that faith is possible. In this way, the resurrection is the historical reality establishing the incarnation and cross, and more importantly confirmation of the confession and kerygma of the Church.[343] Pannenberg claims:

> Only by his resurrection from the dead did the Crucified attain to the dignity of the Kyrios (Phil 2:9-11). Only thus was he appointed the Son of God in power (Rom. 1:4). Only in light of the resurrection is he the preexistent Son. Only as the risen Lord is he always the living Lord of his community.[344]

Pannenberg claims the departure from the historical from below method has been through the development of theology and doctrine, a process of development which has given precedence to the incarnation.[345] The essence of his claim stems from the period of the "second century onward," and how Christology has developed out of the need to relate the "preexistent Son to God himself, and his preceding from the Father."[346] Part of this was out of necessity as the needs of the early church were to relate the message and historical acts of Jesus to those in a polytheistic world whose thinking was through the lens of a polytheistic world-view.[347] From this point of departure, it is plausible that the from above logos methodology would continue to be the position from which the Church defended its Christology. Beyond the early Church, the Roman Catholic Church of the Middle Ages, and into the period of modern theology, Pannenberg contends that whereas Ritschl called for the appeal to the history of Jesus and a Christology from above to below,[348] from the time of Schleiermacher forward, the appeal to the

---

[343] This fits within the corpus of the presuppositions from 2.1.1, namely the utilization of the indirect revelation of God as the unfolding of history between God and Israel that is accessible by all humanity, and the direct and final act of self-disclosure that is proleptically revealed in the resurrection of Jesus Christ from the dead. A from below methodology begins to build upon these presuppositions. This also stands in contrast to Schleiermacher, Barth and Bultmann. See Pannenberg, *JGM*, 33. See also Olive, *Wolfhart Pannenberg*, 55-56. See Pannenberg, *ST II*, 282-297.

[344] Pannenberg, *ST II*, 283.

[345] See Pannenberg, *JGM*, 35.

[346] Pannenberg, *ST II*, 278. Mentioned briefly before in chapter three, Pannenberg gives credit for this move to Ignatius of Antioch who reinterpreted Son of Man in such a way that the humanity of the Son was expressed and thus led to a from above Christological concept. He describes that a "fateful shift" occurs in this movement as the incarnation replaced Easter to describe the union of the Son of God with humanity. Pannenberg argues that the process of unification is not just a singular event in the incarnation but rather an ongoing process of his earthly history. See Pannenberg, *ST II*, 382-384. See also Pannenberg, *ST I*, 297-304, 379-389. This has been disputed by Barth in his argument for the "Way of the Son into a Far Country" and the doctrine of election that he proposes. See Pannenberg, *ST I*, 377-378. See Barth, *Church Dogmatics IV/1*, 182-183.

[347] See Pannenberg, *ST II*, 278.

[348] This is quoted in Pannenberg, *ST II*, 278. Original source: F.H.R. Frank. *Zur Theologie A. Ritschl's*, 1888, 27.

history of Jesus was exchanged for the anthropocentric faith-consciousness approach in which one considers the from above rational approach to the divine logos.[349]

Whereas a theology from above presupposes Trinity, there are three reasons that there is an issue with this. First, there is an issue with presupposing the divinity of Jesus as one must establish why history has proven Jesus to be Christ and thus the divine Son. Otherwise, can one properly confess faith in Jesus Christ? Secondly, the from above methodology supports a divine logos theology, undermining the historicity of Jesus Christ, even making the assumption of the union between humanity and God. In this way, the life and message of Jesus are not "crucial for the basic Christological questions."[350] Without the historicity of Jesus Christ, can one properly claim that the future of humanity lies in Jesus and in God, and can one say that humanity is able to have union with God in Jesus Christ? To press the point further, Pannenberg claims the death of Jesus is important only insofar as one can answer why Jesus is subjected to "the universal human fate of death."[351] Perhaps Anselm understood this when he wrote his *Cur Deus Homo* and this is why he approached it from the perspective of Jesus Christ making a satisfactory payment for humanity to properly satisfy the offended honor of God. And thirdly, the issue with this methodology concerns how it would be necessary for humanity to stand in the "position of God himself," which is impossible because humanity cannot escape the human condition and know fully the nature of the divinity of Jesus Christ.[352] Clearly, this is an issue that does not need much delineation, as if one presupposes classical theism, one would have difficulty saying that one stands in the position of God to understand the nature of the divinity of Jesus Christ. The human condition has inescapable limitations due to the finitude of humanity and the infinite nature of God.

Finally, the theology from above proposal has as a key issue how one can presuppose the divinity of Jesus of Nazareth as the Christ without historical acts to confirm or establish his divinity. More importantly from the perspective of humanity, can humanity properly have faith in Jesus of Nazareth if he is not proven to be the Christ through the acts of God in and through him resultative of the long-standing messianic promise? Can humanity properly claim that their future is founded in Jesus Christ who has claimed union with God if indeed Jesus Christ has not indicated through any acts that he has union with God? These types of questions set the stage for the theology from below proposal for which Pannenberg argues.

---

[349] See Pannenberg, *ST II*, 280-282.

[350] Pannenberg, *JGM*, 35.

[351] Pannenberg, *JGM*, 35. Pannenberg takes care to investigate the soteriological Christology of Anselm and notes that his approach is different from the patristic church as Anselm places emphases upon "satisfaction and penance rather than the deification of humanity." Pannenberg, *JGM*, 42-43.

[352] See Pannenberg, *JGM*, 34-35.

Christology from Below

Given the realities of a theology from above which have now been presented, what is the theology from below proposition Pannenberg offers, and more importantly, what issues are inherent within this methodology? Beyond the acts of Jesus, the kerygma of Jesus, or even later Christological doctrines and confessions of Jesus Christ, concerns the relation of Jesus Christ to God, and according to Pannenberg, the evaluation of the former proceeds in light of the latter.[353] He contends one cannot simply rely upon Christological doctrines or the Christological confessions of the creeds, as these are not the sources for the grounding of Christology, they are merely confessions that form the outcomes of Christology.[354] Rather than presupposing the unity of Jesus Christ with God, Pannenberg contends that through a theology from below, Jesus is indeed shown to be the Christ of God. In this way, whereas the from above methodology looks to confirm "Christ is Jesus of Nazareth (Pannenberg looks to) confirm that Jesus of Nazareth is the Christ."[355] At the heart of his proposal of a theology from below is the resurrection of Jesus Christ as the historical reality confirming the unity of Jesus with God, and the reason the Gospel writers claimed that Jesus was the promised Messiah of God. This central theme of his proposal is the means by which Pannenberg builds his methodology. This methodology looks to the history and message of Jesus of Nazareth and how he is confirmed to be the Christ of God in the Christ-event.[356] It cannot be stressed enough that Pannenberg not only places incredible value upon the resurrection, but also claims the resurrection is a historical act happening within the fabric of other historical acts. He contends that the resurrection is equally as probable as any other historical act, forming the locus of his from below eschatological Christology.[357] From the outset of the from below methodology

---

[353] This is to say that it is the question of how the acts, teachings, kerygma, and most importantly the Christ-event are evidences for the relation of Jesus and God, not vice versa. Whereas a theology from above assumes Jesus is united to God in the incarnation and thus the work and message are from God above, the theology from below evaluates this on the basis of the resurrection as the establishment of the relation between Jesus and God. See Pannenberg, *JGM*, 36-37.

[354] See Pannenberg, *JGM*, 28-29.

[355] Olive, *Wolfhart Pannenberg*, 55.

[356] Pannenberg, *JGM*, 36.

[357] See Grenz, *Reason for Hope*, 148-149. The importance of this is the challenge it presents to Bultmannian theology and the host of other theologians from the time of Hume forward who have denied the historicity of the resurrection because it is a unique and miraculous event which cannot be proven according to historical-critical methodologies or Cartesian rationalism. These theologies have claimed the resurrection is not a historically verifiable event and have tended to view the resurrection as an existential event rather than a historical one. That he posits such great value upon the resurrection could potentially invalidate portions of his systematic theology, especially given the great value he places upon the need for coherence.

Pannenberg employs, there is stress upon the Christ-event, most particularly from the point of the resurrection – which confirms the work of the cross and the incarnation.[358]

His from below methodology is guided by the key presuppositions offered above: how history is the indirect revelation of God, how revelation needs to be subjected to scrutiny for the testing of its veracity, and how it is in the Christ-event that Jesus Christ has opened up the future to humanity. A historically oriented methodology from below achieves these three elements by means of the historical and indirect self-revelation of God, subjected to scrutiny and historical-critical methodologies. His Christology is cast in light of historical probabilities and conclusions from the Christ-event which interpret previous historical events as well as the life and ministry of Jesus. It is also cast in light of the proleptic Christ-event which opens the future to humanity because it is in and through Jesus Christ that humanity is able to discern the process of history and their relationship to God through the process of reconciliation in Jesus Christ. Pannenberg claims this in his from below proposal:

> For this purpose dogmatic Christology must go behind the New Testament to the base to which it points and which supports its faith in Jesus, that is, to the history of Jesus. Christology has to ask and show the extent to which this history substantiates faith in Jesus.[359]

The essence of his from below Christology is simple at face value: the methodology looks chiefly to the historical acts of Jesus. The unity of Jesus Christ with the God he called Father is founded in the history contained within the message, ministry, and established by the Christ-event. Contra modernistic methodologies, Pannenberg creates a methodology that does not utilize a corpus of statements independent of the relationship between Jesus and God.[360] For Pannenberg, the history of Jesus illumines the unity of Jesus

---

[358] See Pannenberg, *JGM*, 33. Again, the contrast to Anselm here is how Anselm built a Christology from a *remoto Christo* methodology via the cross and the incarnation which provided for a satisfaction to answer the problem of sin and the offended honor of God. Whereas Anselm looked to logic, conversely Pannenberg claims it is from history and from the resurrection that the unity of Jesus with God in the incarnation and the work of the cross is established.

[359] Pannenberg is quoting Althaus here in the context of how the Christological tradition grew out of thinking about Jesus from first impulse, and how dogmatics must not presuppose the historical result of this as being self-evident, but rather investigate the Christological statements themselves through the history of Jesus Christ. Pannenberg, *JGM*, 29. Original Source: P. Althaus. *Die Christliche Warheit*, 6*th* Ed. Gütersloh: 1962, 424.

[360] This is not to say that the Christological confessions and creeds are not normative for Christian faith but rather Pannenberg sees these confessions and creeds as being derived from their historical content. It is not the confessions and creeds that form the content of faith, but the historical acts of God in Jesus Christ which are established by means of his resurrection from the dead and thus give rise to the confessions and creeds. This differs from noted sources above as in Kähler, Barth,

with God, not the from above incarnational act, or whether or not it is rational to believe this unity, or whether or not Jesus is conscious of his unity with God. Ultimately, his from below proposal does not look to soteriology as the proper avenue for a Christological methodology either. Pannenberg claims:

> The divinity of Jesus remains the presupposition for his saving significance for us and, conversely, the saving significance of his divinity is the reason why we take interest in the question of his divinity. Since Schleiermacher the close tie between Christology and soteriology has won general acceptance in theology.[361]

Here there is an important point to be made. Whereas Pannenberg claims that Schleiermacher is the genesis of the close tie between Christology and soteriology, Anselm has already made such a move in the *Cur Deus Homo*. Chapter three (1.2) described how Anselm looks to create his Christology from above via the cross and the incarnation, and thus made soteriology the focus of his Christology. This happened in part because of methodological decisions Anselm made, but nonetheless the point remains that soteriology was the Christological locus in Anselm just as much as Schleiermacher. This point shall be explored more later.

Critical to his methodology from below is the second presupposition discussed above, namely the necessity of subjecting truth claims to the process of scrutiny. If the history of Jesus Christ is the source of his method, the scrutiny of this source provides its source of confirmation. Rather than accepting Christological doctrinal statements or titles as means of confirmation to the divinity of Jesus Christ and his unity with God, Pannenberg sees the need for subjecting the history of Jesus as well as these statements and titles to scrutiny.[362] Only in the subjecting of these statements, titles, and the like to historical-critical inquiry can Jesus become the basis for faith. His process of scrutiny with respect to the resurrection looks to "the appearances of the resurrected Lord and the idea of Jesus' empty tomb."[363] These events include 1st Corinthians 15 and how Paul is not inventing his own kerygma but recapitulating the kerygma that had been in existence, as well as the tradition of the empty tomb and how the earliest tradition of the New Testament, Jewish polemic of the empty tomb, and the proclamation of the resurrection all provide substantive witness to this event being a historical event.[364] The process by which he scrutinizes these events

---

Bultmann, and the like who tied faith to kerygma rather than to historical content. See Pannenberg, *JGM*, 36.

[361] Pannenberg, *JGM*, 38. This is a key point respective to Anselm. It shall be argued later that Anselm also established his Christology via the cross and incarnation. Schleiermacher also followed this methodology.

[362] See Pannenberg, *ST II*, 282-283.

[363] Olive, *Wolfhart Pannenberg*, 57.

[364] Don Olive provides a precise recapitulation of the very complex argument Pannenberg makes concerning the validity of the resurrection of Jesus Christ. Rather than deal with all the minutiae in the argument concerning the resurrection of Jesus

occurs by challenging that the resurrection is validated when it is not *a priori* disregarded, and when it is considered to be historically probable.[365] These two presuppositions to his method are critical for the success of his from below proposition, as it is by scrutiny of the life, message, and Christ-event that Jesus of Nazareth is shown to be the Christ of God. Pannenberg claims historical research should not rule out possibilities *a priori* such as miracles because even the laws of nature are not thoroughly known. Even modern science itself is built on well-tested hypotheses, although these hypotheses are not fully known and even change over time. Such is the case in the progression from Newtonian Physics to the Einsteinian Theory of General Relativity.[366] One can look to the shift from a closed system of causality to the now unexplainable and predictable subatomic particle theories which hold potential for systemic chaos to exist that is random and utterly unpredictable. If science is built upon hypotheses, the proposition Pannenberg argues for of not eliminating historical possibilities *a priori* has value. Moreover, when one views the events of the resurrection of Jesus Christ and one takes into consideration the contextual factors of the history of Israel, the prophetic and apocalyptic predictions in the history of Israel, the message and ministry of Jesus, and the response of the disciples and subsequent early Church – if Ockham's Razor is right, it seems probable the resurrection of Jesus did occur.[367]

---

and the Pannenbergian methodology from below it is much easier to see the overarching tenets of his argument. See Olive, *Wolfhart Pannenberg*, 57-64. For the complete delineation of the argument for the validity of the resurrection of Jesus, see Pannenberg, *JGM*, 88-114.

[365] See Olive, *Wolfhart Pannenberg*, 57-58.

[366] See Wood, *God and History*, 233-308.

[367] Pannenberg notes that it is impossible to be without presuppositions and that his position is even "scandalous" amidst the positivistic theologies from theological modernity. See Pannenberg, *BQT I*, 66-67. Pannenberg has been widely contested here. Klooster who has been mentioned above is one important source as he claims Pannenberg is guilty of allowing for a duality in historical-critical methodologies – that theology can claim a slightly different model than any other discipline and this is why he differs from Troeltsch, Barth, and Bultmann (who in his estimation are correct). Moreover he claims that without the apocalyptic presupposition of Pannenberg, his theology will fall. Fred Klooster, "Historical Method and The Resurrection in Pannenberg's Theology." *CTJ 11/1*, 1976, 5-33. Barth, Moltmann, and Bultmann also differ here and such differences are illumined by Daniel Migliore who utilizes a narrative dialogue to illumine such differences. See Daniel L. Milgliore. "How Historical is the Resurrection." *Theology Today Vol. 33*. Princeton: 1976, 5-14. See also Burhenn who challenges the historical and methodological premises of Pannenberg and is critical of the possibility of a truly empty grave and contends that Christian faith should not be tied to a historical argument, especially given that historians have to depart from historical procedure to even consider the resurrection as there is not the historical evidence necessary for such inquiry. Moreover, he challenges to what degree God is able to work within the confines of the historical condition. See Herbert Burhenn. "Pannenberg's Argument for the Historicity of the Resurrection." *Journal of American Academy of Religion, 40*. Oxford: 1972, 368-379.

Pannenberg utilizes the pressures of historical research and historical-critical methodologies to his advantage despite criticism. While others have made the distinction of the historical Jesus and the historic biblical Christ and of the Christ of faith coming alive in the preached kerygma, Pannenberg claims that it is the history of Jesus which proves him to be the Christ and it is that history which is contained in the Scriptures.[368] Thus faith is not only a present experience, but a present experience on the basis of what happened historically in the past and more notably what will happen in the future; only in the past events of Jesus Christ is humanity able to presently and indirectly experience Jesus Christ and enter into his future, and only when humanity is met by Jesus Christ in the future will they be able to fully and directly experience the presence of Jesus Christ.[369] Faith is derived from his theology of history as revelation, the indirect self-revelation of God in history, and the direct self-revelation of God that will occur in the eschaton. Through worship, hearing the Gospel, and by trusting in the resurrection of Jesus Christ, humanity presently encounters the risen Lord, and will know him directly and fully in the eschaton.[370]

While Pannenberg distinguishes his methodology from below in a contrasting manner compared to from above Christological methodologies, there are some potential hazards to such an undertaking. In beginning, one might say that the polar extremes of above and below are the improper place to construct a Christology and it seems that to the extreme of from above, Pannenberg aims his from below proposal. Concurrently, Pannenberg understands that these two extremes form a complementary Christological approach. In his estimation the from below methodology forms the content, while the from above forms the primary material. Thus the polar extremes of this methodology posit, on the one hand (i.e. the from above position), too much emphasis on the assumed divinity of Jesus Christ, and on the other (i.e. the from below position), too much emphasis upon a generalized anthropology that does not find its source in God.[371] Moreover, while the presupposition of divinity is the assumption of a Christology from above, there are presuppositions regarding the person of Jesus in a from below position as well. This is the reason why Pannenberg sees the necessity to maintain "the classical Christology of the incarnation."[372] For example, Jesus had to have some conception of who he was in his divinity in order for his message to have accuracy and understanding. Even more, unless there is someone above to as-

---

[368] See for example Kähler and Bultmann, who Pannenberg disputes in his work. See Pannenberg, *JGM*, 20-25.

[369] See Tupper, *The Theology of Wolfhart Pannenberg*, 130-131. See also Pannenberg, *JGM*, 27-29.

[370] It should be added that Pannenberg also claimed it is because of the reliability of the resurrection that people are able to worship Jesus Christ and have a present experience with Jesus Christ. See Pannenberg, *JGM*, 28-29.

[371] See Pannenberg, *ST II*, 290.

[372] Pannenberg, *ST II*, 288.

cend toward (i.e. God), then a theology from below quickly disintegrates.[373] The issue, claims Pannenberg, is that classical Christology has presupposed the revelatory history of Jesus Christ, without offering support or explanation for it.[374]

Similarly, others have taken issue with Pannenberg because, in their estimation, it is the teachings and acts of Jesus which "disclose his divine being."[375] This is slightly ironic as it is only possible to regard those teachings and acts as divine *a posteriori* from the resurrection. Others have claimed that Pannenberg does not give enough primacy to the Christological titles, which again is not entirely accurate given his theology of "the New Adam." Specifically, Grenz notes that some liberation theologians have leveled an important question against his proposal:

> Pannenberg returns to the old Christology by beginning with the question of the relationship of Jesus to God, a question for which Jesus himself had no answer.[376]

Finally, and most notably, some have challenged his methodology claiming that soteriology is divorced from Christology or that Pannenberg utilizes historical-critical method inconsistently and does not (at least in his earlier work) maintain consistency of his methodological position throughout his proposal of a Christology from below.[377] Mentioned above, Pannenberg contends that since Schleiermacher, soteriology has taken a key methodological emphasis in Christology, and as shall be delineated in chapter seven (2.2.1), soteriology is the improper place to begin Christology as the unity of Jesus is not determined by soteriology, but is established through the resurrection. This challenge to the Pannenbergian soteriology is born out of the lack of experiential dimension to his Christology at first glance – from the human need for Christ into a more objective knowledge of the history of Jesus Christ. This, Grenz claims, is due to his desire to overcome Feuerbach, identify the source of the soteriological experience, and the rejection of experiential Christology.[378] This is an important claim. While some Christologies

---

[373] This is a critique offered by Otto Weber. See Weber, *Grundlagen der Dogmatik*, Vol. II, 26, 34. See Pannenberg, *JGM*, 35-36.

[374] See Pannenberg, *ST II*, 288-289.

[375] Carl Henry takes exception to the Pannenbergian methodology for this reason as he claims that the very teachings and acts of Jesus are the revelation of God to humanity. Henry argues that one is able to see that Jesus is the Christ through this teaching and in these events. Grenz, *Reason for Hope*, 181. Original Source: Carl F.H. Henry. *God, Revelation, and Authority*. Waco: Word Publishers, 1976, 2:302-308.

[376] Juan Luis Segundo. *The Historical Jesus of the Synoptics*, trans. by John Drury. Maryknoll: Orbis Books, 1985, 30.

[377] The methodological challenges are especially of Burhenn and Klooster. See Burhenn, *Journal of American Academy of Religion*, 40. See also Klooster, *CTJ 11/1*, 5-33. See also Klooster, *Septuagesimo Anno: Festschrift for G.C. Berkouwer*.

[378] See Grenz, *Reason for Hope*, 184. The original claim against Pannenberg was made by McGrath. See Alister E. McGrath. "Christology and Soteriology: A Response

begin from the place of the human need for a transaction which effects salvation, Pannenberg looks to see how God has provided a solution to this need by confirming Jesus Christ to be the author of history and thus of new life. For Pannenberg, experience is grounded in objectivity not vice versa.[379] Ultimately, whether it is the reality of a God above or influence from above throughout the life of Jesus and his ministry, it is impossible to make claims that a theology from below does not begin with its own presuppositions which have issues, and even more, one cannot claim that the from below position is entirely without some elements of a from above methodology with some *a priori* assumptions.

Logos Christology or Historical Christology?

Whereas a theology from below proposal attempts to demonstrate the unity of Jesus with the God he called Father in and through the process of historical revelation and coming to a penultimate climax in the resurrection – a historical Christology – what then of logos Christology? Even Pannenberg claims that logos Christology has been prevalent for the majority of Christendom. His contention is that the logos Christology was born out of the need of the Apologists in the second century who needed to differentiate Father and Son, and then the third century marked the "upsurge of logos Christology." His estimation is that it was this decision that began the movement toward Christologies from above.[380] The primary purpose of the logos, then, was to differentiate the God Jesus called Father, and Jesus as the Son, while at the same time showing the unity between the two so that Jesus was not less than God so as to diminish the work occurring in the Christ-event. The terms "Father" and "Son" are relational titles dealing with "mission, trust, and obedience," and even more differentiation so as to show the unity of God while maintaining the work of the Son as being different from that of the Father.[381] Of primary importance is that the biblical concept of logos is seemingly different from the Greek philosophical one; whereas logos in John is simply the God who works in the world and in history, in Ignatius and the Apologists the logos is equated with speech, reason, middle positions, and universally systemic principles which unify separate realities born out of Stoicism and the like. When applied to a Greek-speaking world that was filled with Greek philosophical categories, it became a bridge to "unity and plurality."[382]

---

to Wolfhart Pannenberg's Critique of the Soteriological Approach to Christology." *Theologische Zeitschrift* 42. 1986, 222-236.

[379] See Grenz, *Reason for Hope*, 184.

[380] See Pannenberg, *JGM*, 159-162. Pannenberg contends this was a transformation in Christology from this moment forward. As shall be momentarily delineated, Pannenberg contends that the logos Christology from Ignatius forward began a new manner of Christological development.

[381] Pannenberg, *JGM*, 159.

[382] Pannenberg, *JGM*, 163.

This logos theology that developed had benefits and disadvantages. Whereas Greek philosophy claimed the logos is said to appear, it was said that in Jesus Christ, "the whole logos appeared."[383] An advantage to this statement was its unity and differentiation in a language that was easily transmittable to most people in the second and third centuries, as the concept of the logos was not foreign. Moreover, this posited that the same divine power which manifested creation was present in Jesus of Nazareth, a fully human being who was also fully God. These advantages are concurrently disadvantages, Pannenberg claims. The unity of the logos with God is bathed in Platonic language. The logos is seemingly subordinate to God, an issue of ontological subordinationism, which was later undone by some of the Christological elements within the creeds. In this regard, while the reality of the unity of Jesus as the Son of the Father may be understood in a preexistent manner, Pannenberg claims:

> Such concepts, contradictory when taken for themselves, are meaningful only when they are *not* taken from themselves but are understood in their connection with their basis in the event of God's revelation in Jesus.[384]

This leads to the most important issue, the "precarious loosening of the connection of the Son's divinity with Jesus of Nazareth, God's historical revelation."[385] Pannenberg contends the divinity and unity of Jesus and his Father is founded in the Trinitarian relation in the power of the Spirit, and it is this unity that can only be conceived in and through the history of Jesus of Nazareth who was revealed as the Christ of the God. Ultimately, the differences between a Jewish history of the self-revelation of God, and the Greek philosophical category of an unchangeable principle are seemingly at odds – one is concerned with history, personhood, and relationship with humanity, whereas the other is concerned with an order of things that is universally accessible although not relationally necessary.[386]

The above premise in mind, the theological commitments explained at the outset of this chapter respective to the historical and indirect revelation of God, and the schema of a from below method, Pannenberg makes a bold but natural move: whereas some have continued to appeal to Logos Christology, Pannenberg dialectically combines the two as a "historicized logos" proposal fitting into his overall theological schema. Appealing to Ritschl, Pannenberg claims Christology begins with the person of Jesus

---

[383] Pannenberg, *JGM*, 163.
[384] Pannenberg, *JGM*, 183.
[385] Pannenberg, *JGM*, 165.
[386] See Pannenberg, JGM, *165-166*. See also Larry Wood who is helpful in demonstrating the difference between the Jewish revelational content of salvation history and how Greek philosophical categories were infused within it. One provided the content of revelation, the other provided a categorical accessibility to a predominantly Greco-Roman world that was well aware of such categories. See Wood, *God and History*, 1-50.

Christ and these statements can only be viewed in the context of history.[387] This claim marks an important movement positing value not in the movement of the logos from above to below, nor in the faith-consciousness of humanity, but in the historical acts of the logos. Essentially, Pannenberg contends his proposition is for knowing God in and through Jesus Christ the divine logos whose human history unfolded the reality and personhood of God to humanity. Only in the historical acts of Jesus Christ, the divine logos, can humanity posit proper faith, and therein lies the connection for Jesus Christ as the Son of the Father. Stanley Grenz claims:

> The historicization of the logos concept found in the dogmatics is also prefigured in the afterward to the monograph, where Pannenberg suggests that Christology speaks of the election of Jesus in whom all of salvation history is recapitulated....
>
> Because Jesus reveals the proper relationship of the human person to God, he is the logos. But as Pannenberg repeatedly asserts, the self-differentiation of Jesus from the Father belongs to the intratrinitarian life as the self-differentiation of the logos (i.e. the Son) from the Father, which in turn is the basis for creation. [388]

The combination of historical and logos Christology is guided not only by his presuppositions respective to history, its scrutiny, and the unity of Jesus with God, but how those presuppositions find their way into the methodology from below. Pannenberg holds the unity of Jesus and God (i.e. logos Christology), in tension with the acts of Jesus of Nazareth which culminate in the Christ-event (i.e. historical Christology), in such a way that the latter confirms the former. Thus, incarnation is not the starting place of his theology, rather incarnation is established via the resurrection.

Conclusion: A Theology from Below

Having considered the Pannenbergian Christological methodology, what points can be summarized? Even more, how do these points contrast with that of Anselm? In beginning, just as Anselm wrote in response to a context, so too did Pannenberg. His context was formed by the distinction that was influential for theology for some time, concerning the historical Jesus and the historic, biblical Christ in Kähler. His work was situated after the works of Feuerbach and Nietzsche and their forms of modern atheism that flowed from the remnants of supernaturalism that led to claims of the human projection of God. He wrote in response to Bultmann whose *Kerygma and Myth* and *Theology of the New Testament* disputed the historicity of the Scriptures. He wrote in response to Barth whose methodology and theology had gained wide notoriety, even though one could challenge him on whether or not he capitulated to the challenges of his milieu in attempting to shield the Word

---

[387] See Pannenberg, *ST II*, 280-282.

[388] Grenz, *Reason for Hope*, 152-153. This stands in contrast to Barth and the logos Christology he espoused.

of God from historical-critical investigation. In all of these methodological concerns, Pannenberg saw a key and missing ingredient: history. In his estimation, one could not properly confess faith in Jesus Christ by means of titles, doctrinal statements, confessions, or creeds; faith was a response to the historical message, ministry, and Christ-event. Jesus of Nazareth who was killed on the cross on Friday, was confirmed to be the Christ of God via his resurrection from the dead on Easter Sunday.

This emphasis on history is unique to Pannenberg although Ritschl and others have argued for a similar position. Pannenberg grounds the acts of God in history as a process of indirect-self revelation between God and humanity. It is in this historical process of indirect self-revelation occurring in space-time that God is revealing the self-hood of God to humanity and it is within the context of all history that the religions of the world are being scrutinized and debated for their veracity. Pannenberg contends this testing and confirming of the self-revelation of God is best served by historical method and historical-critical methodologies. Most importantly, Pannenberg lobbies for a final and direct act of self-disclosure that has been already proleptically revealed in the resurrection of Jesus Christ from the dead. This brings the future into the present as an anticipatory event. It will be this final eschatological event in which God is revealed to be the God of the world and all history, thus confirming the process of indirect revelation throughout history. Pannenberg looks to the history contained in the message, ministry, and Christ-event of Jesus Christ which establishes his unity with God. As such, Pannenberg seeks to establish this unity with God within the context of the history between God and Israel coming to penultimate climax in the resurrection of Jesus Christ.

Pannenberg utilized a Christology from below method which has far reaching implications. Mentioned in 2.1.2, whereas Anselm presupposed the divinity of Jesus Christ and therefore his unity with God, Pannenberg sought to establish it through the Christ-event from the resurrection. His emphasis on the resurrection, even subjecting it to historical-critical method is unique, especially for a theologian writing in the twentieth century, as many theologians discounted the resurrection of its historicity precisely because of historical-critical methodologies. Pannenberg looks to the writings of Paul and the empty tomb tradition to confirm his theory and utilizes historical-critical methodology by claiming that one cannot *a priori* disregard a historical event, as the resurrection occurs within the context of history, and even more, one must consider whether the resurrection is the most likely outcome which explains this historical event. His method is carried through to its logical completion when set amidst the context of the history of God and Israel, the prophetic promises and apocalyptic predictions, and the message of Jesus. Amidst this context, it is probable that the resurrection of Jesus did occur which thus confirms his unity with God and the revelation of God in history. His combination of logos Christology with historical Christology is a natural outcome of his from below proposal, as he combines the unity of God and

Jesus in the logos proposal with the historical acts of Jesus Christ as confirmation of such unity.

Finally, the presuppositions and from below methodology will guide the overarching themes of his Christology and provide a Christological alternative to Anselm who constructed his Christology from the cross. Simply stated, Pannenberg provides a Christology via the resurrection. The "from below" proposal Pannenberg offers is guided by his presuppositions of history, subjection of history to scrutiny, and the resurrection which is proleptically revealed in Jesus Christ as the final act of direct self-disclosure to humanity. Given these realities, it is now possible for a deeper look at the retroactive significance of the resurrection and its confirmation of the unity of Jesus with God in the next chapter, chapter seven (2.2).

Chapter 7

The Pannenbergian Retroactive Significance of the Resurrection

The preceding chapter focused upon three key Pannenbergian presuppositions and the *a posteriori* from below methodology he utilizes in creating his Christology from the acts of God in salvation history. This is to say that it is *because* of the historical events happening in Jesus Christ, Christology consequently is formulated. Key to his method concerns how Pannenberg sees Christology as being formulated by the relations of God and the world, by the historical process of truth which emerges from historical debate that must be scrutinized by historical-critical methodologies, and is found in the narrative of salvation history which has been proleptically revealed in the resurrection of Jesus Christ. It is Jesus Christ who reveals the eschatological destiny of humanity. From these presuppositions, Pannenberg forms a "from below" methodology, with the historical acts of God revealing the very self of God to humanity – acts that can be scrutinized for their veracity.

Of all the ingredients to his Christological methodology, one element stands above the rest: the resurrection. Mentioned in the previous chapter, Pannenberg posits tremendous emphasis on the resurrection, building his Christology from what he deems a historical event.[389] Specifically, his systematic theology rests upon the Christ-event, for he believes Christology has to do with not only the confession of Jesus Christ, but more particularly the grounding of Christ in the historical activity of Jesus, and most importantly his resurrection from the dead:

> Only in trust in the reliability of the report of Jesus' resurrection and exaltation are we able to turn in prayer to the one who is exalted and now lives, and thus to associate with him in the present.[390]

---

[389] This is mentioned throughout chapter five and six (2.0, 2.1). As previously noted, Pannenberg is widely contested on this point by those who contend the resurrection is not a historically verifiable event, or even by those who claim that the resurrection should not be subjected to historical-critical methodologies or the scrutiny of historians.

[390] Pannenberg, *JGM*, 28.

Therefore, this chapter illustrates the centrality of the resurrection in Pannenbergian Christology, as his methodology utilizes the resurrection to retroactively establish the person and work of Jesus Christ.

The critical and most central locus of Pannenbergian Christology is his retroactive significance of the resurrection. Pannenberg argues the resurrection of Jesus from the dead establishes the reversal of the cross, the miracles and teachings of the Kingdom, and the very unity of God and Jesus indicating humanity and the world have been reconciled to God through Jesus Christ. While retroactive force or significance shall be explicated more fully later, paramount to understanding this concept at this early juncture concerns how the resurrection retroactively establishes both ontologically and epistemologically the unity of Jesus with God, the reversal of the charges of blasphemy in the cross of Jesus Christ, the authentication of his claims of the Kingdom having come near in him, and finally the implications of salvation and reconciliation of the world and humanity to God through him. Pannenberg contends it is from the resurrection that Jesus of Nazareth is the Christ of God. The resurrection then retroactively casts significance backward upon the whole of the life of Jesus Christ to the incarnation, establishing his identity as the Son of God.[391] Pannenberg contends the incarnation cannot be a presupposition because of the methodological, anthropological, and therefore Christological issues it raises. These issues

---

[391] See Pannenberg, *JGM*, 133-141. See also Pannenberg, *ST II*, 277-396. See also Pannenberg, *BQT I*, 174-182. Pannenberg illumines what was stated in *JGM* in the footnotes of the *ST II* concerning his concept of retroactive force. His understanding is founded in the "hermeneutic of historical experience" that is conceptually borrowed from Dilthey. Pannenberg argues: "...(Retroactive force is a) descriptively demonstrable fact with ontological implications. The significance of an event (as we shall see later in which it is always a matter of its *ti en einai*) is not independent of the events in the light of whose (provisional) conclusion we look back upon it. The thesis of retroactive force corresponds to the constitutive significance of the anticipation." Pannenberg, *ST II*, 303 (ff). This is an Aristotelian concept of something that ontologically becomes what it was intended to be. Pannenberg also demonstrates how the message of the in-breaking of God required divine confirmation because of the implications of the message. Accordingly, Pannenberg argues against Klappert and Moltmann who claim that the resurrection as divine confirmation weakened the crucifixion. Instead, he claims the resurrection is the reversal of the rejection of the Kingdom and the charge of blasphemy that brought about the cross. See Jürgen Moltmann. *The Crucified God*, 173. See also B. Klappert. *Die Auferweckung des Gekreuzigten*. Stutgaart-Berlin: 1971, 54-56. Original source: Pannenberg, *ST II*, 338. See also Wolfhart Pannenberg. *Grundzüge der Christologie*. Gütersloh: Mohn Publishers, 1966, 419-420. There are a number of notable scholars who disagree with Pannenberg on this point. Chapter five and six raised Barth, Bultmann, Klooster, Lewis Ford, and Carl Braaten. Also important is Pinchas Lapide, a Jewish scholar who argues against Pannenberg that his argument, while historically tenable, may also be utilized for Elijah or other biblical figures. See Pinchas Lapide. *The Resurrection of Jesus – A Jewish Perspective*. London: SPCK Publishers, 1984. Also important is McKenzie who argues against his retroactive concept. See David McKenzie. *Wolfhart Pannenberg and Religious Philosophy*. Washington D.C.: University Press of America, 1980.

range from challenges concerning the humanity of Jesus to mythological undertones a presuppositionary incarnation creates.[392]

Moreover, by giving central prominence to the resurrection, this creates soteriological commitments for his Christology. Pannenberg contends Anselm understood the death of Jesus as his own active accomplishment, a result of the Anselmian incarnational emphasis, whereas he (Pannenberg) contends God gave Jesus up as a sacrifice – essentially that Jesus was more passively involved in his own sacrificial death.[393] Whereas Anselm argues for Jesus Christ by means of the need of satisfaction and on the basis of satisfaction the incarnation is a logical presupposition, Pannenberg proposes the proper understanding of Jesus Christ is through the resurrection as divine establishment. As a means of supporting his claim, Pannenberg attempts to utilize the examples of both Anselm and Luther who come to have their methodologies unraveled by the Enlightenment.[394]

Therefore chapter seven (2.2) shall focus on three important realities of the Pannenbergian Christological proposal which finds its central locus in the resurrection: (1) given the premises in his "from below" methodology, the resurrection provides the retroactive establishment of Jesus of Nazareth as the Christ of God and provides a key hermeneutic for interpreting the person and ministry of Jesus Christ; (2) how then through the resurrection and its retroactive significance which establishes Jesus as the Christ, the unity of Jesus with God is revealed, and as the new eschatological Adam, Jesus Christ proleptically reveals the destiny of humanity; (3) and finally, how given the above two realities, both the incarnational and crucifixional questions are answered thus offering the reason why Christology should not begin with the incarnation or crucifixion of Jesus of Nazareth but the resurrection, all of which offers on some level a reorientation of the meaning of the incarnation and crucifixion of Jesus of Nazareth.

---

[392] This is a point raised by Pannenberg concerning how the ministry, message, and death of Jesus Christ can be quickly understood in mythological terms as is the case of Greek Mythology and the like. See Pannenberg, *JGM*, 277-280. See also Molnar, *Incarnation and Resurrection*, 263.

[393] To be fair, Pannenberg recognizes that Anselm found this in the passion predictions in the Gospels. He contends Anselm interpreted them literally instead of symbolically through the "doctrine of penance." See Pannenberg, *JGM*, 277. The medieval penance system was important to Anselm as part of his own feudal context which shaped his writing. The use of *satisfactio* and the active obedience of Jesus in the cross are potential implications of his feudal context which shaped his writing in *Cur Deus Homo*. See especially chapter one (1.0) and chapter three (1.2.2).

[394] Pannenberg, *JGM*, 279. Pannenberg also claims Luther understood the suffering of Christ in terms of its vicarious effect, whereas his predecessors lost this and returned to Anselmian soteriology.

2.2.1 The Pannenbergian Retroactive Significance of Resurrection: Retroactive Significance

Chapter six (2.1.2) illustrated how Wolfhart Pannenberg utilizes a theology from below Christological methodology that looks to the historical acts of God rather than soteriology or kerygmatic confessions of faith. These historical acts contained throughout the whole of the Scriptures are bridged in the person of Jesus Christ, in whom the apocalyptic hopes and prophetic predictions of Israel are embodied and realized. Chapter six also revealed how Pannenberg contends the resurrection is a historical event that can be subjected to historical criticism typical of any other historical event. To this end, Pannenberg looks to the Pauline corpus and empty tomb tradition. His from below process by which he scrutinizes these events contends the resurrection is validated when it is not *a priori* disregarded and when it is considered in light of the consequential outcomes of the resurrection. In this way, the resurrection may be given a status of being historically probable, but not rationally certain.[395] These presuppositions are critical for the success of his from below proposition, as it is by scrutiny of the life, message, and Christ-event Pannenberg claims Jesus of Nazareth is established as the Christ of God.

If his from below proposal succeeds, it is by means of the resurrection and how its retroactive significance is able to establish Jesus of Nazareth is the Christ of God. Pannenberg contends the resurrection establishes Jesus of Nazareth as the Christ, and as such this confirms his pre-Easter message of the Kingdom – the future in-breaking of God in the present, along with his unity with God. Thus, the retroactive significance of the resurrection becomes a hermeneutical key of sorts in the Pannenbergian Christology to interpret the person and ministry of Jesus Christ. These two elements, the retroactive significance of the resurrection which establishes Jesus of Nazareth as the Christ, and its operation as a hermeneutical key to interpret the person and ministry of Jesus Christ are the key emphases of 2.2.1.

---

[395] This is set against Hume whose assertion had in some theological circles prevailed. He contended the resurrection was a miracle and thus was not historically reliable. See Hume, *An Enquiry Concerning Human Understanding*, 169-186. See also Olive, *Wolfhart Pannenberg*, 57-58. The word "probable" is an important distinction in his theology, as Pannenberg deals with probabilities rather than theological positivism. The difference between Pannenberg and his objectors typically relates to one of the following: the miraculous nature of the event, the existential nature of the resurrection as the means rise to preaching and faith, or the divide between revelation and history, leaving the resurrection to be an event God reveals through faith. An especially helpful work to show the difference between important contemporary theologians – Barth, Bultmann, Moltmann, and Pannenberg – is by Migliore, written in the form of hypothetical dialogue. See Migliore, *Theology Today: Vol. 33, No. 1*. Also important is Burhenn, *Journal of American Academy of Religion*, 40, 368-379. See also Dobbin, E. "Reflections on Wolfhart Pannenberg's Revelation Theology." *Louvain Studies No. 4*. 1972, 13-37.

The Epistemological & Ontological Establishment of Jesus Christ

The importance of the resurrection in the Pannenbergian Christology concerns how the resurrection as a historical event provides retroactive significance and establishes Jesus of Nazareth as the Christ of God.[396] His proposal is argued from the perspective of legal terminology and ontology. In terms of legal terminology, Pannenberg contends there are laws and ordinances having "retroactive force" that is *ex post facto* force, and similarly, the resurrection of Jesus casts interpretive force *ex post facto* upon the person and activity of Jesus Christ.[397] The legal concept Pannenberg espouses is readily understandable if one considers how older laws, when changed or updated to consider newer events, may require new elements of law within the corpus of these older laws. This in turn requires that the new laws retroactively apply force upon these older events, which thus provide for new rulings. The future casts force upon past events for the present evaluation of them which in turn creates new meaning and character for them. Moreover, if one considers the nature of technologies and scientific discoveries which are rapidly changing, one might recognize that the future is consistently shaping our epistemological foundations at present to transform the past. Perhaps the greatest example of this concerns the change from a Newtonian model of causality to an Einstenian model of relativity. Whereas the Newtonian model considers the future as being mechanistically derived from the past, the Einstenian model looks to the future and how the future is relative to time at present. Drawing from modern physics, Pannenberg argues the future is open, has priority, and it is ultimately the universality of the future which eventuates the present to transform the past.[398] If one applies this to Christological method, meaning and identity are not determined *a priori* from the incarnation in the assumption that Jesus of Nazareth is the Christ of God and is one with God, but from the future *a posteriori* and the resurrection of Jesus Christ on the third day which reverses the claims of blasphemy and his death on the cross, therefore establishing the incarnation and his Kingdom proclamation.

---

[396] See Pannenberg, *JGM*, 135-141. This is an important distinction governing his Christology that stems from the below-above methodology he utilizes. Whereas the above-below method indicates *a priori* that the Christ is Jesus of Nazareth, Pannenberg seeks (from below-above) to establish that Jesus of Nazareth is the Christ of God.

[397] Pannenberg, *JGM*, 135.

[398] Most helpful here is how Pannenberg sees God as the power of the unbound and ultimate future. This does not mean that God is only relegated to the future but is, as the power of the unbound future, able to move into the present and even in the past. He has been accused of process theology by others, but takes care to refute Whitehead and Hartshorne on this point. See Pannenberg, *Theology and The Kingdom of God*, 61-71, 127-143. See also Wood, *God and History*, 233-308. Wood utilizes these materials to describe Pannenberg and his eschatological theology. Also helpful to describe this is Michio Kaku. *Hyperspace*. Oxford: Oxford University Press, 1994.

While this epistemology is more easily arguable in terms of law and technology, what of ontology? How is it possible for ontology to be changed by a future event?[399] Pannenberg moves the concept forward by arguing how the Greek concept of essence demonstrates that from the future, it is possible to see the essence of something has never changed, but this is only visible from the future. He claims:

> Then the essence of a man, of a situation, or even of the world in general is not yet to be perceived from what is now visible. Only the future will decide it. It is still to be shown what will become of man and of the world's situation in the future.[400]

Contra Bultmann, the thrust of his retroactive significance concerns the manner in which the resurrection establishes the person and work of Jesus Christ preceding the Christ-event. Accordingly, the retroactive significance of the resurrection demonstrates how the logical outcome of his proposal from below manifests itself. The from below method posits the retroactive significance of the resurrection as the lens by which the cross, ministry, incarnation, the very unity of Jesus Christ with God, and the implications for salvation history and humanity are revealed, established, and interpreted ontologically and epistemologically.[401]

---

[399] Timothy Bradshaw captures the essence of his retroactive force argument with an example concerning Wolfgang Amadeus Mozart. Bradshaw argues that at the time of the death of Mozart he was a pauper and died with little notoriety. After his death however, he gained notoriety as the greatest composer and genius. Thus the true identity of Mozart was determined after his death, and was not gleaned from the progression of his life to its end. The influence of this upon time as being determined from the future was indicated in the opening pages of Unit Two. Pannenberg makes the influence of eschatology and the future key to his methodology and his Christology as a whole. This kind of ontology is historical in nature, rejecting the dualistic and Platonic timeless understanding of ontology. See Bradshaw, *Pannenberg: A Guide for the Perplexed*, 78-80. McKenzie has rejected this retroactive force argument calling it, "Process Theology." See McKenzie, *Wolfhart Pannenberg and Religious Philosophy*. Also rejecting this is Bultmann who claimed that the Easter event was a disclosure that already had meaning in the earthly history of Jesus of Nazareth and that the resurrection finds significance in the cross. See Bultmann, *Kerygma and Myth*, 37-40. Barth similarly contends that the resurrection is not a historical event, but differs from Bultmann that it was an event post-crucifixion, and more importantly revealed the events preceding the crucifixion. See Barth, *Church Dogmatics III, II and IV*, 455, 118-131.

[400] Pannenberg, *JGM*, 136.

[401] This concept flows from his theology of history and revelation, as Pannenberg contends revelation occurs within the greater scope of universal knowledge occurring in history. Pannenberg holds the end of history brings the final and direct self-disclosure of truth between Creator and creature. Given the resurrection of Jesus is proleptic in form revealing the eschatological future in the present, the resurrection as a future event is able to create the present to transform the past. Revelation is epistemological as humanity experiences the revelation of God indirectly in history, and the content is ontological having to do with the identity of the truth of Jesus

This is a significant claim Pannenberg makes, as it is by means of a historical event from below – the resurrection of Jesus Christ – the divinity of Jesus is established and not assumed from above via a logos Christology or one beginning in the incarnation.[402] The manner in which the resurrection is retroactively established is important not only as a hermeneutical key for the life and ministry of Jesus of Nazareth, but more importantly to the unity of Jesus with God and revelation of the eschatological destiny of humanity as they relate to God through Jesus Christ.

Therefore, the retroactive significance of the resurrection serves to authenticate and establish the person and the work of Jesus Christ, meaning Jesus has not become someone else, or someone he was previously not, but rather someone who was improperly identified prior to his resurrection.[403] This is an important nuance to understanding the ontological dimension of his thought, as ontology is established from the future, not driven by the past. This critical juncture is of marked contrast to other Christologies claiming the resurrection is a myth of sorts, a mere existential rise for Christian faith, or even Christologies claiming somehow Jesus became someone else in the resurrection.[404] The point of his retroactive significance of the resurrection of Jesus of Nazareth is precisely to show that Jesus is the Christ, the promised messiah, who fulfills the overarching narrative of salvation history which God is guiding to universal historical fulfillment in the eschaton, and which is competing among other truth claims within the scope of the history of world religions.[405] If Jesus is one with God, then the claims he makes about

---

Christ. See Pannenberg, *Revelation as History*, 129-132. See also Nagib G. Awad. *Revelation, History, and Idealism: Re-examining the Conceptual Roots of Wolfhart Pannenberg's Theology*. Theological Review 26, No. 1, 2005, 97-99.

[402] McDermott points to how Pannenberg looked to *communicatio idiomatum* and how it failed to show how Jesus Christ was one with God in the incarnation as the rise of his theology of the resurrection. See Brian McDermott. "Pannenberg's Resurrection Christology: A Critique." *Theological Studies*. 1974, 711. McDermott critiques Pannenberg for a lack of clarity regarding the relation of Jesus and his divinity, an issue which Pannenberg clarifies later in the systematic theology, as he points to the incarnation as being the totality of his life rather than any one distinct moment. See Pannenberg, *ST II*, 383-389. See also Pannenberg, *JGM*, 108-110.

[403] Considering the New Testament is constructed *a posteriori* after the resurrection, it is possible to see how its very construction retroactively established the authority of the teaching and miracles of Jesus Christ on the basis of his resurrection. Pannenberg argues Jesus is Son of God from the beginning which occurs in light of the resurrection, thus proving false the claims of blasphemy by the religious authorities. See Pannenberg, *JGM*, 136-137.

[404] Pannenberg points to Ebeling and Künneth in this regard, and Bultmann and Barth are also significant in this regard, as Pannenberg provides a contrasting proposal to these works. See Pannenberg, *JGM*, 136.

[405] If the resurrection is indeed a historical event as he Pannenberg contends, and if his retroactive significance is correct, then its implications are that God has proleptically revealed the future and as such the course of history from past to the future which has already been revealed and is being brought to its fulfillment by God. Moreover, whereas Pannenberg contends that the history of religions is being tested

God and for God have authority, and the act of crucifixion which seemed to be a failure of another false messiah, is rather the very victory of God in reconciling humanity and the world to God.

His contrasting proposal becomes evident when compared to other Christologies, most notably Christologies whose methodologies are committed to beginning with the incarnation or other from above positions. One of the purposes of 2.1.2 was to provide evidence that his from below methodology seeks to establish Jesus of Nazareth is the Christ whereas other Christologies begin with the presupposition that Christ is Jesus of Nazareth.[406] That is, whereas other Christologies have looked to logos Christology and the incarnation for the divinity of Jesus, whereas others sought to look for the human soteriological need thus positing the divinity of Jesus in the incarnation, Pannenberg turns to the resurrection as the establishment of Jesus of Nazareth as the Christ of God, for it is the Christ-event which is the central historical event from which Pannenberg constructs his Christology.[407] This is the reason why Pannenberg has taken care to lay the framework for the resurrection as a historical event.[408] In this way, the resurrection as a historical event retroactively casts light backward upon the person of Jesus of Nazareth, the

---

and verified, and truth will ultimately be brought to light in the eschaton, resurrection in his Christology claims the central place. Of course, the truth of the resurrection of Jesus Christ can only fully be verified in the eschaton, but his theology makes a strong claim in this regard for the present on the basis of probability. For more on the veracity of truth claims among the religions of the world see, Pannenberg, *BQT I*, 17. See also Tupper, *The Theology of Wolfhart Pannenberg*, 79-81. See also Pannenberg, *BQT. II*, 65-118. See also Pannenberg, *ST I*, 119-188.

[406] See Olive, *Wolfhart Pannenberg*, 55.

[407] Elizabeth Johnson supports this notion claiming this was the concept of the New Testament which "slowly diminished over time." See Elizabeth Johnson. "The Ongoing Christology of Wolfhart Pannenberg." *Horizons 9*, No. 2, Villanova: College Theology Society, 1982, 243.

[408] Pannenberg takes great care to delineate the resurrection as a historical event by utilizing historical-critical methodologies. This is not without contestation. Within the afterward of *Jesus – God and Man*, Pannenberg takes care to reflect upon the challenges of his critics, especially with respect to this issue. Their claims range from the ability to specify the resurrection as a historical event (Hodgson) to the claims of Jesus and its confirmation in the cross (Klappert and Moltmann). See Pannenberg, *JGM*, 401-404. Also Herbert Burhenn is an important voice in the challenges to the Pannenbergian methodology and the historicity of the resurrection. Burhenn contends that the Scriptures account for the resurrection as a vision and as such, it is impossible to claim that faith does not enter into the debate in regard to the resurrection. He challenges Pannenberg on the grounds that the historian must claim there is insufficient evidence for the resurrection if he or she is truly acting as a historian on the basis of the logic that dead men do not rise. Burhenn has built his claim upon the modernistic assumptions of Hume and claims this is precisely the point Pannenberg must concede as a presupposition. See Burhenn, *Journal of American Academy 40*, 369-379. See Pannenberg, *JGM*, 53-114. See also Pannenberg, *ST II*, 325-363. See also Peter C. Hodgson. *Jesus – Word and Presence: An Essay in Christology.* Philadelphia: Fortress Press, 1971.

claims made by Jesus, the miracles and teachings of Jesus, and even the nearness of the Kingdom in him, establishing him as the Messiah and Christ of God despite the seemingly glaring contradiction that the cross of Friday provided. So then, resurrection establishes cross and incarnation, and what Pannenberg provides in the retroactive significance of the resurrection is an important point of coherence for his Christology to reveal mutual complementarity, and the provision of a key hermeneutic for interpreting the person and work of Jesus Christ. Accordingly, the resurrection retroactively establishes the ontology and epistemology of Jesus Christ.

Surprisingly, while his proposal for retroactive significance is of critical importance in his Christology, he relegates a relatively minor amount of space within the corpus of *Jesus – God & Man* to delineate the importance of this. The proposal is treated, in some manner of speaking, as an almost foregone conclusion.[409] The retroactive significance of the resurrection is inherently part of a methodology that is imbued with the historicity of the resurrection as the establishment of the Christ-event. While he does not provide much space to this, he does take care to answer some of the potential criticisms concerning his method.[410] The response Pannenberg provides main-

---

[409] See Pannenberg, *JGM*, 133-141. To be sure, Pannenberg has interspersed this element within the three chapters that are central to his Christology in *ST II*. These chapters include 9, 10, and 11. Within the scope and shape of these chapters, the retroactive significance of the resurrection is not oft mentioned by name, but is recognizable on the basis of the confirmatory/establishing language utilized when speaking of the resurrection. Moreover, the proposal for the unity of Jesus with God and the new eschatological age, are evidentiary on the basis of the resurrection as the confirmatory element of Jesus Christ.

[410] For example see the challenges of Bultmann, Cullmann, Barth, Marxsen, Perrin, and other modern historical-critical challenges. Barth is especially negative toward the historical nature of the resurrection Pannenberg espouses, claiming his position is weaker than the historical Jesus in Vogel. See Molnar, *Incarnation and Resurrection*, 264-265. Original Source: Karl Barth. *Karl Barth Letters 1961-1968*, ed. By Fangmeier, Soevesandt, and trans. by Bromiley. Grand Rapids: Eerdmans Publishing, 1981. Molnar is critical of Pannenberg, claiming there is a detachment of resurrection and incarnation because the pre-Easter appearance of Jesus depends upon a confirmation by God at the end of history. Pannenberg sees this as a confirmation of his unity with God as the unfolding of revelation to humanity, not as some kind of status which Jesus did not previously have as in Kunneth or the like. Concurrently, while Pannenberg utilizes the symbol of adoption, he is very clear to state that he does not receive his divinity on the basis of the resurrection. See Molnar, *Incarnation and Resurrection*, 278-279. See Pannenberg, *JGM*, 135-136. See also Rudolf Bultmann who claims that the resurrection concerns the rise of faith, not a historical event in Jesus Christ. See Bultmann, *New Testament and Mythology*, 41. See John Cobb who claims that the entirety of the Pannenbergian Christology hinges upon the agreement or disagreement of his treatment of the resurrection. See John B. Cobb Jr. *Journal of Religion* 49, 1969. See also John B. Cobb Jr. "Past, Present, and Future." *Theology as History: Discussions Among Continental and American Theologians*, Vol. 3. San Francisco: Harper and Row Publishers, 1967. Also significant here is McDermott and his critique of retroactive significance argument. See McDermott, *Theological Studies*.

tains many points of continuity with the early tradition of the Church and with the witness of Scripture in which Paul argues for the resurrection in 1st Corinthians 15.[411] Pannenberg sees his own methodology as little more than a convention of the early church and the two stage Christology of Romans 1:3 between Son of David and Son of God. He contends the Easter event was understood by early Christians within the scope of relations between God and the world in the context of the apocalyptic hope and promise of Judaism, and in this way, he sees the Easter event establishing by retroactive force the cross, ministry, and incarnation of Jesus illuminating that God is indeed revealed in Jesus, that Jesus is indeed the Son and Christ of God that is one with God, and Jesus has thus revealed the eschatological destiny of humanity in the prolepsis of the Christ-event.[412]

Pannenberg brings his Christology to a penultimate climax as his proposal for revelation as history develops his "from below" methodology to propel his retroactive significance of the resurrection hermeneutic. That penultimate climax is the resurrection of Jesus Christ, a historical event in his theology in which God offers the revelation of the eschatological destiny of humanity and a glimpse of the final self-disclosure of God. This event casts retroactive significance and interpretive light upon the person of Jesus Christ and the ministry of Jesus Christ, showing him to be one with God and the promised Messiah of Israel.

A Key Hermeneutic of Jesus Christ

Now that the retroactive significance of the resurrection has been explored, how does this provide a hermeneutical key to interpreting the person and ministry of Jesus of Nazareth, the Christ of God? Pannenberg contends that the proclamation of the Kingdom which seemingly failed on Friday had been established on Sunday in the resurrection, although the expectation of the general resurrection of the dead as had been apocalyptically expected had

---

[411] This is a point made in Olive. Olive contends the Pannenbergian position is closest to 1 Cor. 15:17. See Olive, *Wolfhart Pannenberg*, 70.

[412] In recent years, the work of N.T. Wright whose biblical basis for the resurrection as being derived from an understanding of resurrection in the Old Testament Scriptures and especially within 2nd Temple Judaism is supportive of the theology of Pannenberg. Wright contends the resurrection of Jesus is best understood as rising out of the historical development of resurrection that is conceptually present in the beginning of the history of Israel which later became a well-developed eschatological and final act of new creation in which God would raise from death to new life those righteous who had died, and enact upon the present age to bring about the eternal age. Wright envisages a two stage process of resurrection as stipulated by Daniel 12:2-3 (some will rise to eternal life and others to everlasting shame and contempt), which the Gospels and Epistolary materials further into first the resurrection of the messiah and then the rest of creation. See N.T. Wright. *The Resurrection of the Son of God*. Minneapolis: Fortress Press, 2003.

only been proleptically revealed.[413] Jesus began a new era, with continuities of the original expectation, although the expression of this new era was discontinuous with many tenets involving the restoration of land, religious life, and socio-political structures.[414] Thus the manner in which the resurrection of Jesus finds meaning for Christology concerns how the crucified one of Friday has been held in tension with the resurrected Lord of Sunday, and how Sunday looks back upon Friday as well as the totality of the life and ministry of Jesus of Nazareth showing him to be the Christ of God and one with God. In this regard, Pannenberg has six themes with respect to the resurrection of Jesus which are helpful to show the meaning of the resurrection and its continuities and discontinuities with the original apocalyptic expectation:

> (1) If Jesus has been raised, then the end of the world has begun. (2) If Jesus has been raised, this for a Jew can only mean that God himself has confirmed the pre-Easter activity of Jesus. (3) Through his resurrection from the dead, Jesus moved so close to the Son of Man that the insight became obvious: the Son of Man is none other than the man Jesus who will come again. (4) If Jesus, having been raised from the dead, is ascended to God and if thereby the end of the world has begun, then God is ultimately revealed in Jesus. (5) The transition to the Gentile mission is motivated by the eschatological resurrection of Jesus as the resurrection of the crucified One. (6) Particularly the last consequence throws light on the relationship between the appearances of the resurrected Jesus and the words spoken by him: what the early Christian tradition transmitted as the words of the risen Jesus is to be understood in terms of its content as the explication of the significance inherent in the resurrection itself.[415]

Essentially, these six themes Pannenberg offers demonstrate the continuity between the retroactive force or significance the resurrection provides and its ensuing consequent: a key hermeneutic of the Christ-event and person of Jesus Christ. He does this by locating the meaning of the event

---

[413] See Tupper, *The Theology of Wolfhart Pannenberg*, 146-147. Tupper relies upon a variety of sources, among them Pannenberg, *JGM*, and also Wolfhart Pannenberg. *The Apostles' Creed: In the Light of Today's Questions*, trans. by Margaret Kohl. Philadelphia: The Westminster Press, 1972.

[414] In this regard, the work of N.T. Wright is important as he argues the resurrection of Jesus being set against the contextual backdrop of 2nd Temple post-exilic Judaism. Pannenberg is similar in this regard as he views it as a historical problem fitting within salvation history as contained in the Scriptures and the apocalyptic framework. See Wright, N.T. *The Resurrection of the Son of God*, 32-200. See Pannenberg, *Jesus – God and Man*, 74-105.

[415] Pannenberg, *JGM*, 66-72. These six theses recapitulate the significance of the resurrection of Jesus in the overarching consideration of the knowledge of Jesus' divinity in the work of Pannenberg. See Pannenberg, *JGM*, 66-73. Awad comments Pannenberg is interested not in "philosophical presuppositions but Scriptural hermeneutics..." In this regard, Awad claims his interest is to show how the cross and resurrection concern the fulfillment of history in Jesus Christ. See Awad, *Theological Review 26, No. 1*, 100.

within the context of its own history from salvation history, apocalyptic hope, and prophetic tradition to its embodiment and expression being fulfilled eschatologically in Jesus of Nazareth, the Christ of God.[416] This is to say that in light of the activity and indirect self-revelation of God in history, in light of the prophetic promises and apocalyptic predictions, and in light of the meaning of resurrection as developed from within the context of post-exilic Judaism and among other religions, the resurrection of Jesus finds its expression.

Pannenberg designates the resurrection as a "metaphor," which is understandable insofar as it relates to the context of post-exilic Judaism, but as he claims this occurs in a very different manner in Jesus Christ.[417] "Metaphor" is at first glance problematic because of potential to deny the resurrection of its historicity, but Pannenberg utilizes the term metaphor expresses a real historical event, points to the contextual examples and partial meaning of this event, while at the same time offering nuance that the resurrection of Jesus Christ is an event unlike any other event for which humanity is able to directly and fully understand at present. This, of course, is derived from his understanding of the future creating the present to transform the past, and the final and complete direct self-disclosure of God in the eschaton in which God will offer the meaning of history. Thus, his hermeneutical key is driven by the direct/indirect revelation presupposition discussed in 2.1, as the resurrection although proleptically revealed, is still yet to come for humanity in its fullest sense.[418] How one utilizes this hermeneutical key from the perspective of the metaphor nuance comes to expression in the experience of the risen Christ for the Church against the backdrop of the expected general resurrection. In this way, the person of Jesus Christ as the resurrected Lord, and the Christ-event finds meaning for past, present, and future. Moreover, it merges salvation history and
universal history, positing God to be the author of history who has through a new and unique event through Jesus Christ made a decisive movement in the reconciliation of God and humanity.[419]

---

[416] Pannenberg claims this is a feature he follows on the basis of the importance of the eschatology of Johannes Weiss and later Jürgen Moltmann. Pannenberg further claims that Barth, despite his strong words for the need of eschatology within Christianity, fell prey to the tenets of modernity along with Bultmann. See Wolfhart Pannenberg. "Constructive and Critical Functions of Eschatology." *Harvard Theological Review* 77, No. 2, 1984, 119-121. See Johannes Weiss. *Die Predigt Jesu vom Reiche Gottes*. Gottingen, Vandenhoeck, and Rupert, 1964.

[417] See Pannenberg, *ST II*, 346-348.

[418] See Pannenberg, *JGM*, 74.

[419] Obayashi claims that Pannenberg is unique in positing the resurrection as revealing the meaning of history and does so by merging universal history and salvation history together. Obayashi contends that whereas Plato contemplated the cosmos, Pannenberg contemplates eschatology. See Hiroshi Obayashi. "Pannenberg and Troeltsch: History and Religion" *Journal of American Academy of Religion* 38 no. 4d. 1970, 402-403.

The treatment Pannenberg gives to the retroactive significance of the resurrection stems from how he sees the early Church having understood the resurrection of Jesus as the "decisive point in the history of his relation to God," which furthers the case for retroactive significance of the resurrection forming a key hermeneutic to establish Jesus of Nazareth as the Christ of God.[420] In this regard, the key hermeneutic functions by casting interpretive light from the resurrection retroactively upon the claim to unity with God which Jesus made. So, while there are titles given to Jesus such as Son of God, while Jesus claimed unity with God, and the presence of God was present to those who believed his message, the titles and events seemingly create "tensions between the physical basis of the divine sonship through Jesus' divine procreation and the idea of the installation as the Son of God through the resurrection..."[421] The question Pannenberg seeks to answer concerns whether or not these titles/events are exclusionary:

> Do these various conceptions exclude one another in the sense that Jesus became the Son of God only at his baptism, through the particular event of transfiguration, or through his resurrection, or that he already was the Son of God from the beginning, from his birth or even a preexistent being before his earthly birth? Or can a material relationship among all these conceptions be shown?[422]

While some have claimed the message and its revelation of the rule of God in human life was enough to make the authoritative claim that the future of the salvation of God was operative in Jesus, Pannenberg argues the message alone is not enough as it does not bring the entirety of the future of God into the present of humanity.[423] Rather, he argues the resurrection of Jesus from the dead was for the early Christian community "the decisive point in the history of his relation to God."[424] This is a key claim Pannenberg levels in his systematic theology as it forms the basis for which the resurrection becomes the key hermeneutic in which Jesus is established to be one with God and the agent of reconciliation between God and humanity. In

---

[420] The key hermeneutic concerns how the resurrection casts retroactive force upon the person and work of Jesus Christ. It is both epistemological and ontological in this manner, and establishes the claims of unity with God, the miracles as signs of the future in-breaking of the Kingdom, and is indicative of reconciliation on the part of God reconciling the world and humanity to God. See Pannenberg, *JGM*, 134.

[421] Pannenberg, *JGM*, 133.

[422] This is an important point. Whereas those who espouse a from above theology claim that the titles, claims, or even incarnation is enough to claim the divinity of Jesus Christ and his unity with God, Pannenberg claims it is from the resurrection that these are authenticated and established. See Pannenberg, *JGM*, 133.

[423] In this regard, Barth is most significant. See Barth, *Church Dogmatics*. Pannenberg is utilizing his from below position against those who take a from above position. Pannenberg claims that the early Church stands in continuity with this position, although he sees there being a change or progression by the time of Ignatius. See Pannenberg, *ST II*, 329-330. See also Pannenberg, *JGM*, 33.

[424] Pannenberg, *JGM*, 134.

so doing, Pannenberg argues the rejection of Jesus at the cross and its reversal at the empty tomb was the purpose for the proclamation, celebration, and community called the early Church, and the early Church saw that Jesus was who he claimed to be because of his resurrection from the dead. This also provided future reality of eschatological expectation to a present reality called the Church, in whom the risen Lord was operating for the expansion of the Kingdom and transformation of the world. Although the incarnation, baptism, and ministry of Jesus revealed the rule of God in human life, and although Jesus kept in step with the prophetic and apocalyptic predictions by making this a feature of his message, in the estimation of Pannenberg, because of the resurrection of Jesus of Nazareth, the early Church saw the rejected Messiah of God revealed, and that this same Jesus who was Son of David was also Son of God, Lord and Messiah, the judge, and hope for the world.[425]

Therefore, Pannenberg contends it is through his resurrection from the dead that Jesus of Nazareth is established to be the Christ, not simply because of the titles ascribed to him:

> The earthly Jesus was not yet designated as "Son of God," but this title was, rather, attributed to him only on the basis of his resurrection and exaltation.[426]

The early Church saw the issue between pre-Easter Jesus who "was already set apart from the multitude of other men," and post-Easter Jesus who was exalted to the right hand of God.[427]

Attempting to capture this from the early Church, Pannenberg presents a potential threat to his Christology through the insertion of the word "adoption" respective to Jesus being the Son of God, although to his credit he takes time to nuance this word in a manner that does not connote the same sense as the Christological controversies of the Early Church. In this way the divinity of Jesus is not something conferred post-resurrection, nor is his divinity an epistemological reality, but an ontological one as well. The divinity of Jesus Christ was established via the retroactive significance of the resurrec-

---

[425] See Pannenberg, *ST II*, 326-327. Pannenberg creates some level of challenge in his Christology concerning how "Jesus could hardly identify himself as the messiah" on one hand, with claims on the other hand of the implications of his message and titles allowed him to emerge more readily as the reconciler and enabler of salvation through the eyes of his hearers. This, he contends, led to the claims of blasphemy and the cross. The manner in which Jesus emerges is the establishment of his unity with God and his message in the resurrection, and the negation of claims of blasphemy which led to his rejection in the cross. See Pannenberg, *ST II*, 334-343.

[426] Pannenberg, *JGM*, 134. This statement has been debated since it emerged in *JGM*. Beyond others who have been mentioned in chapter six (2.1) and chapter seven (2.2) thus far, Stanley Grenz points out that his historical approach has been widely questioned, especially by the likes of Carl Henry who challenges that the teachings and deeds are enough to disclose his deity. See Grenz, *Reason for Hope*, 180-181. See Carl F.H. Henry. *God, Revelation, and Authority*. Waco: Word, 1976.

[427] Pannenberg, *JGM*, 135.

tion, and it this hermeneutical key that casts light from post-Easter Jesus to pre-Easter Jesus. The resurrection casts epistemological and ontological establishment and illumination upon the person and ministry of Jesus of Nazareth as the Christ of God who claimed unity with God and the advent of the Kingdom in him. Accordingly, Pannenberg is able to maintain continuity with the Greek tradition of ontology in that things in their essence remain what they are in their essence, while at the same time recognizing that the priority of the future eventuates the present to transform the past.[428]

This distinction Pannenberg has created between a pre and post Easter Jesus, as well as Son of David and Son of God is also not without criticism. Some have claimed nestorianism against Pannenberg, as the two natures are irreconcilably divided.[429] However, Pannenberg is precisely against such a claim; the issue is not how the divine/human natures are divided or in competition, but rather how the resurrection establishes the activity and divinity of the pre-Easter Jesus. In this spirit, Pannenberg argues that the improper way to understand the distinction between the two is through Künneth who indicates "divinity was conferred upon Jesus only through his resurrection."[430] To make such a statement is to change the divinity of Jesus from prior to the resurrection in his ministry, and to activate that divinity only in and through the Christ-event. Pannenberg rejects this, espousing the meaning of the resurrection is not in a change of divinity but the establishment thereof. Similarly, Pannenberg points to the baptismal tradition of the Gospel of Mark, and claims while there is an important pre-Easter claim, it can only be understood from the perspective of a post-Easter Church who recognized Jesus had been crucified but raised from the dead.[431] Pannenberg answers his critics through his methodology from below, the retroactive significance of the resurrection, and its resultative key hermeneutic.

The Retroactive Significance of the Resurrection Conclusion

In sum, Pannenberg finds the impetus to retroactive significance of the resurrection through his methodological proposal from below that looks to

---

[428] See Pannenberg, *JGM*, 135-136. See also Pannenberg, *Theology and The Kingdom of God*, 51-71, 127-143.
[429] For example see Molnar, *Incarnation and Resurrection*, 265-272.
[430] This is a point Pannenberg makes by looking to the work of Künneth in *Theology of the Resurrection*. See Walter Künneth. *Theology of the Resurrection, trans. by James W. Leitch*. St. Louis: Concordia Publishing House, 1965, 114. Original Source: Pannenberg, *JGM*, 135. Pannenberg guards against this by stating that one cannot simply disregard the methodology from above as if it were "a mistake." In this regard, he looks to Weber who claims, "No one can ascend from a 'below' which is somehow given toward an 'above' without holding this 'above' to be likewise at least potentially given in or with the 'below.'" Pannenberg, *JGM*, 34-36. Original Source: O. Weber. *Grundlagen der Dogmatik, Vol. II*, 35.
[431] See Pannenberg, *JGM*, 138.

history as the means of doing theology. In this way, the resurrection of Jesus Christ establishes Jesus of Nazareth as the Christ of God, and casts a key hermeneutical force back upon the person and ministry of Jesus Christ. Pannenberg utilizes the lens of metaphor by nuancing the Christ-event as metaphor in the sense it has not happened to anyone else and cannot possibly be univocally understood, and yet the Christ-event has revealed the unity of Jesus with God and has thus proleptically revealed the future eschatological destiny of humanity by reconciling humanity to God in Jesus Christ. This will be directly disclosed by God in a final act of self-disclosure in the future eschaton. Pannenberg finds the validity of his retroactive significance theology in and through the early Church.

What then does this retroactive significance mean for his Christology? His chosen Christological methodology from below looks to the historical acts of God as the outworking of the relationship between God and humanity and the self-revelation of God finds its genesis in the resurrection and this is the reason for his careful delineation of the resurrection. His Christology posits the resurrection of Jesus Christ as central, as is history. This does not mean that at some point Jesus became divine, meaning that at another point Jesus was not divine. This is an important distinction that will be delineated momentarily, that is, that Jesus is one with God from the beginning just as he is one with humanity in the incarnation. In terms of the oneness of Jesus with humanity, while Pannenberg claims the resurrection is a metaphor insofar as it is a unique experience that has no other human experiences offering replication, it is not limited to the resurrection of Jesus being a metaphor for authentic human existence God longs for humanity to have as in Bultmann. Rather it means humanity comes to experience fulfillment in being united to God through Jesus Christ presently as a result of the future eschaton. Furthermore, it means the incarnation of Jesus of Nazareth, the claims of Jesus of Nazareth, the ministry of Jesus of Nazareth, and the cross of Jesus of Nazareth have been established by God in the resurrection of his Christ, revealing Jesus of Nazareth to be the promised Messiah and Christ. Finally, Pannenberg attempts to maintain continuity with the early Church and its emphasis upon the resurrection as a hermeneutical key to understanding the person and ministry of Jesus Christ, which confirms his pre-Easter ministry and proclamation.

2.2.2 The Pannenbergian Retroactive Significance of the Resurrection: The Unity of Jesus with God and The New Eschatological Adam

The scope of 2.2.1 provided an understanding of the retroactive significance of the resurrection as establishing Jesus of Nazareth as the Christ of God, which also offers a key interpretive hermeneutic of the ministry and person of Jesus Christ. This retroactive significance is born out of the desire Pannenberg has to do Christology by means of a methodology from below which utilizes history and historical-critical methodologies placing the

Christ-event and most particularly the resurrection as central to his Christology. Given the retroactive significance and its key hermeneutic in his Christology, what exactly can be said about Jesus Christ because of his resurrection? While Pannenberg has much to say about this, there are two points of major significance: (1) the revelation of the unity of Jesus with God and (2) how Jesus Christ is the new eschatological Adam who proleptically reveals the eschatological destiny of humanity because of his unity with God. From this basis, Pannenberg then distinguishes Christology as the forerunner of soteriology because the resurrection reveals Jesus is united with God, and on this basis, humanity receives the benefits of eschatological salvation. Thus the historical act of God is not only a process for God, but for humanity and the world. Through this act there is a retroactive establishment of the process of history between God and the world while at the same time revealing the future of the world.

The purpose of 2.2.2 is to illustrate how the retroactive significance of the resurrection of Jesus Christ and its key hermeneutic from 2.2.1 not only establish Jesus of Nazareth as the Christ of God but also reveals the unity of Jesus with God. Because of his unity with God, Jesus Christ is the new eschatological Adam who proleptically reveals the future of humanity and the world, fulfilling the human soteriological need through relational unity with God. The implications of this concern shows how Pannenbergian Christology via resurrection answers the incarnational and crucifixional questions and fulfills the human soteriological need by means of reconciliation.

The Unity of Jesus with God

The structure of the preceding work in 2.2.1 revealed how the retroactive significance of the resurrection in Pannenbergian Christology establishes Jesus of Nazareth as the Christ of God. Moreover, the retroactive significance of the resurrection is the product of his method from below which, from the outset, places emphasis on the historical events of God and humanity in space-time.[432] Accordingly, the retroactive significance of the resurrection provides a key hermeneutic for interpreting the person and work of Jesus Christ – the events and teachings throughout his incarnation, ministry, and death. Thus, the function of the retroactive significance of the resurrection of Jesus Christ is not just to epistemologically establish the work of Jesus Christ but also ontologically establish the person, and more specifically, the grounds of his unity with God. Ultimately, if God is the unbound power of the future as Pannenberg contends, then it is this future which has been proleptically revealed in the resurrection of Jesus Christ from the dead, and it is this future which is eventuating the present to transform the past.[433]

---

[432] This was the premise of the preceding material in chapter seven (2.2.1).
[433] Again, important to his Christology is the claim Pannenberg makes regarding God as the unbound power of the future. His Christology is eschatological in nature and it is the future eschaton which has proleptically been revealed in Jesus Christ that is already transforming the past in the present. The manner in which to view this is

The Pannenbergian Christological concern to show the ontological unity of Jesus with God does not utilize the presupposition of incarnation, but rather begins from an epistemological basis in the historical event of the resurrection.[434] The resurrection as a historical claim to the divinity of Jesus and the Kingdom which has already broken through from the future in Jesus as an anticipatory event of the future as the basis by which Jesus is shown to have unity with God is a very different proposal than Anselm of Canterbury who utilizes the incarnation in the *Cur Deus Homo* for Jesus *a priori* to have unity with God.[435] How then, does Pannenberg arrive at such a conclusion? Specifically, Pannenberg looks to how the resurrection is a historical claim revealing the divinity and unity of Jesus Christ with God which Jesus began in his proclamation of the Kingdom of God having come presently in him; how then the cross and death becomes the fate of Jesus of Nazareth because of the affront he made toward the religious authorities concerning a proclamation of the future Kingdom having come in him in the present age; and how while his death seems to at first glance negate his proclamation of the Kingdom having come in him it is affirmed and established in his resurrection from the dead so that the future Kingdom has been presently and proleptically revealed in Jesus Christ.

In beginning, Pannenberg looks to salvation history and apocalyptic promise which Jesus related to God on the basis of his own context as being that of the expectation of the Kingdom or divine rule.[436] The history of Israel rested upon the hope of the rule of God, especially in post-exilic Israel. Post-exilic Israel hoped for the day when they would be free from foreign oppressors and she would be saved to be in renewed covenant with her God. Pannenberg

---

through the indirect revelation that occurs throughout history and the final and direct self-revelation of God in the eschaton. Therefore it is this future event at the end of history that is eventuating the present and transforming the past. See Pannenberg, *Revelation as History*, 1-26.

[434] This is the point Pannenberg makes out the outset of chapter nine of volume two in his systematic theology, namely that Christology deals with a "methodological problem" revolving around the choice of beginning in the incarnation or the historical event of the resurrection. See Pannenberg, *ST II*, 277. See also Iain Taylor. *Pannenberg on the Triune God*. London: TandT Clark Publishers, 2007, 107-113. Concurrently, Pannenberg sees need for the incarnational "from above" Christology to provide balance to the issue so as not to focus on only the humanity of Jesus or the historicity of Jesus alone. This is offered in Pannenberg, *JGM*, 131-132. This is set in marked contrast to the post-Ignatian Church which began constructing Christologies from the incarnation to demonstrate how Jesus was the logos and incarnate Son. This is also contra Barth whose Christology holds the incarnation of the pre-existent logos as central.

[435] See especially chapter three (1.2).

[436] This is a feature discussed in chapter six (2.1.1). Pannenberg contends history is formed by the relations of God and humanity in the world. Inclusive of this history concerns the apocalyptic predictions and prophetic promises of the coming of the messiah and the restoration of Israel. In this way, Jesus related to God on the basis of salvation history and such predictions and promises. This is the point made by Pannenberg in Pannenberg, *ST II*, 326.

claims within the teaching and ministry of Jesus of Nazareth are claims regarding the Kingdom of God that had come or were coming in him, and as such, Jesus is making a claim that the future salvation of God had entered into present history and reality.[437] The difference, Pannenberg claims, concerns the nature of the Kingdom Jesus preached:

> Jesus himself did not preach the coming of God's rule as salvation for the covenant people as a whole (on the basis of his covenant relation to God), but as salvation only for those who set their hope wholly on the imminence of the future of God, whether in response to the appeal of his own message or for some other reason, as in the case of those whom he called blessed. For those people the salvation of God's rule was already present and at work.[438]

Accordingly, the future Kingdom is present in Jesus, and as such, the message and miracles of Jesus are born out of the future; it is the future of God proleptically present in the resurrection of Jesus Christ that establishes his unity with God, and it is that future which is in-breaking the present in the pre-Easter activity of Jesus so salvation is a present reality to transform the past. Again, this stems from his understanding of God as the unbound power of the future and from the retroactive force of the resurrection that imbues his Christological proposal.

Pannenberg takes care to delineate some of these Kingdom teachings from the Gospels, and claims the Kingdom concerns the "in-breaking of the future of God, but we must understand this future itself as the dynamic basis of its becoming present."[439] Moreover, this claim of the in-breaking of the Kingdom in him is a question Jesus poses concerning commitment to God that was bound up with the first commandment of the Decalogue, and that the singularity of human commitment which God seeks in this com-

---

[437] See Pannenberg, *ST II*, 327-329.

[438] Pannenberg, *ST II*, 327. Ted Peters agrees with this Pannenbergian concept claiming that God creates from the future and it is the future of God that is actively working in and through Jesus Christ. See Peters, *God: The World's Future*, 188-195. Conversely, George Murphy has written an article that argues against the work of Ted Peters and this Pannenbergian concept entitled "Prolepsis and The Physics of Retrocausality." In the article Murphy argues against Peters who claims one can understand a God who works from the future rather than the work of God in a Newtonian based causal chain from past to present to future. Citing Einsteinian physics, dark matter, and cosmic string theories and also looking to predictive prophecy and the ability of God to bend time without violating the laws of physics, Murphy argues the difficulty of this concept when viewed against Genesis 1-2 and how God created in the beginning. Peters, however, argues that resurrection is incorporative of the history of creation in totality and the manner in which the Christ-event correlates to the history of the created order and its transformation. The issue here concerns time and the manner in which resurrection proleptically occurred in Jesus Christ and not yet for the universe. Thus, creation itself is an eschatological reality which Murphy has not accounted for in the theology of Peters. See George Murphy. "Prolepsis and The Physics of Retrocausality." *Theology and Science, Vol. 7, No. 3, 2009*, 213-225. See Peters, *God: The World's Future*, 189-192.

[439] Pannenberg, *ST II*, 329.

mandment is now coming to present expression in the unity of God and humanity in Jesus.[440] The ultimate expression of this is found in the future salvation God offers to those who are united to God by participating in the presently available Kingdom, or the rule and reign of God that has come in Jesus Christ. This is why the teaching and ministry of Jesus emphasizes the inclusion of those thought to be outside the rule of God or united with God. Those who were once thought to be outside of God experience forgiveness and redemption precisely because they seek in Jesus Christ what the first commandment of the Decalogue asks. In so doing, those who participate in the Kingdom are not only experiencing the future salvation of God in the present, but come to recognize the future is the unity of God and humanity which is presently available to those who are ready to respond to the call of the Kingdom. So then, it is the very reality of the unity of Jesus with God that leads him to make the claims he does concerning the in-breaking of the Kingdom and the present reality of future eschatological salvation. This stands in contrast with the religious authorities that once called the outcast community as being outside the potentiality for oneness with God; now they are confronted with the need for salvation because they are the outcast who stand outside of oneness with God. Even more, it is not simply because Jesus claimed unity with God that these gifts are presently available. Rather it is from the future of the resurrection which is breaking into the present that allowed Jesus to make such powerful claims.

The implications of such claims were an affront to the religious authorities of his milieu and accordingly made for a response from these religious authorities, seen throughout his ministry encapsulated in the gospel narratives. For the religious authorities, the struggle revolved around how the future salvation for all of Israel could have possibly arrived when her oppressors remained in power. The affront to the religious authorities concerning his authority, stems not only out of his claim to authority as was shown above, but more importantly on the basis of the content of his preaching on the Kingdom and the miracles which accompanied his preaching on the Kingdom. Simply put, Jesus makes the claim he is the one to bring their salvation.[441] The affront to the religious authority begins in their calls of blasphemy, and climaxes in the crucifixion as they hand over Jesus to the Romans to decide his fate.[442] The death of Jesus of Nazareth would have made the point that his unity with God was obviously a prevarication, and this is the point of capturing the religious authorities making a mockery of Jesus during the crucifixion.[443] The religious authorities ultimately misunderstood the unity of Jesus with God which was precisely embodied within the scope of the proclamation of the Kingdom which Jesus made, and how the future salvation promised to post-exilic Israel had indeed come in him and was available to all. This availability to all was regardless of their present standing with

---

[440] See Pannenberg, *ST II*, 330-331.
[441] See Pannenberg, *ST II*, 335.
[442] See Pannenberg, *JGM*, 251-253. See also Pannenberg, *ST II*, 336-339.
[443] See Pannenberg, *ST II*, 333-334.

God and the religious system; all that was required to participate was repentance and faith.[444]

This proclamation and teaching, which are the statements and embodiment of the authority of Jesus brings us to the second issue, the death of Jesus of Nazareth, the Christ of God, which made for an entire departure from the preaching of Jesus of Nazareth concerning the Kingdom of God to the hearers of his message. If the Kingdom had come in him, and Jesus died on the cross, indeed his claims of unity with God were false – especially to his hearers of his message. This is at least one reason for the struggle of Peter with the passion predictions of Jesus, the mockery of the crowds and religious authorities, and the thief on the cross who tells Jesus to save himself. The cross was and is entirely related to the claims Jesus made, for it is only in the rejection of those claims that the cross comes to expression. The Scriptures record the trial by the high priest, the mockery of onlookers and the religious community, and the interactions both pre and post crucifixion with the Roman soldiers.[445] But what does the cross mean for Pannenberg? How does he bring the death of Jesus Christ into union with the proclamation of authority embodied in the Kingdom teaching that had come near in Jesus?

The answer comes in form of vindication. Jesus is the Christ of God over and against those who executed him. Pannenberg finds meaning in the cross through the resurrection:

> Jesus' death on the cross is revealed in the light of his resurrection as the punishment suffered in our place for the blasphemous existence of humanity.[446]

Pannenberg contends for Jesus, the crucifixion and resurrection were events placed before him – a fate of sorts to be "suffered and accepted,"[447] and notes the Scriptures indicate the cross is not clear without the resurrection that brings clarity to the cross. He delineates this point by offering the ransom sayings of Jesus in the Gospel of Mark, the Emmaus Road experience of Cle-

---

[444] See Pannenberg, *ST II*, 340-343.

[445] See Pannenberg, *ST II*, 362-364.

[446] Pannenberg, *JGM*, 245. Whereas Anselm saw the cross as being part of the active obedience of Jesus Christ to the will of God in providing a *satisfactio* for the offended honor of God and the salvation of humanity, Pannenberg views this as a passive obedience. Jesus is indeed part of a divine plan but is being subjected to the fate of death and betrayal by the religious community, the political community, and humanity in general (represented by the crowds). Moreover, salvation is (in his estimation) the ending of the present age via the cross and the beginning of a new one via the resurrection that enables future salvation now. This is the reason why Pannenberg utilizes reconciliation rather than *satisfactio* as a central concept to the atoning work of Jesus Christ in the Christ-event. The issue for him is not so much satisfying the offended honor of God through active obedience but through the rejection by the world of the future of God in-breaking the present, he passively accepted the work of reconciling the world to God. See Pannenberg, *ST II*, 397-464.

[447] See Herbert Neie. *The Doctrine of the Atonement in the Theology of Wolfhart Pannenberg*. New York: Walter DeGruyter Publishers, 1979, 6.

opas and his companion in the Gospel of Luke, or even the rejection of the messiah which happened in the same manner that the prophets of old were brought to their deaths. He further points to the Suffering Servant of Isaiah 53:10, the typology of the Passover Lamb and its consequent the Lord's Supper, the new covenant, and even the new eschatological era of the end to the law.[448] He ultimately claims the way the disciples and early church made meaning of the cross was from the perspective of vindication of the innocence of Jesus on the basis of his claims to authority and oneness with God. The reversal of the charges of blasphemy, messianic pretending, and those who disavow his Kingdom teaching occur because of the establishment of Jesus as the Christ of God in the resurrection. Moreover, the manner in which the cross had meaning for humanity was that the death of Jesus was for the sins of humanity in an expiatory sense, albeit "not yet as expiatory *sacrifice* in the cultic sense."[449] Therefore the meaning of the cross is established through the resurrection so that his unity with God and humanity is revealed, so the claims of the nearness of God and the forgiveness of sin have real merit, and so the future salvation which God offers now in the present is not just specific to one person or a people group, but are now universally available and applicable to those who desire such a gift.[450]

This is the juncture at which Pannenberg utilizes the term substitution or representation for his doctrine of reconciliation. In this regard, he argues akin to Luther for the understanding of inclusive substitution. In essence, Pannenberg argues the work of Jesus Christ is for all insofar as he is representative humanity, who was given up to death by God. More importantly, Jesus Christ dies a death that all humanity dies. It is in his death that he is united to humanity and in his resurrection that humanity is united to him in the hope of the future salvation of God in the eschaton. Stanley Grenz has pointed out that the way Pannenberg does this is by showing the death of Jesus Christ to be the universal consequence of sin while Jesus concurrently accepts his death as the "sealing of his own self-differentiation from the Father, constitutive of his differentiation from other creatures as well."[451] In this way, Jesus is as representative humanity the originator of a new hu-

---

[448] See Pannenberg, *JGM*, 246-249. Pannenberg utilizes Mark, Luke, Acts, Romans, and 1 Thessalonians.

[449] Pannenberg, *JGM*, 247. Neie is also helpful here, demonstrating the Pannenbergian concept of the death of Jesus as being expiatory although not in a cultic manner. Neie claims the two pillars of the Pannenbergian understanding of the death of Jesus concerns humanity who deserves to die for their rejection of Jesus and the substitution that is possible. The doctrine of substitution Pannenberg espouses is slightly atypical in that it concerns vicarious suffering and representation, but inclusive substitution as Jesus died a death that all people must die. By his sharing in our death and rising from death we share in his resurrection. In this manner, persons attain the resurrection of Jesus – the future salvation of God in the eschaton – that is already present, active, and working in him. See Neie, *The Doctrine of Atonement in the Theology of Wolfhart Pannenberg*, 180-206. See also Pannenberg, *ST II*, 419-437.

[450] See Pannenberg, *JGM*, 252-254.

[451] Grenz, *Reason for Hope*, 172.

manity as the "last Adam."⁴⁵² This allows Pannenberg to link Jesus as God-Man to the Triune relation and humanity, and show how the substitutionary nature of the death of Jesus is linked to his own identity as Son of God and to the identity as second Adam and author of new humanity. Thus the sacrifice of Jesus on the cross has universality and totality whereas cultic sacrifice does not.⁴⁵³

The soteriological question for Pannenberg which arises concerns how soteriology is related to Christology, or how the cross is related to the historicity of Jesus Christ in his life, ministry, claims of unity with God and the establishment thereof. Pannenberg claims the manner in which these two are united is through the resurrection. This occurs on the basis of the Kingdom teachings of Jesus and how the expectation of the resurrection of the dead comes to expression through the cross which was the rejection of the future Kingdom that had come in him. The cross has meaning insofar as Jesus Christ is the one who vicariously identifies with and is identified by humanity as the expiatory sacrifice for sin. This in turn allows the future to break into the present so that the apocalyptic hope of Israel comes from the future into the present vicariously through him to humanity.⁴⁵⁴ Without the retroactive significance or force of the resurrection, the person and ministry of Jesus of Nazareth as well as the soteriological implications of the cross quickly change the scope of Christology.⁴⁵⁵

For this reason, Pannenberg claims the cross is not something Jesus does, but something which happens to Jesus. To be sure, Pannenberg recognizes the acceptance of Jesus of his fate, but it is not a fate he actively sought. Jesus accepted his death through "passive obedience," which he claims is markedly different from the obedience that satisfaction claims.⁴⁵⁶ Pannenberg claims it

---

⁴⁵² See Pannenberg, *ST II*, 304-315. See also Pannenberg, *JGM*, 258-268.

⁴⁵³ See Pannenberg, *JGM*, 248-250. Pannenberg points to how the cultic notion of sacrifice is ongoing, whereas the sacrifice of Jesus is "ultimate" and "final." Moreover, he distinguishes the universality of this to show the marked contrast with cultic sacrifice being for Israel. This stands in continuity with the rejection of his proclamation of the Kingdom by the religious authorities, as it was precisely because Jesus made such claims that the religious authorities and Romans crucified him.

⁴⁵⁴ This combines a few different elements in the Pannenbergian Christology, most particularly his theology of expiatory sacrifice, vicarious suffering, and the historicity of Jesus. See Pannenberg, *JGM*, 245-282.

⁴⁵⁵ Given what has already been said about the theological assumption of miracles Hume argued for in theological modernity, and those who deny the resurrection of its historicity, this is a bold claim by Pannenberg. It finds contestation by the same parties listed above. Bultmann specifically denied the historical claim of the resurrection for an existential rise of faith, and Barth was unsympathetic to the view Pannenberg takes here as well. Others have challenged Pannenberg on this element, specifically on historical grounds. These have been mentioned throughout this chapter and chapter six. The point to be made here is the weight Pannenberg gives to the resurrection and to its historicity as establishing the cross, the reconciler of humanity to God, and the unity of Jesus with God.

⁴⁵⁶ See Pannenberg, *JGM*, 195.

is not so much incarnation which functions as the purpose for the cross – that a perfect sacrifice was actively seeking to make this sacrifice – rather, it was later determined that in fact, the perfect sacrifice had been made. In this respect, the cross is the rejection of the proclamation of the future Kingdom present in him, and the meaning of the cross emerges from the resurrection.[457] This is, of course, not without contestation. If Jesus did not have an idea of his mission or the tangential aim of his ministry, is it possible for him to reconcile humanity to God? Or is such a limitation a Triune schism? Key to this is how passive obedience does not mean that Jesus did not actively accept his death, but that it was not a death that he actively sought from the beginning of his ministry.

Finally, the future Kingdom is proleptically revealed in the resurrection of Jesus Christ through the cross. The teachings of Jesus in revealing the future of God, the very claims Jesus made that were embodied in his teachings including their accompanying miracles, and the cross which was seemingly the negation of his teaching and claims to be one with God are overcome and established in the resurrection. The resurrection therefore retroactively casts force from the future backward upon past work and person of Jesus to establish his unity with God. The resurrection was the vindication of the crucified messiah whose teaching was the embodiment of his authority and unity with God, and the future hope that had been proleptically revealed. Through cross and resurrection, eschatological salvation is available to all, with the immanent rule of God a reality still to be fully realized in the final act of self-disclosure in the eschaton. Now, a message is to be proclaimed to all:

> For Christian faith it is not a matter of indifference of who it was that was raised from the dead, namely the Crucified (Mark 16:6; cf. Acts 2:36; 4:10; 1 Cor. 1:13). Nor was this just any person crucified but the crucified Jesus of Nazareth. Hence the Easter faith of Christians is linked for all time to the earthly history of Jesus of Nazareth, who proclaimed to his people the nearness of the rule of God, who was rejected by his adversaries as a deceiver and handed over to the Romans for execution, who was raised from the dead by God, and who was thus instituted as Messiah (Acts 2:23f., 36; cf. Rom. 1:4).[458]

The triune God established and authenticated the teachings and person of Jesus of Nazareth as the Christ of God, indicating the rule of God was active in him and could be active in the lives of humanity as hearers and witnesses of Jesus Christ. Pannenberg brings forth an important claim at this juncture that the resurrection of Jesus Christ is a claim to historicity, and it is because of this claim that the battle for truth claims being debated for their veracity among the scope of the world religions emerges. Pannenberg ulti-

---

[457] See Pannenberg, *JGM*, 277. The divine hiddenness of God is an expression that mirrors the words of Paul in Ephesians 3, and is a contribution Luther made at various points in his theology. See also John Calvin who refers to God as *deus incognitus* in his work.

[458] Pannenberg, *ST II*, 344.

mately claims if the resurrection of Jesus Christ includes the implications of historicity and the eschatological future of God as being proleptically revealed and available to all humanity because Jesus Christ is representative humanity, then Jesus Christ is a figure whose historicity bears impact on all history.[459]

The New Eschatological Adam & The Eschatological Destiny of Humanity

Now that the unity of Jesus with God has been explored above, it is possible to take this to a deeper level, which indeed Pannenberg does in the remainder of chapter ten of *Systematic Theology Volume II*. The second Adam inclusive substitutionary soteriology Pannenberg espouses has been briefly mentioned above, but the importance of this is founded in what Stanley Grenz termed the "eschatological new human" Pannenberg utilizes in his Christology. This emphasis is the outcome of his proposal for the centrality of the resurrection in his Christology, uniting both the unity of Jesus with God and the soteriological human need for salvation in the person of Jesus Christ. Grenz notes:

> Pannenberg looks to the Spirit as the link between anthropology and Christology. On this basis he speaks of Jesus as the embodiment of the human destiny definitive for the determination of the nature of humanity.[460]

The unity between God and humanity in the person of Jesus is embodied in his message of the Kingdom, his miracles that accompany this teaching as signs and acts of the Kingdom, and in the death and resurrection that proleptically reveals the future of God and the future fulfillment of the destiny of humanity. Therefore this section shall emphasize how Pannenberg arrives at this juncture through two emphases: (1) the concept of the second eschatological Adam and (2) through linking salvation history with the logos. These elements demonstrate the unity of Jesus with God, and also indicate how humanity is the beneficiary of eschatological salvation through the new eschatological Adam who is one with God.

In beginning, Pannenberg gives Pauline thought important weight in his concept of the new eschatological Adam by utilizing the Adamic metaphor from Romans 5 and 1 Corinthians 15. The linear movement of this occurs in his thinking by his pointing to Jesus as:

> The fulfillment of the human destiny to community with God happening in three stages: (1) Dedication to his office, (2) the acceptance of his fate, and (3) his glorification by God.[461]

---

[459] Pannenberg, *ST II*, 359-362.
[460] Grenz, *Reason for Hope*, 151.
[461] Pannenberg, *JGM*, 195.

The dedication to his office comes through the Kingdom teaching he shares to illumine the reality that future eschatological salvation has presently come to humanity. The expression of the acceptance of his fate is understood in terms of passive obedience, seen by Pannenberg as bringing about the resurrection and consequently the resurrection as unfolding the fulfillment of human destiny.[462] This is how he is able to point to Paul and the distinction between the first and second Adam. Jesus as representative humanity is the second eschatological Adam through his resurrection.

Pannenberg then moves from the second Adam to show through the concept of the Logos that Jesus is the one who has become fully indwelled by the Logos, and accordingly has, through his striving, fulfilled obedience to God. This is what characterizes him as the "prototypal man" who calls humanity to believe that the Kingdom is indeed near.[463] It is for these reasons Pannenberg points to Paul and the ontology of the second eschatological Adam regarding the person of Jesus Christ. For these reasons one can epistemologically relate that if the person of Jesus Christ is the long anticipated second eschatological Adam, then there is universal significance in the death and resurrection of Jesus Christ as the fulfillment of eschatological hope. Thus the second eschatological Adam begins with ontology and anthropology, relating this universally to human soteriological need. Because of the retroactive significance of the resurrection there is, according to Pannenberg, the fulfillment of human hope.

Pannenberg quickly moves into the classic theology of the logos and the link to salvation history. Pannenberg contends the Christology of the Church from the second century forward developed from the perspective of the preexistent Son of God and ultimately the link between the preexistent Son of God and creation through the incarnation.[464] This is partly the reason for his from below proposal which contrasts with the preexistent Son Christology that is a from above. He does so precisely through the from below proposal that is grounded in the historicity of the resurrection which establishes the preexistent Son of God in Jesus of Nazareth. Pannenberg furthers this by also arguing for the logos, relating the concept of differentiation in human anthropology as the outworking of the theology of self-distinction within the Triune relation.[465] To be sure, Pannenberg realizes one cannot construct this

---

[462] See Pannenberg, *JGM*, 196. This is contra Anselm and Barth who claim an active obedience. The terms here of active and passive obedience are from F. Schleiermacher. *The Christian Faith*, ed. by H.R. Mackintosh and J.S. Stewart. Edinburgh: T and T Clark, 1928, 452.

[463] See Pannenberg, *JGM*, 198-199.

[464] See Pannenberg, *ST II*, 278-279. Mentioned before, Pannenberg attributes this primarily to Ignatius and the 2nd century apologists. For Pannenberg, the link between logos and salvation history is grounded in the reality of Jesus who was fully human and fully divine by way of his resurrection from the dead. See Pannenberg, *JGM*, 323-324.

[465] See Pannenberg, *ST II*, 291-293. See also Wolfhart Pannenberg. *Anthropology in Theological Perspective* trans. by Matthew J. O'Connell. London: T and T Clark Publishers, 2004.

entirely from below as there has to be some *a priori* concept of God and the preexistent Son.

Demonstrating the logos and inter-Trinitarian relationship, he continues his delineation of the link between the second eschatological Adam and salvation history by moving to how the incarnation of the logos becomes the outworking of the logos and "completion of creation."[466] In this regard, the logos is not only one with God but has eschatological significance for creation, as it is the logos which becomes manifest within the process of history and as the fulfillment of history and human destiny.[467] This is why Pannenberg claims:

> The relation of our created destiny to the incarnation of the Logos in Jesus of Nazareth is not, then, a direct one of disposition and actualization. The way from disposition to actualization is broken by sin. Because we are alienated from the Logos, we learn to know the Logos – who is still the origin of our life and the light of our consciousness – only through Jesus….Only through Jesus, however, do these general concepts acquire their true content. It is herein that the specific person and history of Jesus have universal relevance.[468]

This is the juncture at which the second Adam takes root. The second Adam is the divine logos incarnate that has defeated sin and the alienation of humanity from God via the cross and in the establishment of Jesus as this second Adam through the resurrection. As such, humanity becomes the beneficiary of future eschatological salvation and unity with God.[469] Whereas Adam was disobedient, Jesus Christ was obedient to God; whereas Adam failed and brought death, Jesus Christ through sharing in the death that all humanity dies and by his resurrection from the dead as vindication of the charges of blasphemy brings life. Here one sees the incarnation of the Logos, but from the basis of the resurrection which connects the purpose of the incarnation as the completion of creation, most notably having effect upon humanity.

This is the real beauty in what Pannenberg offers, and also the real difference in his doctrine of reconciliation. Pannenberg makes God the reconciler through Jesus Christ to humanity and the world. God is not the

---

[466] Pannenberg, *ST II*, 293.

[467] This is an important piece of his argument as it ties eschatology to the incarnation. Utilizing Rahner, he points to the incarnation as the fulfillment of humanity. Pannenberg then contends that the resurrection is the future in-breaking the present, and it is from the resurrection to incarnation which reveals the fulfillment of humanity and the future eschatological destiny of humanity. Thus resurrection, cross, and incarnation are held in dialectical tension through his retroactive theology of the resurrection. See Karl Rahner. "Jesus Christus, III B." *Lexikon für Theologie und Kirche*, Volume Five. Freiburg: 1957-1965. See Pannenberg, *ST II*, 293-294.

[468] Pannenberg, *ST II*, 295.

[469] See Pannenberg, *ST II*, 295-297. Again, one sees here how the from below proposal which centers upon the retroactive force of the resurrection is manifested into his theology of the incarnation and of Jesus as second Adam.

object but subject of reconciliation and the divine logos is the self-actualizing principle of this work.[470] So it is the pre-existent Son of God being sent in the power of the Spirit to the glory of the Father to accomplish the work of reconciliation as the new eschatological Adam. This work occurs through obedience to God even unto death on a cross in the face of the charges of blasphemy and the rejection of the Kingdom proclamation for which the Son was sent. This work is established through the resurrection, which establishes the incarnation, and thus enables the eschatological destiny of humanity that is of universal significance to all humanity. What salvation history claimed would happen did so in the second Adam, the pre-existent Son who is Jesus of Nazareth, the Christ of God.[471] The greater implication is that the expectation of the resurrection – a future event – has now happened in the present which indicates future salvation has entered the present. And the greatest of implications is that humanity now presently has unity with God on the basis of faith and accepting the Kingdom message in Jesus who is declared Son of God on the basis of his resurrection, and who has reconciled the world and humanity to God through the cross and the resurrection to begin the new and future age.

The Unity of Jesus with God and The New Eschatological Adam

It is this issue, the unity of Jesus with God and Jesus as the new eschatological Adam as the fulfillment of salvation history toward which his methodological proposal points. The previous chapter illustrated how Pannenberg contends truth is being debated and scrutinized in historical processes among competing religions, and how history is the outworking of the relationship between God and humanity. Whereas that relationship and history form the core of salvation history, how Jesus Christ is related to God will be the rise or fall of the significance of Jesus Christ among the competing religious claims. The Pannenbergian solution is that Jesus is the second eschatological Adam that is united to God, a reality established by his resurrection from the dead. It is this reality which reveals the future of God and the world proleptically in

---

[470] This is an important nuance as chapter three (1.2.2) argued for the work of the *Cur Deus Homo* as being one in which the work of Jesus Christ on the cross concerned a crucifixional transaction which could easily posit Jesus Christ as the object of reconciliation rather than the subject of it. While it is true that Anselm holds this in tension with the active obedience of Jesus Christ, in some manner of speaking if the *satisfactio* is made to God by Jesus Christ than this more easily puts him in a position of object rather than subject. The Pannenbergian Christology posits Jesus Christ as the one who passively receives a fate but actively accepts that fate – the rejection of the religious, political, and human communities. The difference is that Pannenberg makes Jesus Christ the subject of reconciliation as part of the divine community via his resurrection from the dead. Jesus Christ is reconciling the world to the divine community of which he is concurrently part of both.

[471] See Pannenberg, *ST II*, 320-321.

the present. Pannenberg begins from the perspective of the Christ-event and whether or not Jesus has unity with God, and if so, how the history of Jesus Christ has universal significance as the new eschatological Adam. Moreover he illustrates how Jesus Christ is divine by means of the resurrection which retroactively establishes the incarnation. And finally, he illustrates salvation to be a relational unity by means of reconciliation: the Christ-event inaugurates eschatological salvation in the present.[472]

2.2.3 The Pannenbergian Retroactive Significance of the Resurrection: Responding to the Crucifixional and Incarnational Questions

This chapter has argued thus far that the retroactive significance of the resurrection functions in such a way that Jesus of Nazareth is established to be the Christ of God, that Jesus Christ is united with God, and as such is the new eschatological Adam. Through the utilization of his from below methodology, Pannenberg looks to the resurrection as the historical confirmatory event vindicating Jesus of the charges of blasphemy by the religious authorities, Romans, and human community (crowds) who executed him upon the cross, and establishes him as being one with God. Because Jesus Christ is united with God, this has universal significance for humanity. The Pannenbergian proposal provides an answer to the incarnational and crucifixional questions and fulfills the human soteriological need by looking to resurrection, to the future, and to human destiny proleptically revealed in this historical event. According to Pannenberg, humanity experiences the eschatological future and its destiny of oneness with God through Jesus Christ. This methodological emphasis via resurrection in his Christological proposal forms the concluding unit (2.2.3) of this chapter.

Accordingly, the final section of this chapter (2.2.3) shall focus on two inter-related issues: (1) Given the retroactive significance of the resurrection which reveals the unity of Jesus Christ with God and his significance for humanity as the new eschatological Adam, what are the Christological implications for the incarnation and the cross, and then subsequently, why according to Pannenberg, Christology should begin with resurrection and not incarnation or crucifixion; and secondly (2) how this Christology offers a reorientation of the incarnation and cross of Jesus. These two concluding issues shall complete this study of Pannenberg and prepare the way for how Pannenberg offers a dialectical unity of incarnation, cross, and resurrection and how this unity emphasizes salvation via relational reconciliation and restoration. This final implications of this contrast shall be the potentiality for a Pannenbergian voice in the non-violent atonement onversation occurring within post-modern theology in chapter eight.

---

[472] See Pannenberg, *ST II*, 425-427. Pannenberg delineates the various views of representative salvation while at the same time recognizing that his death concerns the eschatological message and salvation of Jesus Christ.

Incarnation, Cross, and Christology

In beginning, it comes as no surprise at this juncture that Pannenberg places the Christ-event as central to his Christology, and orients the resurrection as having retroactive significance which establishes the work and person of Jesus Christ. This is the outcome of his methodology from below to above, as the historicity of Jesus Christ answers the question regarding the unity of Jesus with God. More specifically, the historical event of the resurrection of Jesus Christ serves not only as the establishment of his unity with God, but also the confirmation of his message that expresses his personhood. Stanley Grenz notes:

> Pannenberg does not limit the reflective confirmation character of Easter to epistemology, however, but views it also ontologically, asserting that without Easter Jesus would not be the Son of God.[473]

Therefore, the historicity of the resurrection is of both epistemological and ontological significance; Pannenberg demonstrates this significance not only as it relates to the unity of Jesus with God but also the unity of Jesus and humanity. The latter concerns establishing the vicarious suffering of Jesus which has universal human significance. This universal significance comes in the form of the proleptically revealed promise of hope which concerns the eschatological future of humanity and intended destiny for humanity. Whereas death meant separation from God, now through the new eschatological Adam who is one with God and died as the vicarious sacrifice for all humanity, all may come to enter into reconciled relationship with God through Jesus Christ. Death becomes the loss of finitude, the resurrection the eschatological future of humanity, and the message of the Kingdom that was rejected in the cross, is established in the resurrection. Given the Christ-event is held in tension and confirmed in the resurrection, Pannenberg claims that the New Testament finds its basis in this central event.[474]

That the resurrection establishes the personhood, history, and unity of Jesus with God, there is then an important implication for his Christology, chiefly as this relates to the incarnation. Whereas other Christologies begin with the incarnation or crucifixion, Pannenberg begins with history and the universal significance of this historical event for humanity because Jesus Christ is united with God. For Pannenberg, the incarnation is not to be considered an *a priori* epistemological presupposition of the ontology of Jesus as the Christ of God, but is rather established retroactively through the resurrection.

This is to say that without the history of the resurrection, the incarnation cannot show that Jesus is one with God and is Christ from his birth. The gospel is related to the Christ-event and the message of the gospel is established from the event. This, according to Pannenberg, is the primary reason why the early Church developed Christology from the point of the resurrec-

---

[473] Grenz, *Reason for Hope*, 160.
[474] See Pannenberg, *JGM*, 66-73, 133-141.

tion and connected the historical chronology of Jesus to develop an understanding of Jesus altogether:

> [Without this historicity] the church's doctrine of a divine saving event in the person and history of Jesus prior to faith in him, and serving as the basis of that faith would be robbed of its substance.[475]

Accordingly, Pannenberg argues the early Church developed its Christology from the basis of Old Testament expectation, then from the basis of the pre-existent logos, from the perspective of the two substances of spirit and flesh united in one person Jesus, until the work of Ignatius where there was a shift of sorts that occurred in Christology.[476] Pannenberg contends that ultimately the logos took precedence regarding the divinity of Jesus, and that the two substances referred to the historicity of Jesus "after the flesh and after the spirit...his earthly path to the cross and his exaltation by the resurrection."[477] Pannenberg claims Ignatius emphasized the incarnation and relatedness of the Father and Son through obedience:

> A fateful change thus took place, or at least a fateful shift of emphasis, when, as in Ignatius Eph. 18.2, the birth of Jesus instead of the Easter event became constitutive for the union of deity and humanity in him.[478]

This is the reason why Pannenberg places the whole life and union of Jesus with God in the incarnation, and not just the conception and birth of Jesus as the incarnation.[479] This feature follows his methodological proposal – it follows from the history of Jesus in its entirety. More importantly as it relates to humanity and its future eschatological destiny, Pannenberg claims that humanity comes to be filled with the divine life of the Son, who is the logos that is one with God the Father and yet stands in distinction from the Father. This feature posits the incarnation as climactic, for it is the union of God and humanity in Jesus that is revealed proleptically in the resurrection which casts retroactive force upon the incarnation that the future eschatological destiny of all humanity is revealed.[480] This fits neatly with his theology of

---

[475] Pannenberg, *ST II*, 379-380.
[476] See Pannenberg, *ST II*, 380-382.
[477] Pannenberg, *ST II*, 383.
[478] Pannenberg, *ST II*, 383.
[479] There is an important point Pannenberg notes here. He shares that his work *Jesus – God and Man* related the incarnation exclusively to the beginning of life for Jesus, and that Christology does not find its genesis here but its climactic moment. By the time of the Systematic Theology, he shifts positions to be more on par with his methodological proposal of below to above, and how the incarnation finds expression in the whole history and its process that happens in Jesus Christ. He argues that his former statement on this point placed Jesus in the role of "mere man and then would later become the Son of God by union with his human person." See Pannenberg, *ST II*, 384-385 (f 73).
[480] See Pannenberg, *ST II*, 224-226. Pannenberg makes an important point about this as it relates to Barthian Christology, claiming that the two agree in the retention of "creaturely correspondence to divine destiny" but the manner in which they go

Jesus as the new eschatological human: the resurrection establishes incarnation and incarnation becomes the promise of the future that has already come proleptically in Jesus.

To be sure, Pannenberg recognizes that the interpretation of the incarnation must be a Trinitarian act. However, the manner in which he arrives at this Trinitarian act comes precisely in the form of the historical acts of God from the resurrection which has direct benefit for humanity, rather than as an *a priori* presupposition. Whereas those who begin with the incarnation presuppose God and the unity of Jesus with God in the incarnation, Pannenberg demonstrates that the incarnation is indeed the Trinitarian act of God for the reconciliation of God and humanity – but the manner in which he does this is based upon the history of Jesus Christ and in the Christ-event that gave rise to the early Church and the gospel itself.[481] So then, as mentioned above, the incarnation is not just a Trinitarian act, but *the* Trinitarian act in which the incarnation of Jesus Christ is the "completion of creation."[482] Thus, the incarnation concerns the logos made incarnate in Jesus Christ, and it is through the logos made incarnate that new humanity is revealed. Through Jesus Christ, the logos made flesh, the new eschatological Adam, humanity enters into future eschatological salvation, and where sin and death reigned through the disobedience of the first Adam, reconciliation and life comes through the obedience to God even unto death, and resurrection of the second Adam.[483] In this, the destiny of humanity as bearers of the divine image is founded in the incarnation of the logos as the completion of creation but only insofar as the resurrection was the proleptic event which revealed the future of human destiny and established the unity of Jesus and God. The future of human identity finds its origin in its oneness with God, just as Jesus was one with God.[484]

---

about this is entirely different. Whereas Barth presupposes the truth of God, Pannenberg looks to historicity. See Pannenberg, *ST II*, 226-227. Pannenberg is further challenged on this by Molnar who defends Barth by claiming that Pannenberg is too close to adoptionism and too binding upon the Trinity in his doctrine of the incarnation. Molnar claims that existence creates revelation and not vice versa. What Molnar has missed is the notion that while Pannenberg is thoroughly committed to his methodology, he nonetheless realizes a certain concession for the need of a corresponding theology from above. The two are complimentary, although the from below which establishes incarnation through resurrection is a more tenable position in light of the historical-critical methodologies Pannenberg seeks to combat. See Molnar, *Incarnation and Resurrection*, 279-280. See Pannenberg, *ST II*, 288-290.

[481] See Pannenberg, *ST II*, 289-297. In this regard, Pannenberg claims that Christology cannot allow "statements of the Christian confession to retain the status of a presupposition that is external to itself." (289-290). In other words, one cannot simply accept the claims of Christian doctrine because they are doctrine – they must have some historical referent by which they are made tenable.

[482] Pannenberg, *ST II*, 293.

[483] See Pannenberg, *ST II*, 289-297.

[484] See Pannenberg, *ST II*, 202-231, 386-389.

Secondly, the Pannenbergian Christological emphasis on the resurrection also bears weight upon the cross. This has in part, been touched upon briefly earlier in this chapter (2.2.2), as the cross concerns vicarious suffering and inclusive substitution. The cross and death of Jesus Christ is vindicated in the resurrection in terms of his unjust execution, and in the face of what seems to be dereliction by God there is on Easter the revelation of his unity with God. The cross is then not the only salvific moment, but rather one part of it. Rather, it is the totality of the history of the Son of God – the divine logos incarnate in Jesus of Nazareth the Christ of God who proclaimed the future of God as having arrived that was raised from the dead– that becomes constitutive for salvation. Whereas satisfaction theologies posit weight upon the cross, the *a priori* assumption of the incarnation, and satisfying the injustice done unto God or the wrath of God, Pannenberg posits weight upon the history of Jesus Christ from the resurrection which enables salvation through reconciliation and entry into the future Kingdom of God – human participation in the future power and presence of God at present through the one who was crucified and risen from the dead. It is that word "reconciliation" which one finds regularly in the work of Pannenberg, along with the biblical reference of 2 Corinthians 5:19. For Pannenberg, the cross which is established by the resurrection is for the purpose of God reconciling the world to the self of God in the process of history through the Son who is the divine logos made incarnate and in the power of the Spirit. Rather than a Christology that has the cross or human soteriological need at its core, Pannenberg posits the history of Jesus Christ and most notably the resurrection of Jesus Christ in the Christ-event as being central. Ultimately it is not soteriology that drives Christology in his proposal, but Christology that drives soteriology.[485]

The cross is an act of the Triune God to reconcile the world through the Son. Jesus Christ by means of passive obedience accepts the will of the Father, so it is the Father who reconciles the world to God through Jesus the Son in the power of the Spirit. Whereas some could raise the issue of ontological subordinationism or even perhaps divine child abuse on the part of the Father in sending the Son, one must keep in mind that there is a factor of obedience and active cooperation on the part of the Son and an empowerment through the Spirit in this regard.[486] The cross is the suffering of Jesus

---

[485] See Pannenberg, *JGM*, 38-40. See also Pannenberg, *ST II*, 397-398, especially 398 where his first footnote describes this exact point of how Ohlig claimed Christology is a function of soteriology. Schleiermacher also formed his Christology from a similar method. While Anselm was not a systematic theologian per se, it is possible to see how the *Cur Deus Homo* and its soteriological line of reasoning proceeded from theological tendencies to posit Christology as a function of soteriology. Anselm sought to explain why the need for the God-Man beginning from a soteriological need, rather than from the salvation history of Jesus Christ. This is not to say that Pannenberg is not interested in the human soteriological need. However, the expression Pannenberg takes in the human need for salvation comes in the form of hope that is gained in the resurrection and it is precisely because of the resurrection that humanity can have hope for it sees its future eschatological destiny and final unity with God.

[486] See Pannenberg, *ST II*, 438-442.

for us (i.e. *pro nobis*) as a vicarious representative of humanity for human blasphemy and the rejection of the future Kingdom Jesus claimed was present. And whereas Luther held the cross as being of a penal nature and the sacrifice of Jesus as being an expiation for such a penalty, Pannenberg sees the vicarious suffering of Jesus as being representative of humanity for the purpose of reconciliation. This reconciliation is achieved through the resurrection that gives retroactive significance to the cross; the blasphemy of humanity is reconciled, as is the death that is part of the condition of human finitude through the separation between God and humanity. Through the death and resurrection of Jesus comes the death of these elements, the reconciliation of God and humanity, and a regaining of the divine image as the eschatological human destiny.

Ultimately, as has been noted throughout this chapter, the cross must be understood in light of the resurrection, Pannenberg argues. The resurrection reveals the cross to be for us, and the purpose of the cross and the resurrection is to reconcile humanity to God and proleptically reveal the eschatological future destiny of humanity that he had been teaching about in his message of the Kingdom. The destiny of humanity is forever tied to Jesus and the Christ-event, the one who is united with God for us and it is this claim which is being debated and tested in the history of religions for its veracity and shall be until the final and direct act of self-disclosure by God in the eschaton.

The Pannenbergian Reorientation of Incarnation and Crucifixion through Resurrection

Ultimately, Pannenberg places Christological centrality to the resurrection with the incarnation and crucifixion establishing their interpretation and meaning from the resurrection. The Pannenbergian Christology via the resurrection not only answers the incarnational and crucifixional questions in an alternative way to those who espouse a from above Christology, but also fulfills the human soteriological need by means of an eschatological unity. Therefore, it is not only the retroactive force of the resurrection which establishes the cross and the incarnation of Jesus Christ, but it is also the impetus of the future in the present that has salvific implications for humanity.

The struggle with beginning solely at the juncture of the incarnation stems from the fact that it is an *a priori* presupposition with no historical grounding. Whereas one may disagree with the great lengths Pannenberg goes to show the mythological and unverifiable nature of the incarnation as the Son of a peasant girl named Mary who is a virgin, his claim nonetheless rises from historical verifiability through historical-critical methodologies.[487] Must one pin all of Christianity upon the incarnation? If the incarnation or even cross is the central point of Christology, then this seems necessary. Revealing the sinless, miraculous nature of the incarnation becomes critical, especially as it relates to a Newtonian based understanding of causality from

---

[487] See Pannenberg, *ST II*, 302-304.

past to present to future. In this model the incarnation is critical to the crucifixion of Jesus, because for the crucifixion to have validity as the perfect satisfaction to appease the wrath or offended honor of God, it must be established from the past that Jesus is sinless, and more importantly, one with God. Accordingly, there is a critical *a priori* presupposition here that must be maintained or the validity of the sacrifice can too easily be diminished or challenged.

Moreover, can one be certain that Jesus is the Christ if it is assumed that he is the Christ on the basis of Christological creedal formulae or on the basis of what others have said about him? To be sure, faith is elemental in all of this as is the necessity of God revealing Jesus Christ to humanity. However, where those who have espoused the from above theology have missed the mark, concerns that faith itself must be grounded in reality itself rather than confessions or doctrines that are not necessarily the product of reality. In other words, faith must be grounded in actual history for it to be reasonable to believe. The early Church had reason to believe that Jesus was the logos incarnate, the Christ, and Son of God on the basis of his resurrection, otherwise the New Testament Scriptures, the Christological controversies that led to the creedal statements of faith would likely have never occurred. Where Bultmann seems mistaken in this regard was his claim that those living in a second temple Judaic context would have an existential "rise of faith" based upon some kind of mythical or visionary experience. This is a faulty modernistic assumption based upon a time frame that posited epistemology above ontology. Larry Wood has demonstrated in *God & History*, the earlier period in which the early Church began its rise was more concerned with ontology. Accordingly, for the disciples to have faith would require an ontological distinction that Jesus Christ was indeed raised from the dead and while this had not happened in step with the general resurrection expected at the eschaton, his resurrection indicated that the future of salvation had entered the present age, indicating him to be one with God.[488] Pannenberg is not claiming that until the resurrection Jesus is one with God, but rather it is because of the resurrection that the incarnation is established as the Triune act of God in reconciling the world to himself through the Son.

Similarly, the crucifixion has its own issues if it is to be the sole center of Christology. Perhaps an important issue even at the outset is how it has the tendency to push soteriology to the center of Christology. This occurs in some Christologies as the product of the significance of the crucifixion as the means of salvation for humanity. Christology is then subverted as secondary to soteriology, an issue Pannenberg challenges: "Has one said anything about Jesus Christ at all, if this is the central place from which Christology is formed?[489] This is a capitulation to the same methodologies that bifurcated the historical Jesus and the historic biblical Christ, as Kähler once relayed, and later in Schleiermacher who constructed a Christology that was

---

[488] See Wood, *God and History*. See also Wood, *Theology as History and Hermeneutics: A Post-Critical Conversation with Contemporary Theology*.

[489] Pannenberg, *JGM*, 47.

heavily grounded in human experience.[490] Pannenberg challenges that the issue here is how Christology should concern more of its subject matter – Jesus Christ and his history – and then secondarily his significance for us.[491] If Jesus Christ has claimed unity with God and has claimed that the future Kingdom and salvation have come in him, and if Jesus Christ has shown the eschatological destiny of humanity and this has universal significance for humanity, then the former must precede the latter. Without the historicity of Jesus Christ and the soteriological meaning within his history, it is unlikely his universal significance for humanity can be gleaned.

Consequently, if the cross is the central point of Christology then this raises questions if the nature of the sacrifice alone was efficacious for humanity. How, without the incarnation could one say that the sacrifice was made by the right God-Man? How without the resurrection could one say that the sacrifice was acceptable to God? Clearly, this creates issues. Moreover, is the cross the product of an active and willing role of Jesus Christ in this form of Christology, and how does this relate to reconciliation being a Triune act of God? It would seem that the cross in such a Christology could easily become an act of the Son to appease a wrathful and angry Father whose honor has been treated unjustly, and who consequently requires that satisfaction be made to restore this honor through a proper victim. This of course, shall be challenged later, but the issues it raises is a potential schism within the Triune community. The cross is the vicarious identification of Jesus Christ with humanity in its suffering, the fulfillment the climactic events of salvation history, and the reconciliation of the world and humanity to God. The event and hermeneutical key that establishes all of this is the resurrection that has proleptically revealed the future eschatological destiny of humanity through its new eschatological Adam. Without the resurrection and the vindication of Jesus Christ to reveal his unity with God then the cross is simply another crucifixion on any given day of either a religious traitor, political rebel, or helpless victim who fell prey to the power of the Roman Empire and/or religious leaders.

Finally, what is revealed is a dialectical tension with an eschatological progression from the future to the past: the center of Christology is formed through the resurrection, which retroactively establishes the cross and incarnation, both also rightfully at the center. Because of these historical events, the early Church has reason to believe, reason to share the gospel, and reason to go and make disciples of all nations. Because of the resurrection, Jesus is crucified and risen, the new era of future salvation that Jesus spoke of in his teaching about the Kingdom which had arrived in him is indeed a present reality, and humanity gains reconciliation and unity with God through Jesus Christ the Son of God, and in the power of the Holy Spirit. Resurrection is the central premise of the Pannenbergian Christology, although with a small caveat: it is bound in dialectical tension with the crucifixion and incarnation

---

[490] See chapter three (2.0, (83-88)), for the discussion regarding these issues.
[491] See Pannenberg, *JGM*, 48-49.

of Jesus Christ. Because of the incarnation of Jesus Christ, the destiny of humanity is fulfilled; because of the cross of Jesus Christ humanity is reconciled; and because of the resurrection of Jesus Christ, the unity of Jesus and God and the unity of God and humanity through Jesus Christ in the power of the Spirit for future eschatological salvation at present is indeed reality.

Summary

The retroactive significance of the resurrection is paramount to the Pannenbergian Christology. It is this element in his Christology that establishes the cross and incarnation, an element that is derived from his methodology from below and the presuppositions noted in chapter six. Methodologically speaking, Pannenberg does not presuppose the divinity of Jesus Christ, but rather by examining the history of Jesus of Nazareth who by means of the resurrection is established to be the Christ of God, he is able to establish the incarnation and descent of the logos as well as the hypostatic union of God and humanity. This is the reason why history and the historical investigation into the person and work of Jesus Christ is a critical element to the centrality of the resurrection in his systematic theology. Pannenberg contends that the resurrection is the reason for the rise of faith and why the Easter community took the message of the Christ-event to the whole world. As such, Jesus Christ is not only one with God but the reconciler of the world to God, proleptically revealing the eschatological destiny of humanity.

Clearly, context had much to do with this, as Pannenberg wrote in response to his milieu of modernistic assumptions including the claims and challenges of Barthianism, Bultmannianism, as well as the prior claims of Nietzsche and Feuerbach that had long challenged theology. While his theology from below methodology has potential issues that have been noted above, it is possible to see the great value in offering historical grounding to the divinity of Jesus Christ to enable a properly grounded and historical faith. Can one simply accept creedal formulae or other faith propositions because of the traditions and experiences of earlier faith communities as evidentiary to the veracity of Christian faith claims? Pannenberg thinks not. Moreover, Pannenberg sees the value in the from above proposition, noting that it is necessary to recognize that without some from above notion of the Triune God, it is nearly impossible to construct a Christology from below. Now as this work now presses toward its last two chapters, it is possible to see the contrast in Christologies by offering a Pannenbergian alternative to the Anselmian question, and hearing a Pannenbergian voice in the present day atonement conversation.

Part Three

A Critique of Anselm from a Pannenbergian Perspective

Chapter 8

A Pannenbergian Engagement with Anselm and the Implications for the Contemporary Atonement Conversation

This work has considered how the Anselmian Christology utilized a presupposition that was compromised through a methodology from above, and was derived from the cross and incarnation. These commitments relegated resurrection to the periphery. Thus, Anselmian Christology is expressed via the cross. Conversely, Pannenbergian Christology is derived through a from below methodology, positing resurrection and especially the retroactive significance of the resurrection as central to his Christology. This decision shaped his soteriological commitments, forming a hermeneutical key to interpret the cross, incarnation, and very person of Jesus Christ and his unity with God. The Christological programs and outcomes of these two revered theologians (one of whom is considered a saint of the Roman Catholic Church) form a noteworthy contrast. While both are of different eras, and while Anselm is clearly unable to offer commentary on Pannenberg, it is also curious that Pannenberg has offered some, yet not an extraordinary amount of commentary on Anselm.

Accordingly, this work turns to chapter eight which emphasizes the Christological contrast between Pannenberg and Anselm, and how a Pannenbergian alternative to the question *Cur Deus Homo* provides a potentially fruitful voice in the contemporary atonement conversation. Chapter eight shall be divided into three portions, the first of which (2.3.1) considers a Pannenbergian engagement of Anselm as noted in both *Jesus – God & Man*, and *Systematic Theology Volume Two* in terms of merit and obedience, satisfaction and reconciliation, and penitential and eschatological soteriology. This can then be pressed forward into the second portion of the chapter (2.3.2), and a consideration of the implications of the Pannenbergian proposal as it relates to holding key Christological elements of incarnation, crucifixion, and resurrection in dialectical tension with time – future, past, and then present. Finally, the third portion of the chapter (2.3.3) proposes that the Pannenbergian Christology might provide a fruitful voice in the ongoing debates that challenge Anselmian and post-Anselmian metaphors of the cross, as resurrection enhances the meaning of the cross.

2.3.1 A Pannenbergian Engagement of Anselm

Given the outcomes of the first four chapters, it is now possible to illumine the contrast between Pannenberg and Anselm. Pannenberg utilized the from below *a posteriori* methodology positing the retroactive significance of the resurrection as central to his Christology. Conversely, Anselm considered an *a priori* presupposition of the unity of Jesus and God and utilized a *remoto Christo* methodology. This posited the cross as the central reason for the incarnation and the means by which satisfaction was made for human sin and the offended honor of God. While Anselm provides a reason for the incarnation via the cross, presupposes the unity of Jesus and God, and considers the active obedience of Jesus Christ in his penitential act of supererogation on the cross, Pannenberg establishes the unity of Jesus and God and human salvation as the outcome of the resurrection. More importantly, while Anselm certainly believed in the resurrection, Anselmian Christology was methodologically expressed from the cross. This demonstrated the reason for the incarnation, the satisfaction made unto God through the cross, which moved resurrection toward the periphery. Conversely, Pannenbergian Christology features resurrection as its central element, and this is held in tension with the crucifixion and incarnation of Jesus Christ. So, whereas Anselm emphasized the crucifixion and incarnation in his *a priori* from above methodology that presupposed Jesus was one with God. Whereas Anselm sought to resolve human soteriological need and the need of God for satisfaction because the honor of God had been offended, and whereas that need can only be satisfied through a magnanimous act – i.e. the crucifixion of Jesus Christ – Pannenberg offers a differing proposal *a posteriori* from below to establish the unity of Jesus and God via the resurrection, which reconciles humanity to God, and invites humanity into its intended eschatological destiny.

Therefore 2.3.1 shall consider how Pannenberg offers a differing Christological proposal than that of Anselm via three key avenues: (1) the Anselmian concept of active obedience and merit and the Pannenbergian concept of passive obedience and reliance, (2) secondly, a critique of the Latin (Anselmian) view of the cross as satisfaction through the lens of Gustaf Aulén, and the Pannenbergian concept of reconciliation, and finally, (3) soteriology as penance in Anselm and soteriology as future eschatological destiny in Pannenberg. These contrasts have some level of engagement by Pannenberg himself in both *Jesus – God & Man*, and *Systematic Theology Volume Two*. This section (2.3.1) shall illumine and prepare the way for the following section that describes the dialectically oriented Christological proposal Pannenberg provides.

Active Obedience and Merit or Passive Obedience and Reliance?

It is now appropriate to consider the first area of contrasting significance between Anselm and Pannenberg, as illumined by *Jesus – God & Man*, and *Systematic Theology Volume Two*. This first area of significance concerns the nature of active obedience and merit, and passive obedience and reliance. Key to this discussion is the issue of whether Jesus was actively or passively pursuing the cross, and related to this is whether or not the cross is a meritorious act (as in active obedience), or an act of reliance (as in passive obedience). Anselm espouses the active obedience of Jesus Christ and his meritorious act on the cross, whereas Pannenberg espouses the passive obedience of Jesus Christ and his reliance upon the Father in his being subjected to the human fate of death on the cross.

In beginning, Anselm believes Jesus actively pursues the cross, demonstrating a meritorious act by seeking in his human will to satisfy the offended honor of God for the sake of humanity.[492] Anselmian Christology proposes that Jesus Christ has two wills and two natures, a Dyothelitist position that (as shall be illumined momentarily) Pannenberg claims is problematic. Anselm claims humanity suffers from a lack of obedience to God in showing honor due unto God, and this places humanity squarely within the position of salvific need. This need can only be satisfied by Jesus Christ as the God-Man through active obedience which creates merit. As such, Jesus learned perfect obedience, and it is the obedience in his divinity that is upheld in his humanity. Through the active obedience of Jesus Christ in his meritorious act of penitential supererogation on the cross, the sins that have left humanity in a state of utter helplessness are forgiven, and humanity receives the benefit of salvation.[493]

Anselm contends that the human will of Jesus was desirous to participate in the divine will, and thus the human will is now able to be subordinated unto God. Accordingly, obedience has been restored through the first one who was not made to die, but was freely willing to be obedient even unto death itself. This, in turn, posits the salvific act of the cross as an act of satisfaction, especially given that the incarnation is assumed *a priori*. Yet there are potential issues with this Christology: if it is assumed that

---

[492] See CDH 1.8-1.10, 2.11, and most notably 2.16-2.19. See chapter three for a discussion of the active obedience of Jesus Christ, (1.2.1 (63-71)). See also Pannenberg, *JGM*, 42-43.

[493] Mentioned in 1.2.1, this is a position that I have recapitulated from Deme: "We can speak about genuine obedience when one person, from his own free initiative, internalises about someone else's will, in which case the plurality of wills will be eliminated in their identity." See Deme, *The Christology of Anselm*, 164. Sonderegger agrees with the language of obedience position, claiming obedience is important to the whole of the CDH demonstrating the proper response of humanity to God. She illustrates this is important to the Anselmian theology of satisfaction. See Sonderegger, *International Journal of Systematic Theology Vol. 9, No 3*, 352-354.

Jesus is one with God, it seems unrealistic to say that Jesus Christ in his human will became subordinated to the divine will – was his meritorious act truly an act of the human will giving way to the divine will, or was it the divine will superseding the human will to fulfill the eschatological plan of salvation?

Whereas Anselm held Jesus was actively looking to make the sacrifice on the cross to fulfill what he assumed in the incarnation, Pannenberg claims Jesus only passively does so, and that it is not until after the resurrection that one can say the sacrifice was indeed made on behalf of all humanity by Jesus Christ who is one with God.[494] In this regard, Pannenberg views the passion predictions in light of the resurrection, and the cry of dereliction from the cross by the abandoned one of God as an act of passive obedience.[495] Pannenberg claims that at first glance Anselm seems correct in finding the character of the death of Jesus as something he actively seeks, not as something that happens to him. He also notes that at first glance, the passion predictions in the Gospel narratives suggest the active obedience of Jesus Christ, which Anselm literally incorporates into his thinking.[496] However, Pannenberg claims the passion predictions are not written prior to the resurrection, they are established on account of the resurrection. Had Jesus not been raised from the dead, the passion predictions would have proved false. Thus, there is an inherent question which arises from the concept of Anselmian active obedience: if Jesus did not have some element of passive faith and obedience in his offering to God, and if Jesus possessed total knowledge that he was one with God and his sacrifice was being made on the basis of such knowledge, then the resurrection would have mere epistemological or interpretive significance and not ontological priority. This is partly the challenge in the from above methodology Anselm utilizes. Anselm posits that in knowing his identity, the resurrection has only an epistemological distinction of sorts for Jesus Christ. Therefore, for Anselm the cross is based upon an *a priori* knowledge of the incarnation, the active obedience of Jesus Christ, and his meritorious act of satisfaction, and for Pannenberg, the cross is established *a posteriori* by means of the passive obedience and reliance upon God the Father because of his oneness with God. This fulfills the eschatological plan of salvation.

For Pannenberg, the issue concerns the complete reliance and passive obedience of Jesus Christ upon God the Father to fulfill the eschatological mission at hand. Essentially, he takes a patristic view that the freedom of Je-

---

[494] This is central to his thesis in *Jesus – God and Man*, as Pannenberg contends that it is only in light of the resurrection that the blasphemous death of Jesus Christ has consequence for humanity. See Pannenberg, *JGM*, 245.

[495] This is an element of his form-critical analysis which he utilizes as part of his from below methodology. Pannenberg is almost excessive in what he will concede as being legendary in this regard. Methodologically speaking, Pannenberg contends that the construction of the New Testament occurs in light of the resurrection, and so these sayings of Jesus which are passion predictions are recorded from this *a posteriori* perspective. See Pannenberg, *Revelation as History*.

[496] See Pannenberg, *JGM*, 277.

sus is not an independence from God, but a unity within God.[497] This is different from Anselm who according to Pannenberg presupposes a Dyothelitist Christology, namely that the human will with which Jesus offered himself to God was independent of the divine will.[498] So whereas for Anselm, Jesus Christ creates *merit* in his offering himself to God by demonstrating the kind of active obedience that humanity is intended to give unto God, for Pannenberg, the *reliance* of Jesus Christ upon God in passively receiving his death on the cross is established via the resurrection showing him to be one with God. The death and resurrection of Jesus Christ through his complete reliance upon the Father is the model for the eschatological destiny of humanity. This is markedly different, as the issue is not so much a freedom to choose independently of God in the human will, but a freedom of unity within God through Jesus Christ who invites humanity into the divine life of God.[499] Essentially, the reliance of Jesus Christ upon God the Father through passive obedience to the eschatological mission at hand is the very possibility that creates the merit that Anselm attempted to forge in his argument, albeit in a different form. As such, the Pannenbergian concept of the ontological and epistemological establishment of the unity of God and Jesus Christ through the resurrection reveals that the passive obedience of Jesus Christ in freely accepting the human condition of death came to pass through his perfect reliance upon the Father. Anselm sets his proposal through active obedience and merit, whereas Pannenberg sets his proposal through passive obedience and reliance upon God that is retroactively established in the resurrection.[500]

The Cross as Satisfaction or Reconciliation?

Having looked to the passive obedience of Jesus Christ and his reliance upon God, now it is possible to demonstrate another key distinctive of Pannenbergian Christology and Anselmian Christology in the nature of the cross as satisfaction or reconciliation, and illumine this through a critique of the Latin View of the cross by pointing to the work of Gustaf Aulén. The Anselmian concept is to view the cross as satisfaction, whereas the

---

[497] See Pannenberg, *JGM*, 349.
[498] See Pannenberg, *JGM*, 293-295.
[499] The key here is a revelation of true being in the unity of essence of Jesus and God. This is proleptic or anticipatory (a key word given the manner in which anticipation is related to how the future determines the present through anticipation) of the eschaton and how God will make a final and direct self-disclosure to creation to end the temporal age and begin the eternal one. Related to this is his understanding of the Hegelian dialectic which showed essence and appearance as being dialectical so that essence was making its way into appearance – or hence, the future was appearing in the present. See Pannenberg, *Theology and The Kingdom of God*, 127-143. See Pannenberg, *Revelation as History*, 1-21. See also Pannenberg, *BQT II*, 15-80. See also Pannenberg, *ST I*, 63-73, 189-257.
[500] This was the purpose of chapter seven, 2.2, namely that the resurrection both ontologically and epistemologically establishes the unity of Jesus and God. See also Pannenberg, *JGM*, 349-351.

Pannenbergian concept of the cross is understood in terms of reconciliation by way of inclusive substitution.

Perhaps the most significant of the Pannenbergian engagements with Anselm comes in *Jesus – God & Man*, as he delineates the Anselmian concept of vicarious satisfaction and the manner in which it is linked with the concept of merit that has been offered above.[501] Pannenberg describes the Anselmian Christology typical of the *Cur Deus Homo* argument, namely that satisfaction is something that the sinner is required to make unto God because of his or her condition before God. Moreover, he adds it is only possible to make satisfaction in a work "that goes beyond his obligation, that is, in a merit."[502] He goes on to say:

> Thus here also Jesus is the representative of men before God – however, not in their striving after the good, toward *homoiosis theoi*, but in offering the satisfaction owed in penance for sin. This satisfaction, which is accomplished in the gift of Jesus' life, is universally effective because Jesus is at the same time God, and the life he offers has, therefore, infinite worth.[503]

Pannenberg offers criticism of this approach, noting that the patristic church and Anselm are quite different in their orientation of the saving significance of Jesus Christ, and that in this view, salvation is related to satisfaction and penance and no longer the deification of humanity. He further claims that Luther and others developed this stream of thought in later days.[504]

Pannenberg offers an approach more typical of Gustaf Aulén and his work *Christus Victor: An Historical Study of the Three Main Types of the Idea of Atonement*. Aulén establishes the Anselmian understanding of the cross as "the Latin view," primarily because it was developed on Western Latin soil and utilizes legal terminologies of satisfaction, substitution, or sacrifice, whereas (in his estimation) the classic view of the atonement has a variety of forms that stem from an idea of victory over sin and death, the devil, etc., all of which predate the Latin view.[505] In his estimation, Anselm is the one who

---

[501] See above (2.3.1, (173-175)). See also, for example, Pannenberg, *JGM*, 42-43, 48, 198, 276-279.

[502] Again, this is connected with active obedience and merit, as was previously demonstrated above (2.3.1, (173-175)). See Pannenberg, *JGM*, 42. Sonderegger has also demonstrated that active obedience and merit are closely tied with the theology of satisfaction that is derived in Anselm. See Sonderegger, *International Journal of Systematic Theology Vol. 9, No 3*, 352-354.

[503] Pannenberg, *JGM*, 42.

[504] See Pannenberg, *JGM*, 42-43. It is of further interest to note that Pannenberg claims that the divinity of Jesus Christ is important only insofar as his life has infinite worth, so as to make a satisfaction of infinite value. Thus, in the judgment of Pannenberg, sinlessness and divinity are of indirect value to the argument, whereas in the patristic church, this was of direct importance. This fits within the purview of his retroactive significance of the resurrection.

[505] Pannenberg quotes Aulén at a number of different points, agreeing with his classical soteriology, especially at the beginning of chapter two of *JGM* in preparation

fully establishes the Latin view of the atonement, and does so by means of satisfaction. The satisfaction that must be made unto God for sin is required of humanity, and it is the God-Man who makes this satisfaction. This, according to Aulén, disconnects what was organically connected in the classic view, that is, the incarnation and atonement.[506] For Anselm, the cross is central to Christology and is the just victory of God which establishes the necessity of the incarnation, and it is for this reason that Aulén claims Anselm has broken with the Early Fathers of the Church who posit the incarnation for the purpose of redemption.[507] The ultimate expression of the Latin view of the atonement is the juridical merit earned by Jesus Christ on the cross, which is the victory of God that satisfies the offended honor of God and achieves salvation for humanity.

There have been many critiques of the Latin view, and they continue in the present era.[508] For example, one might consider primary emphases of justice and satisfaction, the contradiction of God concurrently acting as the reconciled and reconciler, the penitential nuance that deals with the necessary punishment for sin but not an answer to the problem of sin itself, or even the challenge of a disconnect between atonement, justification, and sanctification.[509] Beyond these critiques, an even more important challenge to the Latin view emerges: the resurrection is far from central in the argument. Justice, satisfaction, penance, establishing salvation and even the incarnation are well within the purview of the Latin view, but resurrection is an almost ancillary concept, perhaps to some degree, even superfluous. Mentioned before, Anselm surely believed in the resurrection of Jesus Christ as he was a highly orthodox theologian, but the Latin view which he developed has a notable absence of the resurrection with the exception of CDH 2.3. The reason for this is quite simple: the cross represents the necessary meritorious penitential act that satisfies the honor and justice of God that has been offended by the sin of humanity, and it is the atoning nature of the death of Jesus Christ which through faith justifies humanity before God.

Pannenberg, in the same manner as Aulén, offers a critique of the Latin view of the cross, but does so from the perspective of the resurrection. He indicates the Latin view does not consider as the Early Church Fathers did, the necessary eschatological significance of the Christ-event and the required future sanctification/deification of humanity. More significantly, his critique of the Latin view claims a disparity between the proclamation of Jesus and his death as a vicarious sacrifice. In the Anselmian view, the mission of God is solely related to the death of Jesus Christ, and seemingly unrelated to the resurrection. Pannenberg claims that Anselm overlooked the

---

for his recapitulation of soteriological motifs in the history of Christology. See Pannenberg, *JGM*, 39, 274. See Aulén, *Christus Victor*, 1-16.

[506] See Aulén, *Christus Victor*, 86-87.
[507] See Aulén, *Christus Victor*, 88-90.
[508] See for example, the concluding work of this chapter (2.3, (201-209)).
[509] See Green and Baker, *Recovering the Scandal of the Cross*, 116-152. See also Aulén, *Christus Victor*, 90-92, 150.

importance of the resurrection, as it is in the resurrection that the death of Jesus emerges as being expiatory.[510] Accordingly, Pannenberg asks the question, "Why was Jesus Christ the representative of humanity whose life led to the cross?"[511] He illustrates that the cross comes to pass partly due to the statements of Jesus Christ being equal with God, a chargeable offense of blasphemy under the Mosaic Law. He further argues it is only from the retroactive significance of the resurrection that these statements can be established as valid and not transgressions against the law. Pannenberg claims that meaning is created out of a sense of vicarious expiation, "but not as expiatory sacrifice as in the cultic sense."[512] Jesus died bearing the punishment of those who unjustly condemned an innocent man; those who condemned an innocent man to die were the true blasphemers, and Jesus was the one who died on their behalf.[513] In this sense, the death of Jesus, while retroactively ordained by the Triune God, is through passive obedience – Jesus accepts the eath that is brought about through the social, religious, and political community, and more importantly, all humanity. Whereas the religious authoriies and Rome represented universal humanity, the charge of blasphemy was universal in scope, just as the death and resurrection of Jesus is universal in cope. The religious authorities acted upon Mosaic Law, and the Romans acted upon their laws. The guilt of both the religious and political authorities is established through the retroactive force of the resurrection, as the resurrection retroactively establishes that Jesus is the Christ of God and one with God, and that the actions of the religious authorities and Rome were blasphemous, thus changing the law(s) and power of such laws. Israel is blasphemous against the backdrop of their own salvation history and an inability to recognize that Jesus is the Christ of God. Similarly, Rome whose political power is the prideful effect of believing the state has equality with God (i.e. the sin of blasphemy), acts blasphemously in condemning Jesus Christ to die. In this way, the Mosaic and Roman Laws that condemned Jesus Christ to death (which condemned them to death), are fulfilled through the cross and resurrection of Jesus Christ to reconcile humanity to God, and as second eschatological Adam, Jesus reveals the future eschatological destiny of humanity.[514]

Therefore, given what has been illumined above, rather than pointing to satisfaction as the proper understanding of the cross, Pannenberg offers a contrasting proposal by claiming that the cross when retroactively

---

[510] Pannenberg, *JGM*, 277-278.
[511] See Pannenberg, *JGM*, 246-247.
[512] Pannenberg, *JGM*, 247.
[513] See Neie who carefully delineates Pannenberg on this point. See Neie, *The Doctrine of the Atonement*, 136-137. See Pannenberg, *JGM*, 258-274.
[514] See Neie, *The Doctrine of the Atonement*, 138-139. Neie challenges Pannenberg on this and claims that it is not so much the human failure as it is the failure of the Mosaic Law which Jesus is at odds with.

established by the resurrection is best understood as reconciliation.[515] Claiming that the Anselmian convention of satisfaction theory was destroyed by the Protestant enlightenment, Pannenberg illumines that the Pauline conception of God acting in Jesus Christ to reconcile the world unto himself is the manner in which the resurrection establishes the cross as being efficacious and expiatory.[516] In this way, the reconciliation of the world and humanity is the means by which the human eschatological destiny intended at creation which shall be the eschatological reality in the future, begins its process at present.[517] Therefore, the Pannenbergian Christology that is developed from the resurrection, enhances the meaning of cross and incarnation. This dialectical tension of resurrection, cross, and incarnation is the future eschatologycal revelation of God, proleptically revealed in Jesus Christ, to eventuate the present and transform the past. More shall be offered with respect to this below in 2.3.2.

Within his concept of the cross as reconciliation is also the notion of inclusive substitution. Pannenberg applies the retroactive significance of the resurrection and claims Jesus is the second eschatological Adam whose death has vicarious significance for humanity.[518] He contends that the transferability of guilt is the "fundamental concept underlying the Israelite institution of the sin offering," which is an understanding of substitution.[519] Where he differs, however, concerns the change in post-exilic Israel who cannot identify with the past sins of Israel as a theocracy, and the inability for the individual to reconcile the guilty deeds of the community. This posits the reality of the future resurrection of the righteous and the nature of the post-exilic community to view sinful deeds as a social construct rather than an individual one. And yet, Pannenberg claims it is misguided to think that individual guilt does not bear weight upon the entirety of humanity – in his estimation whether good or bad, all human interactions have a substitutionary character in that there is transference of them onto all.[520] It is only in this manner in which Pannenberg nuances substitution as being inclusive. Moreover it is only in this manner of inclusive substitution, that he agrees with a *pro nobis* understanding of the atonement.

In sum, the Pannenbergian understanding of the cross while embracing of substitution is only insofar as there is a shared anthropological nature of guilt and a substitutionary character to relationships. Only through this understanding of a shared guilt and substitutionary character to relationhips

---

[515] On this point, Aulén and Pannenberg are similar. See Pannenberg, *ST II*, 412. Pannenberg notes that "Aulén advanced the idea of a divine victory over sin, death, and the devil as a third type of teaching about reconciliation that the Greek fathers favored, an alternative both to the Anselmian satisfaction theory and to the Abelardian subjective doctrine that many moderns adopted."
[516] See Pannenberg, *ST II*, 404-416.
[517] See Pannenberg, *ST II*, 412-413.
[518] See Pannenberg, *JGM*, 260-266.
[519] Pannenberg, *JGM*, 260-265.
[520] See Pannenberg, *JGM*, 265-268.

can one claim the death and resurrection of Jesus Christ as having a reciprocal substitutionary effect. Whereas Jesus was judged and rejected as a blasphemer in the cross, in his resurrection those who judged him as blasphemous are shown to be the true blasphemers. And whereas those who judged Jesus a blasphemer rejected God and deserved death under the law, Jesus in bearing their death bore the death of all humanity and by his resurrection grants unto them new life and forgiveness of sins.[521] Ultimately Pannenberg understands the Christ-event, that is the resurrection, death, and incarnation of Jesus Christ, as reconciliation by means of inclusive substitution. His Christology stands in contrast to Anselmian Christology, who understands the cross to be an act of satisfaction, which establishes the necessity of the incarnation, and pushes the resurrection toward the periphery of Christology.

Soteriology as Penance or Soteriology as Future Eschatological Destiny?

2.3.1 has thus far focused on the contrast of how Jesus Christ came to the cross – as an active act of obedience which was considered meritorious by God in Anselm, or as a passive act of obedience stemming from the reliance of Jesus Christ upon the Father in Pannenberg. Additional focus has been placed upon how one might understand the cross via the Latin view of satisfaction in Anselm, or reconciliation via the resurrection and inclusive substitution found in Pannenberg. The final element of contrast to be considered is the nature of soteriology in both Anselm and Pannenberg. Anselm views soteriology as penance between God and humanity (i.e. a justification), whereas Pannenberg views soteriology as the impetus of the future eschatological destiny of humanity (i.e. sanctification or even the Early Church Fathers concept of deification).[522]

The Anselmian Christology posits soteriology as being an act of penance. Jesus Christ offers himself as an act of penance to satisfy the offended honor

---

[521] See Pannenberg, *JGM*, 267-270.

[522] Key here is the Pannenbergian critique of the Latin view, or as he describes it, "The Christology of Vicarious Satisfaction." Pannenberg makes a direct claim that the interest of salvation in this view deals with satisfaction and upon penance for the sins of humanity. This stands in marked contrast to the concept of deification which the patristic church espoused. See Pannenberg, *JGM*, 42-43. See also Pannenberg, *ST II*, 404-408. Also important here is the nature of what was raised at the outset of unit two, and especially chapter six (2.1), concerning the Pannenbergian argument that Christology must proceed soteriology and not vice versa. The Anselmian concept of soteriology as penance and a justification of humanity before God through the cross posits the cross as central to Christology. Conversely, if Jesus is the fulfillment of the eschatological plan of salvation as contained in salvation history, and by means of his resurrection, death, and incarnation, invites humanity into this intended destiny, then one is able to properly place Christology before soteriology. See chapter six (2.1.2, (114-127)).

of God which the gravity of human sin has created. This is a function of the Latin view of atonement, which views Jesus Christ as "mediator."[523] God receives this act of penance which Jesus Christ meritoriously performs out of active obedience, an act which restores honor unto God, and it is this act which is then extended to humanity for the benefit of salvation. The reception of this penitential act of Jesus Christ through faith is the penance required by humanity to receive the benefit of salvation:

> What, indeed, can be conceived of more merciful than that God the Father should say to a sinner condemned to eternal torments and lacking any means of redeeming himself, 'Take my only-begotten Son and give him on your behalf,' and that the Son himself should say, 'Take me and redeem yourself.' For it is something of this sort that they say they call us and draw us toward the Christian faith. What also could be juster than that the one to whom is given a reward greater than any debt should absolve all debt, if it is presented with the feeling that is due?[524]

According to the above from CDH 2.20, the act of penance that Jesus Christ offers unto God is to be received as the act of salvation by sinners who are doomed to inescapable destruction. The key here in CDH 2.20 is, "'Take my only-begotten Son and give him on your behalf,' and that the Son himself should say, 'Take me and redeem yourself.'"[525] Perhaps another way this might be stated is for sinners to take his penance (i.e. the penance Jesus Christ satisfies on the cross) and make this act of faith our penitential offering unto God. So it is by the penitential act of faith of sinners to believe in the penitential act of Jesus Christ which satisfies the offended honor of God – this is how one receives salvation according to Anselm. Whereas one stands in condemnation because of sin and the offended honor of God, through the death of Jesus Christ the magnanimous act necessary to alleviate sin is achieved. Yet what remains problematic at the end of the day is not that sins are atoned for, but that the problem of sin altogether has not been transformed.[526] One is justified and in right standing with God under the Anselmian Christology, but what of sanctification and the intended eschatological human destiny of oneness with God?

Conversely, Pannenberg posits soteriology as being the prolepsis of the future eschatological destiny and salvation of humanity, and as such his soteriology flows from Christology. The key nuance here is that Pannenberg moves beyond penance or justification and right standing with God – a forgiving of sin – and emphasizes the reconciliation of God and humanity to transform the problem of sinfulness altogether as the resurrection of Jesus Christ has brought the future eschatological salvation of humanity into the present to transform the past. The nuance of this shall be further developed in 2.3.2. Whereas the Latin view claimed Jesus Christ as "mediator" on the

---

[523] See, for example, Pannenberg, *ST II*, 444.
[524] CDH 2.20, 354.
[525] CDH 2.20, 354.
[526] See Aulén, *Christus Victor*, 84-92.

cross, Pannenberg claims the issue is not so much the mediator being able to make satisfaction for sin, but one whose mission is to reconcile and redeem the world, through his death and resurrection.[527] In this way mediation goes beyond the work of justification and into the work of sanctification, or deification as the Early Church Fathers claimed. This, in turn, qualifies that for Pannenberg soteriology is not just the forgiveness of past sins or even a change or impartation of righteous status, but even more how the future eschatological salvation which humanity is destined for in the future, is now available at present. Jesus Christ as the second eschatological Adam is the first born from the dead, and in being fully God and fully human (i.e. the God-Man), through his passive obedience to human death by way of reliance upon the Father, he is the one who identifies with all humanity inclusively in their death and rises from death to grant everlasting life. This future eschatological salvation is in part present now as humanity is enjoined through Jesus Christ into the divine life of the Triune God. Clearly Pannenberg agrees with the need for justification, but recognizes how the greater salvation history of God points beyond it toward sanctification, or as claimed by the Early Church Fathers the concept of deification. Humanity receives the beginnings of its own new ontological reality as a new eschatological humanity even as all of creation itself is being transformed.

This is of marked contrast when compared to Anselm. For Pannenberg the issue is eschatology, the new eschatological humanity, sanctification and deification, whereas for Anselm the issue is penance and a legally justified standing before God. In this sense, the theme of reconciliation is further imbued in the Pannenbergian eschatological soteriology, as God in Jesus Christ is reconciling the cosmos and humanity to himself, and the future has indeed arrived in Jesus Christ through his resurrection from the dead to eventuate the present and transform the past. In the Pannenbergian corpus, one finds the future at present in the Church of Jesus Christ, preparing for final destiny through worship of the Triune God. It is this preparatory worship that anticipates the eschaton, a time in which sin and death have been fully destroyed, and creation and humanity join in the scene of Revelation chapter five and the worship of the Father, Son, and Spirit. This future has been revealed proleptically in the Easter event of Jesus Christ as his oneness with God is ontologically established, and the eschatological plan of salvation is proleptically fulfilled.

2.3.2 A Dialectical Pannenbergian Alternative: Future, Past, and Present

How then, might the Pannenbergian Christology offer an alternative to *Cur Deus Homo* by holding the incarnation, crucifixion, and resurrection in dialectical tension? The answer to this question forms this second unit of

---

[527] See, for example, Pannenberg, *ST II*, 444-445.

chapter eight (2.3.2). The focus of 2.3.2 concerns how the Pannenbergian Christology offers a dialectically oriented Christological alternative that can be best understood in terms of time: (1) *From the Future*: from eschatology and the future revelation of the eschatological destiny of humanity revealed in the resurrection of Jesus Christ; (2) *From the Past*: by looking to salvation history as contained in the Scriptures, specifically the resurrection as it retroactively establishes the cross and incarnation; and (3) *By Way of the Present*: recognizing that the resurrection, crucifixion, and incarnation of Jesus Christ enables the possibility for faith and present reconciliation and restoration between God and humanity, and that the future eschatological destiny of humanity is proleptically revealed in the present. The manner in which these points converge provide further contrast between the Pannenbergian alternative to *Cur Deus Homo* and the Anselmian proposal.

From the Future: Resurrection & Eschatological Destiny

In beginning, recall that the entire theological enterprise of Pannenberg is committed to the future, and how the future has been revealed in the present through Jesus of Nazareth who by his resurrection is established as the Christ of God. [528] And yet, while Pannenberg is deeply committed to the future in his systematic theology, the future is held in tension with past and present. In essence, his retroactive significance of the resurrection is not only a matter of Christological underpinnings, but this also sets his Christology apart from others, particularly that of Anselm. Whereas Pannenberg looks to the future and how the future eventuates the present to transform the past, Anselm looks to the past and to events which are formed by a causal chain.[529]

---

[528] See chapters six and seven (2.1 and 2.2). Inherent is the notion that the resurrection, if not disregarded *a priori*, is an actual event and it is this event (according to Pannenberg) that bears retroactive force upon the person and work of Jesus Christ. Moreover, Pannenberg argues that it is this event which bears decisive meaning for all of history. See Pannenberg, *JGM*, 74-88, 134-141. This has been contested by others as mentioned throughout chapters six and seven, especially Barr, Barth, Bultmann, Klooster, McDermott, and Pailin. Torrance gives great importance to the resurrection especially as it relates to space-time but is critical of Pannenberg for confusing "historical, logical, and epistemological priorities." Thomas F. Torrance. *Space, Time, and Resurrection*. Edinburgh: T and T Clark, 1976, 34-35. In the opinion of Torrance, Pannenberg misjudged Judaism and its understanding of the resurrection being a decisive event in history. N.T. Wright disagrees with this judgment, as his proposal concerns how resurrection emerges from within the roots of the Israelite religion and especially 2nd Temple Judaism, then as being universally significant in Jesus Christ, the first to be resurrected. See Wright, N.T. *The Resurrection of the Son of God*.

[529] This has already been raised in chapter five (2.0, (91-96)), which stems from his early work *Theology and the Kingdom of God*. Helpful here is Philip Hefner who illumines Pannenberg and his understanding of physics as it relates to contingency, as well as field theory and inertia. Pannenberg draws from an Einstenian view of space-time as

Pannenberg considers how the resurrection is a future event which establishes the person and work of Jesus Christ, and how in the resurrection there is a revelation of the future of humanity insofar as they relate to God in Jesus Christ. Anselm considers how God provides for the present need of human salvation through the satisfaction God received from the death of Jesus Christ on the cross for the past sins of humanity. Through this transaction, one is able to believe and receive the transactional outcome of salvation. Whereas Anselm is concerned with how the past transaction of the cross satisfies the present human need for salvation, Pannenberg is concerned with future salvation and the eschatological destiny of humanity. These elements, how Anselm looks to satisfaction, cross, and the past, and Pannenberg to reconciliation, resurrection, and the future, comprise the present exercise.

Anselm emphasized the cross by means of an intellectual and feudal milieu, a presupposition of the divinity of Jesus, and a focus on satisfying the offended honor of God through a transaction happening in the cross.[530] Central to this was also how humanity stood in need of salvation and Jesus Christ in being incarnate for the purpose of satisfying the offended honor of God via the cross was the divine answer to this need. The intellectual milieu featured the utilization of logic and the cultural milieu that was feudal, sought an answer to the question why the God-Man. Unsurprisingly, the answer was also couched in these terms. Logic, along with feudal, monastic, and medieval penitential terms and imagery are key to the argument. More importantly, it is the past and present that drive the argument of Anselm – the past sins of humanity and offended honor of God, and the past and present changes in society and the needs of that society. This is the reason for emphasis on restoring the past injustices done unto the honor of the ultimate Feudal Lord (God) through one that can claim identification (without having committed

---

being unified and how the contingency of things relates to the future. Given his understanding of God being the unbound power of the future, it is possible to see how Pannenberg has in *Theology and the Kingdom of God* pointed to his understanding of the future eventuating the present to transform the past. From the sciences, Pannenberg gleans that the biblical notion of "all things being rooted in God – not only has a point of contact with scientific understandings of reality but also has something to contribute to those understandings." See Philip Hefner. "The Role of Science in Pannenberg's Theological Thinking." *Beginning with the End: God, Science, and Wolfhart Pannenberg*, ed. by Carol Rausch Albright and Joel Haugen. Chicago: Open Court Press, 1997, 102. As Stanley Grenz notes, process theologians have taken issue with this. See Grenz, *Reason for Hope*, 280-281. See also especially McKenzie who interprets Pannenberg as process theology, Young who interprets this as a form of modified deism as God would have trouble interacting with creation. See McKenzie, *Wolfhart Pannenberg and Religious Philosophy*. See Young, *The Making of the Creeds*. Also significant are John Cobb Jr. and Lewis Ford whose process arguments against Pannenberg (who has critiqued process theology) are important as they contend that a future that is open ended an infinite it preferable to one that is determinate in the final consummation. See Cobb, *The Theology of Wolfhart Pannenberg, Twelve American Critiques*, 58-62. See also Ford, *The Theology of Wolfhart Pannenberg*, 75-94.

[530] See chapter three (1.2.1 and 1.2.2).

the same offenses) with the subjects who have offended that honor (humanity). Through a penitential act of supererogation, the one who identifies with the subjects without sharing in their offenses can satisfy these offenses. Anselm reports that this one is none other than Jesus Christ. Thus the crucifixion of Jesus Christ is the reason or logic of the incarnation, as the Christ and pre-existent Son was born the God-Man for the purpose of being the satisfaction unto God, for the salvation of humanity.

Pannenberg takes issue with the from above methodology inherent in the Anselmian argument by recognizing that people think in terms of their own historical context, and this is a limitation which cannot be overcome. However, it is precisely for this reason that people cannot assume they stand in the place of God and know from the beginning that Jesus Christ is one with God.[531] If the resurrection of Jesus Christ did not occur then it is unlikely the satisfaction or sacrifice was acceptable to God and the cross of Jesus and claims of his incarnation from the beginning would simply be legendary, not atypical of the Maccabaean martyrs and other failed messianic figures in history.[532] If there were other historical figures who claimed a messianic status and whose revolutions died with them, then what sets Jesus apart in his death? Despite the incarnational claim(s), the death of the one united with God would be a rejection of, not confirmation of the divinity or unity of Jesus with God. This is precisely the reason for which Jesus was executed by the religious authorities, political establishment, and crowds. Moreover, this is the reason for the mockery made of Jesus while dying on the cross. Simply stated, without the future value of the resurrection event bearing ontological and epistemological status upon Jesus, one would have difficulty claiming salvific meaning, let alone universal meaning in the event or transaction. This, then, is the perceived weakness of the Anselmian argument as he deals with a past event which one has difficulty claiming meaning of independent of the resurrection. Whereas it is certain Anselm held orthodox belief in the resurrection of Jesus Christ from the dead, it is glaringly absent in the work

---

[531] This is an important piece of his from below proposal as it considers the nature of finitude and the contextually oriented human situation that maintains distinctness between God and humanity. Key to this is how Pannenberg sees the unity of God and Jesus as being the decisive factor for his significance for us. He contends the resurrection is the historical event that establishes this unity. See Pannenberg, *JGM*, 34-35. Mentioned before, Otto Weber has taken issue with this (not to mention others), and Pannenberg takes care to challenge him on this point by claiming that he is not the first to make such a methodological move as Luther and Schleiermacher make some moves in this direction, and especially Ritschl. See Weber, *Grundlagen der Dogmatik Vol. II.*

[532] See Wright, *The Resurrection of the Son of God*, 82-85. This is highly contested by Bultmann and others whose historical-critical methodologies posit the resurrection as being void of historicity. In the case of Bultmann, he contends the resurrection was the rise of faith. What remains unique about those who void the resurrection of its historicity is that in many cases they do not consider the historical context from which resurrection emerged, namely the Israelite religion and 2nd Temple Judaism as Pannenberg and Wright do. See Bultmann, *Kerygma and Myth*.

of *Cur Deus Homo*.[533] For Anselm, the cross is given meaning by the incarnation with some reciprocity being given to the incarnation via the cross – the Christ was incarnate for the purpose of sacrifice to God.

Therefore, the future is the critical factor in the Pannenbergian Christology as it casts retroactive force or significance upon the cross and the incarnation. In the resurrection, the cross in which Jesus identifies with human suffering and suffers on behalf of humanity, and the incarnation in which the logos came to be enfleshed as the completion of creation and future of human destiny, are revealed. More importantly, within the context of salvation history as contained in the Scriptures, the resurrection stands as the end event of salvation, so it is the future coming to expression in the present, rather than the past giving meaning to the present or future of humanity. The Pannenbergian focus on the ontological priority of the future posits salvation as a future happening that has come to expression in the past and in the present even though it is yet to be fulfilled in the future. This is also, according to Pannenberg, the very message of the Kingdom which Jesus Christ preached, namely how the future salvation of God had come near in him and people were called upon to either believe this message and their accompanying signs and acts, or reject it, which they ultimately did by putting Jesus to death as a blasphemer.[534] Whereas Anselm and others held Jesus was actively looking to make the sacrifice on the cross to fulfill what he assumed in the incarnation, Pannenberg claims Jesus only passively does so, and that it is not until after the resurrection that one can say the sacrifice was indeed made on behalf of all humanity by Jesus Christ who is one with God.[535] In this regard, Pannenberg views the passion predictions in light of the resurrection, and the cry of dereliction from the cross as the abandoned one of God through passive obedience.[536]

---

[533] See for example chapter one (1.0). See also Deme who is helpful here, as he notes that the resurrection is almost entirely ignored by Anselm in his work, although references to the resurrection are mentioned in his prayers and devotional material. He is quick to defend Anselm regarding his belief in the resurrection although readily admits that the cross and resurrection are presented in a separate fashion with different meanings. See Deme, *The Christology of Anselm of Canterbury*, 227-235.

[534] See chapter seven, (2.2.2, (145-158)). Also helpful here is Neie who recapitulates Pannenberg and his theology of inclusive substitution and vicarious suffering. See Neie, *The Doctrine of Atonement in the Theology of Wolfhart Pannenberg*, 180-206. See also Pannenberg, *ST II*, 419-437.

[535] This is central to his thesis in *Jesus – God and Man*, as Pannenberg contends that it is only in light of the resurrection that the blasphemous death of Jesus Christ has consequence for humanity. See Pannenberg, *JGM*, 245.

[536] This is an element of his form-critical analysis which he utilizes as part of his from below methodology. Pannenberg is almost excessive in what he will concede as being legendary in this regard. Methodologically speaking, Pannenberg contends that the construction of the New Testament occurs in light of the resurrection, and so these sayings of Jesus which are passion predictions are recorded from this *a posteriori* perspective. See Pannenberg, *Revelation as History*.

The from above methodology Anselm utilizes, and its expression of active obedience and merit, posits Jesus Christ had no ontological establishment in his resurrection; rather only an epistemological distinction emerges from his resurrection.[537] This, then, reveals another key element respective to the future orientation of the answer Pannenberg gives to the question *Cur Deus Homo*, namely, the difference between the cross as satisfaction and subsequently salvation, or the cross as reconciliation which enables the divine eschatological destiny of humanity. As illumined in 2.3.1, the Anselmian answer to this question deals with a present need for satisfaction based upon past sins which have dishonored God, and the Pannenbergian answer to this question deals with divine destiny and emerging the futurity of this destiny into the present. Again, one is oriented toward past action and the human situation, and the other toward the consummation of salvation history and the future of the human situation for God and humanity. Anselmian satisfaction is geared toward satisfying the offended honor of God, acts and events transpiring in the past and leaving humanity in a present state of need for salvation by means of a magnanimous event. To be sure, Pannenberg holds an orthodox view of the need for salvation, but the effects are not just to satisfy the present need of salvation or the past history of sin. Rather, Pannenberg in a move similar to Irenaeus, claims those who are not reconciled to God stand outside of the future eschatological salvation of God, and even more outside of living into their intended eschatological future destiny.[538] So salvation for Pannenberg, while very much something that deals with past and present, is much more constitutive of the future as it relates to the future eschatological destiny of relations between humanity and God, and the future resurrected state of humanity and creation. This is one of the important outcomes of his historical model of doing Christology from below, as it is the future which eventuates the present to transform the past. Conversely, modern theologies take issue with this, as the resurrection is denied historicity because it is a break in the causal chain based upon Newtonian physics emerging from past to present to future.

More importantly, whereas Anselm presupposed the existence of God, and the unity of God and Jesus, Pannenberg claims that it is in the resurrec-

---

[537] The key here is a revelation of true being in the unity of essence of Jesus and God. This in many ways is proleptic or anticipatory (a key word given the manner in which anticipation is related to how the future determines the present through anticipation) of the eschaton and how God will make a final and direct self-disclosure to creation to end the temporal age and begin the eternal one. Related to this is his understanding of the Hegelian dialectic which showed essence and appearance as being dialectical so that essence was making its way into appearance – or hence, the future was appearing in the present. See Pannenberg, *Theology and The Kingdom of God*, 127-143. See Pannenberg, *Revelation as History*, 1-21. See also Pannenberg, *BQT II*, 15-80. See also Pannenberg, *ST I*, 63-73, 189-257.

[538] This is typical of the Irenaeus recapitulation theology. See Pannenberg, *ST II*, 403-405. For more on recapitulation theology see Eric Osborn. *Irenaeus of Lyons*. Cambridge: Cambridge University Press, 2001, 117-142.

tion that all of the meaning of history will be given in a final and direct act of self-disclosure by God to creation. This is not to say that the resurrection is unimportant for Anselm but its methodological relegation to the periphery occurs because the cross is the central element in his Christology. Conversely, the very manner in which Pannenberg intersects resurrection and the history of the world religions whose truth claims are being tested and verified in a process of critically analyzing truth claims, means he has included how the future resurrection of all creation (which he argues has already been revealed proleptically in Jesus) casts retroactive force upon all history. Thus, whereas Anselm has focused on how the cross brings satisfaction for the sins of humanity which have offended the honor of God, Pannenberg focuses upon the resurrection as it establishes not only reconciliation, but the future eschatological destiny of humanity as they relate to God through Jesus Christ – the one made incarnate to complete the process of creation itself.

Ultimately, the Pannenbergian Christological enterprise focuses upon the future and the eschatological destiny of humanity insofar as it relates to the acts of God in salvation history which anticipate that future. Rather than looking to the past and the satisfaction of the lost honor of God, or a singular event in the cross that concerns the restoration of the dignity of God and salvation of humanity for its offenses, Pannenberg focuses upon the reconciliation of humanity and the cosmos to God in Jesus Christ through the resurrection, cross, and incarnation. Through this reconciliation, what has been lost has been regained through the totality of the Christ-event, (resurrection, cross, and incarnation) and in the resurrection of Jesus Christ from the dead, one can see at least in part the future destiny of God and humanity.

From the Past:
Salvation History & Dialectical Unity

Given the future and how the resurrection is the future act of God which is proleptically revealed to eventuate present and transform past, now it is possible to look to the past, and continue to demonstrate the contrast between Anselm and Pannenberg. The manner in which this contrast manifests itself at a past level is two-fold: (1) first, concerning the Anselmian Christology in *Cur Deus Homo* which is rooted in the tools of his era, whereas Pannenberg looks to the past in terms of its meaning that is derived from the future and (2) secondly, how Anselm by looking to the past emphasizes the cross which relegates resurrection and the future to the periphery, whereas Pannenberg holds the past in dialectical tension with present and future. Specifically, the Anselmian Christology remains within an era of monasticism, logic, feudalism, medieval penance, and the like, whereas Pannenbergian Christology emerges from the future to establish the past historical acts of God in salvation history. More importantly, whereas Anselm looked to the cross as a past event that brought about satisfaction relegating resurrection to the periphery, Pannenberg maintains dialectical unity by pointing to the historical nature of the events of incarnation, cross, and resurrection of Jesus Christ. This second point shall be finally developed in the remaining sections of 2.3.2 that illustrates the present implications of Pannenbergian and Anselmian Christology and an alternative to the question, "Why the God-Man?"

The second chapter revealed that Anselm exchanged salvation history for feudal history by means of an intellectual milieu that demanded logic and a cultural milieu rooted in feudalism.[539] The sheer genius of Anselm was to utilize the tools of his day to answer a question for his day. Unfortunately, the sheer genius is also the greatest challenge of the argument. The *remoto Christo* methodology Anselm utilized as part of his presentation might be argued from the perspective of apologetic relevance, but there is also a level of danger in excising Jesus Christ from the salvation history of God. In other words, can one really consider an answer to the question "why the God-Man" without considering the greater history into which the God-Man emerges?[540]

Whereas Anselm has good ground to stand upon with respect to the nature of original sin as being universally relevant to all persons at least insofar as he writes from an Augustinian tradition, one must also consider the context from whence this came, or the universal relevance he claims is too easily lost. In this regard, to excise Jesus Christ from his history is a modernistic assumption that on the one hand demonstrates what one theologian said about the relation of humanity to Jesus Christ which he called, "the scandal of particularity," and on the other hand without any sense of context to consider why this is the right God-Man other than a simple case of authoritarianism or presuppositionary bias.[541] Without the history of God and consid-

---

[539] See chapter three (1.2.1, (54-74)).

[540] This stems from Pannenberg and his proposal from *Revelation as History* in which he argues that revelation has confused meaning given the theologies from Ritschl forward into Barth, but at its core, revelation is self-revelation – that is, the indirect religious experience of Israel and her God in history. This is consistent with Althaus and Brunner and contra Barth who contended that revelation was not an indirect revelation but direct revelation. What is unique about the Anselmian proposal is the potential of extracting revelation from the scope of history and making it a generally accessible principle of salvation in which a transaction logically infers salvation to people. In this way, there is greater potential in making Jesus Christ a principle rather than a person of the triune relation that has been working throughout salvation history. As such, one could question the validity of the Christ-event among the other competing religious claims of salvation in the history of world religions. To be fair, given the milieu of Anselm, the Roman Catholic Church had great power and influence and a predominantly Christian world-view. As such, this issue was not likely considered. However, it is possible to see how a Christology from above emphasizing this methodology could more easily fall into the potential issues named above, especially in the enlightenment. See Pannenberg, *Revelation as History*, 1-21.

[541] See for example Kierkegaard who claimed that it was scandalous for all of history to be connected to one man in history. See David J. Gouwens. *Kierkegaard as a Religious Thinker*. Cambridge: Cambridge University Press, 1996, 128-132. See also Martin Kähler in his attempt to shield the "Christ of Faith" from the "Historical Jesus," and the historical-critical methodologies that were present in which had

eraion of the mighty acts of God in salvation history, one must question whether or not the magnanimous offer of satisfying the offended honor of God through the cross is acceptable to God. Without past context it is slightly difficult to hold anything other than a human need for a God-Man, and while Anselm might have to some degree answered the question that a God-Man is needed to satisfy the offended honor of God, the meaning of the cross is not easily obtainable without any kind of indication that the cross was acceptable and the death of Jesus Christ was atoning. This was a mistake found in theological positivism years after Anselm, as there are few brute or bare facts of information.

Conversely, Pannenberg looks to the resurrection of Jesus as a hermeneutical key that establishes past events of crucifixion and incarnation. Whereas Anselm attempts to demonstrate the incarnation of Jesus Christ on the basis of the event of the cross which satisfies a God who has been dishonored, Pannenberg posits the meaning of the cross and the incarnation as being established within the context of salvation history and by the future of the resurrection that has come proleptically and thus anticipatorily in Jesus Christ at the present. Chapter seven, (2.2) demonstrated how the retroactive significance of the resurrection is a key Pannenbergian distinctive in which he argues that the resurrection of Jesus Christ casts retroactive force upon the past acts, claims, and the very person of Jesus Christ. This is both an epistemological and ontological reality. Thus, as mentioned before, Pannenberg believes Christology has to do with not only the confession of Christ, but with the grounding of Christ in the historical activity of Jesus, most particularly from the resurrection:

> Only in trust in the reliability of the report of Jesus' resurrection and exaltation are we able to turn in prayer to the one who is exalted and now lives, and thus to associate with him in the present.[542]

Mentioned above, the resurrection fits within the context of salvation history positing the future orientation that Pannenbergian Christology claims as being central to its identity. Yet, the power of the future with respect to the resurrection of Jesus Christ is not relegated to the future alone; Pannenberg describes how it is from the future that the resurrection eventuates the present and transforms the past to establish, clarify, confirm, and contrast the meaning of the cross, incarnation, work, and very unity of Jesus Christ with God. This is absent in Anselm, as the claim is always from the past event of the human need for salvation and satisfying the offended honor

---

tendencies to undermine the historicity of the Gospel narratives. This theology became important in some of the modern theologians, especially in Bultmann. See Kähler, *So-Called Historical Jesus and the Historic-Biblical Christ*. This theology is also commonplace in Barth whose theology of the Word has tenets of authoritarianism. See Barth, *Church Dogmatics*.

[542] Pannenberg, *JGM*, 28.

of God, the response to the issue in the incarnation of Jesus Christ, and the resolution of these needs through the cross which satisfies this need.⁵⁴³

The manner in which the first and above issue affects the second issue, namely how Anselmian Christology emphasizes cross and incarnation relegating resurrection to the periphery and how Pannenbergian Christology maintains a dialectical unity, now becomes readily apparent. The Anselmian emphasis upon the past human soteriological need, the past incarnation of Jesus Christ, and the past event of cross which satisfies the offended honor of God, completes the circle for the present human soteriological need which Anselm asserts confronts every human being. This is the Anselmian response to the question raised, *Cur Deus Homo*, a response formulated for an era which demanded logic and structured relationships in terms of feudal hierarchy. For Anselm, the cross provided a satisfaction of sin and a restoration of the honor of God, an event God has very keenly and with active participation provided for humanity. Moreover, chapter three (1.2) further revealed how Anselm resolved the problem of sin, the dishonor of God, and the loss of bliss by humanity by means of the transaction of the cross, but without the full view of the resurrection because his Christology assumes the divinity of Christ *a priori* and attempts to establish the incarnation through the necessity of the transaction of the cross. Essentially, his question "why the God-Man" is methodologically answered in the cross and his Christology proceeds from soteriology, and soteriology looks to how the cross satisfies the needs of humanity and the offended honor of God.⁵⁴⁴

Conversely, Pannenberg provides a dialectical unity within his Christology: resurrection establishes cross and incarnation, and consequently the unity

---

⁵⁴³ To be sure, advances in modern physics as well as the development of modern theology were helpful here as was the ability of Pannenberg to contrast Hegel from that of Aristotle. Mentioned above, the difference is found in his work *Theology and the Kingdom* in which Pannenberg illumines the manner in which Aristotle attacked the divorce between idea and appearance in his notion of substance although he was unable to completely overcome this and still maintained a distinction between substance and essence. Given Anselm utilized Aristotelian logic and dialectic and was himself a realist, one can see why in utilizing the method of argumentation he does (*remoto Christo*) that Anselm would apply reason toward how a transaction of the cross (appearance) would require the a God-Man (essence) to fulfill it, and how subsequently that through this transaction (appearance) humanity could then regain their intended state of blissful existence (essence). Conversely, Pannenberg by utilizing the Hegelian dialectic which claimed that essence and appearance were reciprocal – in fact that "essence must appear" – could apply this to the future (or essence of what shall be in the eschaton) eventuating the present (or the appearance of what is now) so as to have the future establish ontologically and epistemologically Jesus as the Christ of God via his resurrection. Thus the contrast between Pannenberg and Anselm is illumined by way of Hegel who refuted Aristotle, one of the key sources for Anselm. See Pannenberg, *Theology and the Kingdom*, 127-143.

⁵⁴⁴ This was a major premise in Pannenberg, as he claims that Christology should precede soteriology and not vice-versa. See chapter five (2.0). See also Pannenberg, *JGM*, 48.

of God and Jesus flow from this dialectical unity. In this manner, Pannenberg holds not only these events in dialectical unity but also the salvation history of God in dialectical unity as the events are all critical to the person of Jesus Christ and his universal significance for humanity. Whereas Anselm points to the universal significance of Jesus Christ on the basis of universal human soteriological need, Pannenberg points to this same universal significance on the basis of the history, especially as that history is held dialectically in tension between future and past as it relates to present. Mentioned above, it is the resurrection, the future and promised eschatological destiny of humanity as anticipated in the salvation history of Israel, in the teaching of the Kingdom by Jesus of Nazareth, established from the future to transform the past. Thus, to speak of any sort of reconciliation between God and humanity, one must speak of this in terms of the resurrection and the very victory of God over the rejection of the Kingdom in the cross of Jesus, and how since the future Kingdom of God was present in Jesus of Nazareth, that he was indeed incarnate as the logos from the future to complete the work of creation and reveal the future eschatological destiny of humanity. Without the resurrection to establish the cross of Jesus Christ, the soteriological meaning of the cross for humanity is at best epistemologically unclear, as the ontology of Jesus Christ remains unclear. The question from the cross without the resurrection becomes, "Why did Jesus die as the betrayed one, and can humanity safely assume that his death alone atones for any one person and their sins, let alone the sins of all humanity?"

More importantly, without the resurrection, while one could say that it is possible, even plausible that the offended honor of God had been satisfied, it would be difficult *remoto Christo* without its preceding history to determine what present meaning it has for humanity, and would be even more difficult to ascertain what future meaning it has for humanity. If, however, the resurrection is the origin of Christology and is held in dialectical tension with cross and incarnation, is set amidst the context of salvation history, then one can see in the proleptic event of the resurrection of Jesus Christ, the future eschatological destiny of humanity which retroactively establishes the salvation history out of which Jesus Christ emerges.

Thus, as the seventh chapter revealed in 2.2.2 and 2.2.3, Pannenberg has claimed:

> The relation of our created destiny to the incarnation of the Logos in Jesus of Nazareth is not, then, a direct one of disposition and actualization. The way from disposition to actualization is broken by sin. Because we are alienated from the Logos, we learn to know the Logos – who is still the origin of our life and the light of our consciousness – only through Jesus....Only through Jesus, however, do these general concepts acquire their true content. It is herein that the specific person and history of Jesus have universal relevance.[545]

In this manner, while it is true that resurrection should be central to the Christological enterprise for its operation as a key hermeneutic to establish

---

[545] Pannenberg, *ST II*, 295.

the work and person of Jesus Christ and his unity with God, one cannot claim only the centrality of the resurrection for Christology, but concurrently the cross and incarnation. Therefore, central to Christology is the dialectical unity of resurrection, cross, and incarnation, which consequently establishes the unity of Jesus with God. The result is that the future event of resurrection that has been proleptically revealed in Jesus transforms all of the past history – the sins of humanity, the offended honor of God, the enmity between humanity and God, and the creation itself, which longs for redemption.[546]

By Way of the Present: Christology & Reconciliation

Given the two previous sections concerning the future and the past, now 2.3.2 turns to its final aspect, the present, and namely how the present is shaped by the future in the Anselmian and Pannenbergian Christologies. The manner in which the present is shaped by the future concerns (1) the nature of the Christological enterprise and (2) the manner in which the Christ-event or work of Christ has meaning for people in their present human situation irrespective of the era in which they are presently located. This shall proceed along two interrelated arguments, firstly that the Anselmian *remoto Christo* argument in the *Cur Deus Homo* shapes Christology from a soteriological perspective, creating a challenge that logic has proven in the death of God movement to overcome a need for God – an issue which Pannenberg resolves with his *a posteriori* from below methodology; and secondly, how the satisfaction Anselm purports in the cross differs from the reconciliation Pannenberg purports through the dialectical unity of resurrection, cross, and incarnation.

In beginning, chapter two (1.1) demonstrated how the *credo ut intelligam* principle was compromised by means of the *remoto Christo* methodology.[547] While the presuppositionary principle is indeed an important issue, it is the methodological one that is of greater interest, as the methodology Anselm utilized drove the Christological outcomes of his proposal. Whereas he begins from the presupposition of believing so one may understand, he pursues such understanding by means of eliminating the history of the subject of faith – Jesus Christ.[548] In so doing, his Christology is driven by soteriology and situating persons within a logical need for a transaction to satisfy their sinfulness and the offended honor of God – a transaction which they

---

[546] See, for example, Romans 8.

[547] See chapter two (1.1.4, (48-50)).

[548] A careful nuance is to be offered here. There are Scriptural allusions in Anselm, although he rarely quotes Scripture. The key is how salvation history is, at the very least, hidden in the background of the argument as Anselm takes an apologetic and logical line of argumentation for those inside and outside the community of the Church. Here the key is his desire to demonstrate with a commonality or sense of general revelation that is achievable by human logic the reason for the God-Man. See Deme, *The Christology of Anselm of Canterbury*, 9-11.

cannot satisfy given their standing before God.[549] At the end of chapter two (1.1.4), it has been demonstrated that Anselm utilized a methodology that may have pushed the Church beyond its Augustinian tradition by the utilization of Aristotelian logic before the materials of the Church. Now it is appropriate to ask the question, "What were the effects of this methodological decision?"

The milieu and its desire for logic sought an answer to the incarnation and the means by which this occurs is through the methodological elimination of historical materials and consideration of the reason for the incarnation that is based upon the logical satisfaction of sin and human salvation. Key to this is the context of the pre 1066 CE daily supernatural battle between good and evil, and the subsequent post 1066 CE era which began a critically important growth factor toward placing humanity in the center of human existence. This is not to say that humanism had fully taken root, but by this time the human search for how human experience was a vehicle to knowing God became more central to daily life.[550] In short, whereas the previous era looked to the history of God as contained in the Scriptures and then considered how their lives fit into this history for salvation, the post 1066 CE era looked to the human need for God and asked the question, "Why does one need salvation and how does one obtain it?" This is important as the question offers a new approach to salvation that puts soteriology in front of Christology. This also allows for a potential break from the Augustinian tradition for Anselm to feature logic as a primary method for doing theology. Accordingly, Anselm in seeking to meet the resistance and challenges to Christianity utilized a methodology that does not look to the authority of the root materials of Christology but rather to the human need of Christ. For Anselm, the God-Man is needed so that he may complete the task of actively seeking to offer himself as the penitential offering for sin to satisfy the offended honor of God and thus complete the transaction to bring about salvation. Only because he is incarnate as God-Man is the sacrifice satisfactory unto God. It is this methodology which Pannenberg takes issue with in *Jesus – God & Man* as he refers to it as a Christology from above that assumes the divinity of Jesus Christ without ever looking to his history for confirmation of such divinity, and also that this same Christological convention that methodologically places soteriology before Christology.

Anselm sought to answer how the Christ is Jesus of Nazareth, the God-Man, who satisfies the sins of humanity and offended honor of God in the cross, and Pannenberg seeks to demonstrate that Jesus of Nazareth is the Christ in the resurrection that retroactively establishes him to be the God-Man and reconciler of God to humanity. Whereas Anselm places soteriology as primary and Christology as secondary, Pannenberg places Christology as primary and soteriology as secondary. Anselm and the *remoto Christo* method-

---

[549] See CDH 1.5, 1.19-1.20, 1.23-1.24.
[550] See chapter one (1.0).

ology he utilized removed the historicity of Jesus Christ to situate persons into a logical argument which is to be resolved through an act of satisfaction. As such, the concern is for the satisfaction of past sins and present salvation. Pannenberg, conversely, seeks for people to look to the history of Jesus Christ and from this history understand the implications of it as the revelation of the future eschatological destiny of humanity, the confirmation of the activity of Jesus in his proclamation/teachings of the Kingdom and his claims to unity with God, and of the present implication of reconciliation for humanity and the inauguration of a new eschatological era.

It is this last statement with respect to reconciliation as a present implication of the work of Jesus Christ in the incarnation, cross, and resurrection that offers the final point of present contrast that has been highlighted in 2.3.1: satisfaction in Anselm and reconciliation in Pannenberg. The primary means of understanding the cross of Jesus Christ in Anselm is in terms of satisfaction. The understanding is couched in transactionary terms concerning the past offenses of humanity, a God whose honor has been offended, and the satisfaction to satisfy both conditions. In the medieval fief, to not fulfill the contractual agreements of the fief brought grave consequences, and the only manner of making restitution of the *debitum* due the feudal lord was through penance. Anselm presented a case for the God-Man, who actively and willingly offered himself in a penitential act of supererogation to God as the means of satisfying the *debitum* of humanity and restoring the honor of God. It becomes readily apparent to see why the resurrection becomes a more peripheral issue in Anselm, as it is the magnanimous act of suffering and penance which is required to make satisfactory restitution of the debt which required such an act. The present implication Anselm provided is that the honor of God has been restored, and the debt which humanity owes has been satisfied, or as Anselm puts it, "absolved."[551] The required human response to Jesus Christ is even more telling:

> What, indeed, can be conceived of as more merciful than that God the Father should say to a sinner condemned to eternal torments and lacking any means of redeeming himself, 'Take my only-begotten Son and give him on your behalf,' and that the Son himself should say, 'Take me and redeem yourself.' For it is something of this sort that they say when they call us and draw us towards the Christian faith.[552]

From this, one must ask then, "But what does this mean beyond a God who is satisfied and a people who are now required to look to Jesus Christ as the object of their faith?" While God is satisfied, and while the devil has not been the recipient of the ransom or falsely tricked, one must question beyond the penance that has been paid, the satisfaction of God that has been chieved, and the debt of humanity which has been lifted, where exactly does this fit into the larger schema of salvation history that calls for the resurrection of humanity and the fallen cosmos? What of the present state of relationship

---

[551] CDH 2.20, 354.
[552] CDH 2.20, 354.

between God and humanity? What of the proclamation or teachings of the Kingdom? How is the future shaping the present toward the coming eschaton that has been proleptically revealed in the resurrection of Jesus Christ?

Pannenberg, by looking to reconciliation describes how the future Kingdom of God has broken in upon the present, how the future eschatological destiny of humanity is revealed in the present, and how the future unity of humanity and God is shaping the present. The cross and resurrection occur through the passive obedience and perfect reliance of Jesus Christ upon God the Father that comes about as the crowds, Romans, and religious authorities reject the future Kingdom which Jesus taught had arrived in him. The meaning of these events remains unclear until after the resurrection. The ontology of Jesus Christ remains unclear until after the resurrection. The present implications through the future event concern not a satisfaction of the offended honor of God through the event of crucifixion, but rather the revelation of the future of God, inaugurated at present. The future age and the power and presence of God being manifest in all of a fallen creation and fallen Adam are now presently inaugurated through the second eschatological Adam. Thus, the enmity between God and humanity described when the first Adam frustrated and subjected humanity and the creation to it, have come to an end. Satisfaction is not the proper term to describe the present state of affairs for humanity but reconciliation. Reconciliation concerns how through the incarnation and cross, and established by the resurrection, humanity has been reconciled to God by the one who by means of the incarnation, cross, and resurrection brought the past era of suffering to an end by the future act of God, to reshape the present for humanity so that they might live, and move, and have their being in God.

A Dialectical Pannenbergian Alternative: Past, Present, Future— Concluding Observations

Considering the contrast between Anselm and Pannenberg in 2.3.1, and the contrasting elements of 2.3.2 relating to future, past, and then present, Pannenberg offers a fruitful alternative to the Anselmian question. The God-Man is the revelation of the future of humanity, the promised Logos who from the future reveals the eschatological destiny of humanity, establishes the past acts of God in the history which God has been creating from the beginning and reconciles the past sins of fallen humanity. This new Eschatological Adam offers the future reconciliation, power, identity, and hope of God from the future, now, at present, thus transforming the past.

While this is a rather concise alternative, the implications and meaning of it require some level of elaboration to properly conceive of a Pannenbergian approach to the Anselmian question. It is not without irony that the Anselmian presupposition of belief in order to understand is compromised by the *remoto Christo* methodology he utilized and this methodology placed soteriology directly into the center of the Christological question he sought to answer. The question is an incarnational one; the answer is soteriological. For

Pannenberg, the incarnational question is held in a dialectical tension in the history of Christ from the retroactive significance of the resurrection which establishes the cross, the teaching and miracles proclaimed in the Kingdom that Jesus said had come in him, and the incarnation – both epistemologically and ontologically. Chiefly important, is how Pannenberg grounds his Christology in its subject manner, Jesus of Nazareth who is the Christ by means of the retroactive force of the resurrection in history. Thus, Pannenberg conceives of the answer from the outset of the Christological enterprise through an entirely different methodology than Anselm. Whereas Anselm conceives of the question in terms of the human soteriological need from the basis of logic to prove the incarnation, Pannenberg considers it from the perspective of the working of God in history and sees this question in terms of the culmination of history in the reconciliation, restoration, and very future of creation whose chief creature is humanity, made in the image of God. So for Anselm, the question is answered in terms of the penitential meritorious act of satisfaction of God that was logically necessary to set human beings free of their sin and regain the lost honor of God via the death of Jesus Christ, whereas for Pannenberg, the question is answered in terms of history: Jesus Christ is the one expected from within the context of salvation history, and he as the new eschatological Adam proleptically reveals and inaugurates the future in the present by reconciling humanity to God which transforms the past.

The results of this with respect to the death of Jesus Christ are then even more pronounced. Whereas Anselm conceives of the death of Jesus as a satisfaction, Pannenberg conceives of the death of Jesus as a reconciliation via vicarious suffering and inclusive substitution that gives way to the eschatological revelation of the future of human destiny. Perhaps what can be gleaned from this concerns a deep twist that undermines the Anselmian answer to the *Cur Deus Homo* question: the hypostatic union between God and humanity is not the basis of the revelation of human destiny but only for the purpose of satisfying the offended honor of God. It would seem that while Anselm holds satisfaction to put things right between God and humanity, there still seems to be some manner of incompleteness. Even the word *satisfactio* seemingly compromises the purpose of the union, as one could question if the God-Man is only to set right that which was undone by human sin, if it is a payment of sorts as in a legal setting, or a product of the medieval penance system. Pannenberg, conversely, contends the God-Man is not for the purpose of satisfying but for reconciling. In this reconciliation a revelation of the future of humanity is achieved: humanity fulfills its intended destiny that was present in creation – union with God, divine image bearers, the intention for humanity present with God indwelling humanity by the Spirit.

Thus, what comes to expression in the Anselmian answer to the question is not the reason for the God-Man according to salvation history, but the reason for the God-Man in culturally imbued metaphor, an almost foreign concept to the Scriptures which contain the indirect salvation history of God and the relations between God and creation. Pannenberg alternatively opts for the completion of salvation history in Jesus, as the second Adam gains that which was lost by the first Adam. The enmity between humanity and God in the thwarting of creation is not satisfied, but rather reconciled – a relational understanding that depletes the metaphor in which Anselm conceives of God as a feudal lord and of humanity as dishonorable vassal. The Pannenbergian Christology posits that God longs for reconciliation, restoring the lost unity between God and humanity, and humanity regains its intended ontological state that was lost.

Finally, whereas Anselm sought to maintain his presupposition of *credo ut intelligam* and compromised it via his *remoto Christo* methodology, he did so with an *a priori* methodological presupposition. This presupposition was that Jesus was one with God and incarnate because of the human need for salvation which came via his death on the cross to satisfy both the condition of the offended honor of God and the sinfulness of humanity. While his assumptions of needing a God-Man to satisfy the offended honor of God may be tenable, what is problematic is his assumption that Jesus Christ was the God-Man. Other messiahs were claimed historically, why Jesus of Nazareth? Without the resurrection to retroactively establish his divinity, sacrifice, and incarnation, can one offer any kind of definitive statement about whether or not Jesus is the God-Man? Conversely, Pannenberg provides a methodology that provides a *ratio fidei*. One does not come to believe because of the authoritarian nature of kerygmatic confessions as contained in Scripture, creeds, or the like, but rather because set amongst the backdrop of history, it is plausible to see Jesus of Nazareth via his resurrection from the dead, is the Christ of God. The implications of his Kingdom teaching, incarnation, and death, result in the reconciliation of humanity to God, the eschatological destiny of humanity has been revealed in and through him, and he has significance among competing religious claims vying for the nature of reality.

Ultimately, one must remember that Anselm conceived of his work in an era that on one hand faced many challenges to Christian faith, and on the other hand was deeply influenced by the authority of the Church which claimed an Augustinian model of theology that proceeded from belief toward understanding. In an era of sweeping religious, intellectual, and social change, it is unsurprising that Anselm would borrow from the methods and tools of his milieu and structure an argument reflective of these elements. More importantly, as a theologian who lived at the crossroads between a past era in which people were caught between the supernatural battle between good and evil on a daily basis, and the new era of logic and the eradication of the devil from the immediate foreground of theology, one can see why he would attempt to utilize the newer methodologies while attempting to maintain the past Augustinian tradition. So, while the preceding is very much about the contrast between Pannenberg and Anselm, and reveals some matter of preference for the Pannenbergian methodology and Christology, one must recognize the work of Anselm as being unparalleled for its time. In this respect, while developments in knowledge between Anselm and Pannenberg are a rather wide advancement, tenets of the Anselmian methodological program remain in use today, Barth as a good example of this. Thus, while methodologically speaking Pannenberg provides a more fruitful answer to the question, one must also recognize the sheer genius of Anselm who pushed the Church forward by maintaining continuity with the past era and answered the questions and challenges of his era. Through the use of these newer methods and the like, he provided a platform that shaped theology for years to come.

2.3.3 Pannenberg & The Contemporary Atonement Conversation

The preceding material illustrated the contrast between two theologians of marked importance. The bigger question is then, given this contrast, what are the implications of this for Christology today? While many implications could be offered, one potential contemporary avenue for application can be observed within the scope of the present atonement conversation. This conversation typically is focused upon either Anselmian or subsequent metaphors for the atonement that are derivatives thereof. Satisfaction and penal substitutionary atonement metaphors are challenged from a variety of viewpoints ranging from accusations of divine child abuse in feminist studies of atonement, to being overly violent and antithetical to the purposes of God in Christ Jesus in non-violent atonement studies.[553] This final section provides a potential area of further study with the outcomes of this present work.

Accordingly, the primary emphasis of this final section concerns the methodological issue expressed in Anselmian Christology, namely how the Anselmian Christology places the focus upon the cross and relegates resurrection to the periphery, an issue which influences atonement, is present in the contemporary atonement conversation, and would benefit from the Pannenbergian voice in the conversation so as to demonstrate how resurrection enhances cross. Therefore, the final section of this work (2.3.3) shall (1) consider Anselmian and post-Anselmian atonement theologies in the present day atonement conversation and the accusations against them; then (2) how the Christology of Pannenberg provides a fruitful voice concerning the future, the eschatological destiny of humanity, and the victory of God in the future Kingdom present proleptically which retroactively enhances the meaning of the cross.

Anselm & The Present Day Atonement Conversation

From the outset of this remainder of the chapter, it must be expressly noted that the centrality of the cross is not in question as it relates to Christology,

---

[553] See a variety of sources inclusive of these characteristics noted below (201ff).

but rather how the cross operates Christologically. This is an important distinction to make. The reason this is an important distinction centers upon the conversation in atonement theology over the last few years concerning the various atonement metaphors that have gained usage in Christian theology and how some of these models have been accused of being rooted in violence.[554] More specifically, the atonement metaphors that are typically challenged are the Anselmian satisfaction presentation, and/or post-Anselmian metaphors influenced by his theology of satisfaction.

Satisfaction and penal substitutionary metaphors for the atonement focus on the vicarious sacrifice of Jesus Christ who by his death satisfies the debt owed unto God, the wrath of God, the penalty for sin, and forgiveness for sin thus extending salvation to humanity.[555] The emphasis is upon the

---

[554] Specifically, both the Anselmian satisfaction theory of the atonement and subsequent penal substitutionary theory of the atonement are typically challenged as being rooted in violence or divine child abuse. Feminist and liberation theologies are important to some of the initial challenges of these theories although in contemporary theology, there are a number of sources related to this, from the Nonviolence Atonement Conference Project featuring Tony Bartlett, J. Denny Weaver, Sharon Baker, and Michael Hardin, to the London Symposium on the theology of Atonement. See *Stricken By God: Nonviolent Identification and the Victory of Christ*, ed. by Brad Jersak and Michael Hardin. Grand Rapids: William B. Eerdmans Press, 2007. See also *The Atonement Debate: Papers from the London Symposium on the Theology of Atonement*, ed. by Derek Tidball, David Hilborn, and Justin Thacker. Grand Rapids: Zondervan Books, 2008. Marit Trelstad has challenged atonement theology in Marit Trelstad. *Cross Examinations: Readings on the Meaning of the Cross Today*. Minneapolis: Augsburg Fortress Press, 2006. Also significant is J. Denny Weaver. *The Non-Violent Atonement*. Grand Rapids: William B. Eerdmans Publishing, 2001. See Hans Boersma. *Violence Hospitality and the Cross*. Grand Rapids: Baker Academic, 2004. See also Hans Boersma. "Eschatological Justice and the Cross: Violence and Penal Substitution." *Theology Today*, 60, no 2. 2003, 186-199. See also *Atonement and Violence*, ed. by John Sanders. Nashville: Abingdon Press, 2006. See also Anthony W. Bartlett. *Cross Purposes: The Violent Grammar of Christian Atonement*. Harrisburg: Trinity Press, 2001. See also Stephen Finlan. *Problems with Atonement: The Origins of, and the Controversy About, Atonement Doctrine*. Collegeville: Liturgical Press, 2005. See also *Christianity, Patriarchy, and Abuse: A Feminist Critique*, ed. by Joanne Carlson Brown and Carol R. Bohn. New York: Pilgrim Press, 1993. See also Colin Gunton. *The Actuality of the Atonement: A Study of Metaphor, Rationality and the Christian Tradition*. Grand Rapids: William B. Eerdmans Publishing, 1989. This is a small but representative concentration of relatively recent atonement debate works.

[555] While the Anselmian satisfaction oriented understanding of atonement has been delineated in the preceding chapters, the emphasis here is not to delineate, nuance, or debate every nuance of the penal substitutionary models/metaphors of the atonement. What can be said generally is that penal substitutionary understandings are generated from the crucifixion of Jesus Christ as a vicarious sacrifice that appeased the wrath of God to satisfy a penalty which is deserved and fitting for humanity to receive given their sinfulness. While there are biblical tenets of this model as well as theological tenets back to the early Church as some have noted, some scholars turn to Charles Hodge and Benjamin Warfield as being the authors of its present form. See Hilborn, *The Atonement Debate*, 15-28. See also Gordon R. Lewis and Brude A.

active obedience of Jesus Christ to meritoriously provide satisfaction for the wrath of God toward either offended honor or the offense of sin itself, and concurrently a means of extending the salvific benefit of this transaction to humanity. The difference lies in the better-developed nuance occurring from satisfaction into penal substitutionary terms.[556] Specifically, the nuance "in our place" is more developed in penal substitutionary atonement, although tenets of this are present in satisfaction atonement as only the God-Man is able to satisfy the offended honor of God through a penitential act of supererogation that humanity owes unto God. Moreover, in penal substitutionary atonement there is a well-developed sense of wrath that Jesus Christ actively appeases by taking the place of humanity, whereas in satisfaction Jesus Christ is actively satisfying offended honor and not so much wrath. In sum, satisfaction concerns Jesus Christ actively and obediently offering himself as a penitential act of supererogation to repair the offended honor of God which has occurred by human sinfulness, and penal substitution similarly posits Jesus Christ actively and obediently offering himself to God by taking the place (or being the substitute) of humanity who deserves the wrath of God and the death due unto them.

For example, the work of René Girard proves an important voice that is often pointed to in the atonement conversation. His work on mimesis and violence depicts violence being diffused through a scapegoat who was blamed for such violence, and upon whom all of the mimetic violence was then directed toward in an act of retributive violence and murder.[557] As such, Girard claims the idea of the death of Jesus as being sacrificial is a cultural convention, and further claims that Jesus espoused non-violence and the end of violence in human culture. Thus to feature violence in a presenta-

---

Demarest. *Integrative Theology*. Grand Rapids: Zondervan Publishers, 1996, 378-382. See also Aulén, *Christus Victor*. See also Green and Baker, *Recovering the Scandal of the Cross*. See also Hardin who categorizes atonement theologies into two categories, sacrificial and non-sacrificial. While one may not agree with this generalization, it is possible to see the nature of satisfaction and penal substitution theologies as having contrast with other atonement theologies. See Michael Hardin. "Out of the Fog: New Horizons for Atonement Theory." *Stricken by God*, 54-76.

[556] Helpful is the work of Michael Jinkins. See Michael Jinkins. *A Comparative Study in the Theology of the Atonement in Jonathan Edwards and John McLeod Campbell: Atonement and the Character of God*. Lewiston: Edwin Melon Press, 1993. Also helpful is P.T. Forsyth. *The Work of Christ*. London: Hodder and Stoughton, 1910. Also helpful is Swinburne, Richard. *Responsibility and Atonement*. Oxford: Oxford University Press, 1989.

[557] See René Girard. *The Girard Reader*, ed. By James G. Williams. New York: Crossroads Books, 1996, 9-19. See also J. Denny Weaver whose book on Non-Violent atonement looks to utilize Girard in his narrative Christus Victor atonement theology. Weaver points to Girard who contends "there is nothing in the Gospels to suggest the death of Jesus is a sacrifice, whatever definition (expiation, substitution, etc.) we may give that sacrifice." Weaver, *The Non-Violent Atonement*, 48. Original Source: René Girard. *Things Hidden Since the Foundation of the World*, transl. by Stephen Bann and Michael Metter. Stanford: Stanford University Press, 1987, 180.

tion of the cross is foreign to the gospel.[558] Moreover, he argues that individuals are competing for similar realities, and that mimesis is an imitative desire that reciprocally operates to reinforce the desire for such similar realities. This competition eventuates into ritual and religion which attempts to create a satisfactory solution to the problem of such competition and rivalry, often through sacrifice. In this regard, the model of the scapegoat and violence being done unto the scapegoat emerges as a way of pacifying the rivalry – religion ritualizes the need for reconciliation.[559] In addition, Girard also looks to the surrogate victim and the sacrificial act in the biblical texts. For example, Girard points to the themes of brothers in conflict, the substitutionary needs of Abraham and Isaac, and the like. The model of sacrifice is the implication between sacrificer and deity, and how the act of violence upon the surrogate victim is for not only the sacrificer but also for the whole community; in this regard sacrifice helps deal with violence, justice, or the need for reconciliation.[560] In this way, the death of Jesus is not at the hands of the God of love but rather due to the inability of the world to accept his message or personhood.[561] Gunton has similarly noted both satisfaction and penal substitutionary views of the atonement concern the removal of guilt rather than the bestowal of new life.[562] Those who agree with Girard, Gunton, and/or others, claim an inconsistency of these models between Scripture and the death of Jesus Christ.[563] Some claim the cross "isn't a form of cosmic child abuse,"[564] while others point to Alan Mann and his concept of atonement as not being of the concern of appeasing an angry God,[565] while others yet point to biblical examples concerning the suffering servant as being an example of "inclusive place taking."[566]

Notwithstanding the criticisms of Girard, it is possible to see how the idea of mimetic sacrifice is involved in the Anselmian model of satisfaction, primarily because of the methodological decisions he has made *remoto Christo*

---

[558] See especially Weaver, *The Non-Violent Atonement*. Grand Rapids: William B. Eerdmans, 2001.

[559] See Girard, *The Girard Reader*, 9-19. This is potentially problematic as one could question if this is the manner in which one is to understand the work of Jesus Christ. The issue here is namely the lack of sovereignty of God who is not authoring the process of salvation history, which consequently makes this simply a matter of ethics. See Pannenberg who accepts Girard but notes this criticism in Pannenberg, *ST II*, 422.

[560] *The Girard Reader*, 74-88.

[561] See *The Girard Reader*, 178-188.

[562] Gunton challenges Anselmian atonement, even noting that divine sacrifice is an eternal reality rather than only a temporal one. See Gunton, *The Actuality of the Atonement*.

[563] The primary impetus to this concerned the language of penal substitution supported by the Evangelical Alliance of the UK and the London School of Theology. See Hilborn, *The Atonement Debate*, 15-28.

[564] Chalke, *The Atonement Debate*, 34.

[565] See Marshall, *The Atonement Debate*, 49.

[566] See Groom, *The Atonement Debate*, 103. See also Moody, *The Atonement Debate*, 115-129.

that have relegated resurrection to the periphery of his Christology. In a Christology that is methodologically expressed through the cross, Jesus dies because of the offended honor of God and because of the inability of humanity to pay a debt capable of satisfying the offended honor of God. Within the corpus of the *Cur Deus Homo* the emphasis is on the sin of humanity and the offended honor of God, but important is the impasse between both parties – between sacrificer and deity. Humanity needs to make the sacrifice, the deity requires a sacrifice, and so a surrogate victim or scapegoat becomes the natural response to the impasse of one party who requires honor and the other party who refuses to properly give honor. Thus, the sacrifice of Jesus Christ is through an active act of obedience to satisfy God, and in this meritorious act, Jesus Christ freely and willingly gives himself up unto to death. As the God-Man, Jesus Christ is the only one who can meet the requirement and satisfy the offended honor of God and pay the penalty due humanity. The emphasis here is on Jesus Christ relieving the guilt-debt of humanity through a penitential act of supererogation, providing humanity the benefits of salvation. But this raises questions, namely was Jesus Christ delivered unto death by God – is God the one who requires Jesus to make the sacrifice? Is this divine child abuse? Is the violence done unto Jesus on the behalf of God? What might this to say to humanity about ethics if this is merely a legal and transactionary sacrifice to satisfy an angry God? And finally, how does this act fit into salvation history in its entirety? These questions raise an entire host of issues that fit within the range of orthodoxy to more radicalized versions of Christianity. More specifically, these types of questions are at the heart of many feminist and liberation theologians who claim that patriarchy, subordination, oppression, and systems of law which enforce practices that subjugate others to power structures.[567]

While Anselm certainly did not intend for these issues to be raised nor were they part of his milieu, the methodological decision he made *remoto Christo* that expressed his Christology via the cross may indeed have opened the door for penal substitutionary Christologies in the future. If God is the originator of the sacrifice and its violence, what does this say about God and how does this fit within the whole of salvation history as contained in the Scriptures? Moreover, what might be said if the Father seeks justice but only at the expense of the death of the Son? Most importantly, is the Triune relation in favor of the world systems that can oppress and subjugate persons as

---

[567] For example, see the work of Peter Schmiechen who develops a composite portrait of feminist atonement critique. See Schmiechen, Peter. *Saving Power*, 153-163. See also Audrey Lorde. *Sister Outsider: Essays and Speeches*. Freedom: The Crossing Press, 1984. See Audrey Lorde and Carter Heyward. *Speaking of Christ: A Lesbian Feminist Voice*. New York: Pilgrim Press, 1989. See Rosemary Radford Ruether. *Sexism and God-Talk: Toward a Feminist Theology*. Boston: Beacon Press, 1983. See Rosemary Radford Ruether. "Feminist Interpretation: A Method of Correlation." *Feminist Interpretation of the Bible*, ed. By Letty M. Russell. Philadelphia: Westminster Press, 1985. See also Darby Kathleen Ray. *Deceiving the Devil: Atonement, Abuse, and Ransom*. Cleveland: Pilgrim Press, 1998.

the means of bringing about the reconciliation of God and humanity or is it something altogether different? Could it be that the very issues of those who challenge satisfaction and penal substitutionary atonement have illumined a deeper issue, that to subject God and the nature of salvation to be understood according to our own cultural conventions is problematic at best? Perhaps. Consider again how satisfaction and penal substitution motifs find some locus in the Anselmian question posed at the forefront of the *Cur Deus Homo*:

> By what logic or necessity did God become man, and by his death, as we believe and profess, restore life to the world, when he could have done this through the agency of some other person, angelic or human, or simply by willing it?[568]

What the above shows is that the resurrection is at the very least hidden from the overall premise of the argument of God restoring life to the world, God is the originator of the sacrificial death of Jesus Christ, and it is because of this, claims of divine child abuse, violent redemption, little regard for ethical behavior, subjugation, and a methodology that is problematic for salvation history arise. What these claims fail to consider however, is that Anselm has methodologically chosen to do Christology via the cross. Without consideration of the resurrection and the lens by which it establishes the atonement, there arises a serious question of how Jesus Christ comes to his cross: does the cross come about because of divine plan or human rejection of the divine plan? These approaches differ as one has God to be the orchestrator of the cross, and the other has humanity rejecting the proclamation of the Kingdom thus orchestrating the cross.

Pannenberg & A Fruitful Voice in Atonement Conversation: Resurrection Enhances Cross

Given the outcomes of 2.3.1 as they relate to the Anselmian Christology via the cross through active obedience and merit, satisfaction, and penance, and the Pannenbergian Christology via the resurrection through passive obedience and reliance, reconciliation by way of inclusive substitution, and the future eschatological destiny of humanity; and given the outcomes of 2.3.2, as the Pannenbergian Christology provides a dialectical unity of resurrection, cross, and incarnation as it relates to the future, past, and present, now it is possible in 2.3.3 to indicate how Pannenberg might offer a fruitful voice in the present atonement conversation.

Of paramount importance is this consideration: if by means of the resurrection of Jesus Christ God is able to bring reconciliation to himself through the cross and inaugurate the future eschatological destiny of humanity at present to transform the past, then it must be recognized that the resurrection shapes the meaning of the cross. The resurrection is the eans

---

[568] See CDH 1.1, 265.

by which the blasphemous act of humanity in putting Jesus Christ the Son of God to death finds forgiveness, retroactively establishes the cross and the incarnation of Jesus Christ, and reconciles humanity to God to offer a prolepsis of their eschatological destiny. Jesus Christ who is united to humanity and shares in the death of humanity, does so in order for humanity to be united to him so they will share in his resurrection.[569] His conflict with the law, his proclamation of the Kingdom having come in him, and his condemnation to death by the religious authorities and Rome for such blasphemy against their systems desiring total allegiance, relocates true humanity from past to future – from the first Adam to the second and eschatological Adam.[570] While God may have allowed or even ordained it retroactively, the reason for the death of Jesus is not because God initiated it, but because humanity rejected the Kingdom and their own future eschatological destiny as Jesus Christ taught, proclaimed, and embodied. It is Jesus who through perfect reliance upon God the Father, is vindicated from the charges of blasphemy by which humanity put him to death. More specifically the substitutionary guilt that extends to all humanity in his death is due to the nature of human relations.[571] Thus, while Jesus dies, his death is substitutionary in the way that all humanity is subjected to death. Yet in his resurrection, humanity finds its eschatological destiny, as the humanity of Jesus is inextricably bound with his divinity in the hypostatic union of the God-Man. His death has significance, but only as established by his resurrection, and his death can be rejected by humanity just as humanity rejected Jesus Christ by delivering him unto death.

Pannenberg reveals the importance of what should be a more active element within the atonement debate: resurrection. More typical of the critique of the Latin view of atonement by satisfaction Aulén has offered, Pannenberg claims that in the resurrection, the substitution of the resurrected life of Jesus is now made manifest to humanity who is called to share in his life and in their own eschatological destiny.[572] Without this, and especially in the hands of satisfaction or penal substitutionary motifs of the atonement, the claims of feminist, non-violent atonement proponents, and liberation theologians have greater validity. What these specific voices in the conversation typically claim is the problematic issue of mimesis, violence, and the condoning of violence for the purposes of achieving reconciliation. These arguments, in many ways, are admirable. Where these arguments are misguided is that too often resurrection is relegated to the periphery of the argument typical of the Anselmian Christology. As such, precisely because of the *a priori* methodology and the active obedience/merit nuance, Anselm develops an atonement theology that posits all the redemp-

---

[569] Pannenberg, *ST II*, 427.

[570] See Neie, *The Doctrine of the Atonement*, 10. Original Source, Pannenberg, *JGM*, 200.

[571] This was a point made above regarding the difference in Pannenberg as it relates to inclusive substitution. See pg. Pannenberg, *ST II*, 337-338.

[572] Pannenberg, *JGM*, 274-280.

tion of humanity in the death of Jesus Christ via satisfaction, rather than the establishment of a sacrifice that was made because of humanity but for humanity via the resurrection. Conversely, through the retroactive significance of the resurrection, Pannenberg demonstrates how reconciliation is achieved, how humanity is revealed and inaugurated in its divine eschatological destiny, and how the proclamation of the future of God having arrived in him the logos made flesh, are from and of God.

Moreover, if the injustice done to Jesus Christ on the cross by humanity is revealed to be blasphemous via his resurrection, than those who argue against the oppressive systems of humanity come to a more profound expression. If the futurity of humanity and God is without these injustices in the eschaton, and if the resurrection reveals these actions to be unjust, then the ethical imperatives Paul issues throughout the New Testament in light of the resurrection of Jesus Christ are reason enough to live the resurrected life and put to death the same guilty behaviors which are pridefully thought to be individual but are in reality substituted upon all humanity. If resurrection were to take a more active role in the atonement conversation, issues of justice and divine child abuse might find retroactive transformation by the future of God.

Without an active role of resurrection within the atonement conversation, these issues too easily take shape primarily because there are a variety of methodological issues at play. If the center of Christology is the cross, then the implications of Christology lend themselves primarily to soteriology with satisfaction or penal substitutionary emphases. If the center of Christology is the incarnation, a number of historical questions are raised, namely can one assume *a priori* that Jesus is one with God, and that this has any significance for us? When resurrection is more readily pushed toward the periphery, the atonement conversation issues raised begin to surface. More importantly, a key issue respective to Christian faith surfaces altogether which seems faulty from the primary purpose for which the New Testament Scriptures were constructed – a response to the resurrection of Jesus Christ which was good news for humanity as the future salvation of God had been manifested in the present to transform the past. As demonstrated throughout 2.3.1 and 2.3.2, it is the resurrection which enhances the meaning of the cross. Without it, one is left wondering if another failed messianic attempt was made, if a blasphemer died at the hands of the religious community, or if another poor soul or political rebel died at the hands of an oppressive Roman government. With the retroactive significance of the resurrection, there is an epistemological and ontological establishment of the person and work of Jesus Christ for the sake of humanity to reveal their eschatological destiny and inaugurate the benefits of future salvation in the present which thus transforms the past.

Ultimately, what is markedly different about the Pannenbergian proposal is the recognition that the resurrection is the reversal of the cross and that the cross without the resurrection is rendered potentially meaningless. When the Pannenbergian Christology via the retroactive significance of the resurrection is offered as a voice in the atonement conversation, the cross is no longer divine child abuse but the abuse of the divine child by the humanity he came to save; the cross is no longer the unjust treatment of the Son but the injustice done unto him so that the injustices of a fallen world could be declared as such on resurrection day; and the individuality that humanity so desperately wants to maintain is recognized to be a differentiated unity that finds invitation into the divine life through the resurrection of Jesus Christ who shares in this life – the life of God. Finally, a narrative of salvation history becomes not an addendum or antiquated backdrop to the incarnation or the cross but the lens by which the incarnation and cross are understood in light of the resurrection which retroactively establishes both.

Clearly, Pannenberg is not the only or final voice in this conversation but a fruitful one. Others with Pannenbergian tendencies also focus upon the resurrection and the understanding of the cross as not being the will of the Father insofar as it relates to violence but rather to his death as atonement for a world that loves to violently reject and make the object of rejection a scapegoat. What Pannenberg offers is the potential to see the challenges of satisfaction and subsequent penal substitutionary atonement, namely that without the resurrection the cross can easily slip into a convention of violence that raises many questions about the nature of God, the meaning of the cross, the relationship between God and humanity in light of the intentions of God for this relationship, and most importantly, the future eschatological destiny of all creation.

Chapter 9

Concluding Observations

From the outset, this work set out to compare and contrast the Christologies of two important theologians who have shaped theology: Anselm of Canterbury and Wolfhart Pannenberg. When brought into dialogue with one another, their work revealed contrasting Christologies: Anselm of Canterbury utilized an *a priori* from above methodology that emphasized the cross and incarnation, and Wolfhart Pannenberg utilized an *a posteriori* from below methodology which emphasized the resurrection and retroactively establishes cross and incarnation.

Typical of the theological enterprise which is both critical and constructive, both wrote in response to the theological challenges of their milieu. While Anselm faced a host of challenges from those who sought answers to questions such as the degradation of God in the incarnation of Jesus Christ or the challenges of the monastic community who were desirous of logical presentations of faith, Pannenberg faced his own challenges from the historical-critical methodologies and death-of-God theology that theological modernity perpetuated. Both Anselm and Pannenberg utilized the tools of their day, Anselm in logic and deduction, and Pannenberg in historical-critical methodologies and to some degree, modern science.

The point of contrast between Anselm and Pannenberg is predominantly methodological. Whereas Anselm focused on the cross and incarnation by way of a from above methodology, Pannenberg focused on the utilization of a from below historical-critical methodology that emphasized resurrection, and how it retroactively established the cross and incarnation. More importantly, this establishes the unity of Jesus with God and the eschatological destiny of humanity. The programs of Anselm and Pannenberg are important for Christology as one looks to a presupposition of divinity whereas the other seeks to establish it historically by means of probability. One, by means of undermining his presupposition of faith through a *remoto Christo* methodology, assumes Jesus is divine and made a perfect sacrifice, whereas the other seeks to establish the divinity of Jesus who made a perfect sacrifice on the basis of the overturning of the denial of the Kingdom which Jesus proclaimed was present in him in his resurrection. Interestingly enough, one is concerned with the past, overcoming the past sins of humanity, and consequently the past offended honor of God, and the other is concerned with the future, and how God as the power of the unbound future eventuates the present to transform the past. The Christology of Anselm deals with epistemological and ontological presuppositions by means of the incarnation which are necessary to satisfy the pre-existing conditions for God and humanity in a transaction that is based upon feudal and medieval penance related issues, whereas the Christology of Pannenberg establishes epistemologically and ontologically the person and work of Jesus of Nazareth who is vindicated in the resurrection, and retroactively established as the Christ of God in his work and personhood. Whereas Anselm emphasized the cross and by way of the cross the incarnation, resurrection is methodologically relegated to the periphery. And whereas Pannenberg emphasizes the resurrection, he establishes cross and incarnation, holding all three together dialectically.

Clearly, both men were theological geniuses. Both have shaped Christology. Both have works that are being debated and tested even today. The work of Pannenberg may be helpful in the contemporary atonement conversation as he emphasizes the resurrection held dialectically in tension with a reconciliatory nuanced understanding of the cross and incarnation. The present day challenges to atonement as they specifically relate to violence and divine child abuse as some have claimed, might be better understood through the Pannenbergian Christology that emphasizes resurrection. Recapturing the conversation under this Christological emphasis might better enhance the cross through the resurrection so that the world community recognizes its rejection of the future of God that had arrived in Jesus. By sharing in our death – nay, by inclusively substituting himself in our place for the death we deserved for killing him on the cross – Jesus Christ with perfect reliance upon God the Father, invites us by faith into the divine life of God, and into our future eschatological destiny.

It is this life that is yet to come for us in the future that has been proleptically eventuated in the present to transform our collective past. And if Einstein is right about his theory of relativity, perhaps it is simply that our future is not yet moving as quickly as the future of God in Jesus Christ who eventuated the present. To this degree, our future remains a matter of debate until the eschaton and until the history of world religions will determine once and for all the meaning of history. On that great and glorious day, Pannenberg contends:

> The whole path from the beginning of creation by way of reconciliation to the eschatological future of salvation, the march of the divine economy of salvation is an expression of the eternal future of God to the salvation of creatures and thus a manifestation of the divine love.[573]

Accordingly, as the people of God hope, wait, and pray, we do so not blindly but with anticipation, because we have already seen the future in Jesus Christ.

---

[573] See Pannenberg, *ST III*, 646.

Bibliography

Allies, T.W. *The Monastic Life: From the Fathers of the Desert to Charlemagne.* London: Kegan Paul, Trench, Trübner, & Co., 1896.

Althaus, P. *Die Christliche Warheit,* 6th Ed. Gütersloh: 1962.

Anselm & Abelard: Investigations & Juxtapositions, ed. By G.E.M. Gasper & H. Kohlenberger. Pontifical Institute of Medieval Studies No. 19. Toronto: Pontifical Institute of Medieval Studies, 2006.

Anselm of Canterbury, "The Monologion." *Anselm of Canterbury: The Major Works,* ed. by Brian Davies and Gill Evans. Oxford: Oxford University Press, 1998.

Aquinas, T. *On the Truth of the Catholic Faith, Summa Contra Gentiles.* trans. Anton C. Pegis. New York, 1955.

Asiedu, F.B.A. "Anselm & The Unbelievers: Pagans, Jews, & Christians in the *Cur Deus Homo.*" *Theological Studies,* Vol. 62. Hanover: Theological Studies, 2001.

Atonement & Violence, ed. by John Sanders. Nashville: Abingdon Press, 2006.

Aulén, G. *Christus Victor,* trans. by A.G. Herbert. London: SPCK, 1931.

Awad, N. *Revelation, History, & Idealism: Re-examining the Conceptual Roots of Wolfhart Pannenberg's Theology.* Theological Review 26, No. 1, 2005.

Barr, J. "Old and New in Interpretation." *Scottish Journal of Theology No. 19.* London: SPC Publishers, 1966.

Barr, J. "Revelation Through History in the Old Testament and in Modern Theology." *Interpretation 17.* 1963.

Barth, K. *Anselm: Fides Quaerens Intellectum.* London: SCM Press LTD, 1960.

Barth, Karl. *Dogmatics in Outline.* New York: Harper & Row Publishers, 1959.

Barth, K. *Church Dogmatics Vol. I.,* ed. by G.W. Bromiley and T.F. Torrance. Edinburgh: T & T Clark Publishers, 1936-1969.

Barth, K. *Church Dogmatics IV/1.* London: T & T Clark, 1932-1968.

Barth, K. *Church Dogmatics, IV/2.* London: T & T Clark, 1932-1968.

Barth, K. *Karl Barth Letters 1961-1968,* ed. By Fangmeier, Soevesandt, and trans. by Bromiley. Grand Rapids: Eerdmans Publishing, 1981.

Beginning with the End: God, Science, & Wolfhart Pannenberg, ed. by Carol Rausch Albright & Joel Haugen. Chicago: Open Court Press, 1997.

Bloch, M. *Feudal Society*, trans. by L.A. Manyon. Chicago: University of Chicago Press, 1961.

Boersma, Hans. "Eschatological Justice and the Cross: Violence & Penal Substitution." *Theology Today*, 60, no. 2. 2003.

Boersma, H. *Violence Hospitality & the Cross*. Grand Rapids: Baker Academic, 2004.

Böhmer, H. *Kirche und Staat in England und in der Normandie im XI und XII*. Leipzig: Dieterichsche Verlagsbuchhandlung, 1899.

Borst, A. *Medieval Worlds: Barbarians, Heretics, and Artists in the Middle Ages*, trans. by Eric Hansen. Chicago: The University of Chicago Press, 1991.

Braaten, C. & P. Clayton. *The Theology of Wolfhart Pannenberg: Twelve American Critiques with an Autobiographical Essay and Response*. Minneapolis: Augsburg Publishing House, 1988.

Braaten, C. "The Current Controversy on Revelation: Pannenberg and His Critics." *Journal of Religion* Vol. 45. 1965.

Bradshaw, T. *Pannenberg: A Guide for the Perplexed*. London: T & T Clark Publishers, 2009.

Brightman, E. *A Philosophy of Religion*, Englewood Cliffs: Prentice Hall, 1940.

Bultmann, R. *History and Eschatology: The Gifford Lectures, 1955*. Edinburgh: The University Press, 1957.

Bultmann, R. *Theology of the New Testament Vol. I & II*. New York: Charles Scribner & Sons Publishing, 1951, 1955.

Burhenn, H. "Pannenberg's Argument for the Historicity of the Resurrection." *Journal of American Academy of Religion*, 40. Oxford: 1972.

Bury, J.B. *The Cambridge Medieval History, Vol. III: Germany & The Western Empire*. New York: The MacMillan Company, 1922.

Butler, C. *Benedictine Monachism: Studies in Benedictine Life & Rule*. Eugene: Wipf & Stock, 2005.

Calvin, J. *Institutes of the Christian Religion*. Peabody: Hendrickson Publishers, 2009.

Campbell, R. "The Conceptual Roots of Anselm's Soteriology." *Anselm, Aosta, Bec, and Canterbury: Papers in Commemoration of the Nine-Hundredth Anniversary of Anselm's Enthronement as Archbishop, 25 September, 1093*, ed. by D.E. Luscombe and G.R. Evans. Sheffield: Sheffield Academic Press, 1996.

Carre, M. *Realists & Nominalists*. Oxford: Oxford University Press, 1946.

Charry, E. *By the Renewing of Your Minds: The Pastoral Function of Christian Doctrine*. New York: Oxford, 1997.

Christianity, Patriarchy, and Abuse: A Feminist Critique, ed. by Joanne Carlson Brown & Carol R. Bohn. New York: Pilgrim Press, 1993.

Church, R.W. *St. Anselm*. London: MacMillan and Company, 1884.

Clark, F. *The Gregorian Dialogues and the Origins of Benedictine Monasticism*. Leiden: Brill Publishers, 2003.

Cobb Jr., J. "Past, Present, and Future." *Theology as History: Discussions Among Continental & American Theologians, Vol. 3*. San Francisco: Harper & Row Publishers, 1967.

Cobb Jr., J. *Journal of Religion* 49, 1969.

Cohen, N. "Feudal Imagery or Christian Tradition? A Defense of the Rationale for Anselm's *Cur Deus Homo*." *St. Anselm Journal 2.1*. Manchester: St. Anselm Journal, 2004.

Colish, M. *Medieval Foundations of the Western Intellectual Tradition*. New Haven: Yale University Press, 1997.

Cook, W. & R. Herzman. *The Medieval World View: An Introduction*. Oxford: Oxford University Press, 1983.

Copan, Paul H., Tacelli, Lüdemann, and Craig. *Jesus' Resurrection: Fact or Fiction? A Debate between William Lane Craig and Gerd Lüdemann*. Downers Grove: InterVarsity Press, 2000.

Dales, R. *The Intellectual Life of Western Europe in the Middle Ages*. Leiden: E.J. Brill Publishers, 1995.

Darlington, R.R. "Last Phase of Anglo-Saxon History." *English Historical Review, Vol. 22*. Oxford: 1937.

Dawson, C. *Religion and the Rise of Western Culture*. London: Sheed & Ward Publishers, 1950.De Vaux, C. *The Sacrament of Penance*. Glen Rock: Deus Books Paulist Press, 1966.

Deem, M. "A Christological Renaissance: The Chalcedonian Turn of St. Anselm of Canterbury." *St. Anselm Journal 2.1*. Manchester: The St. Anselm Journal, 2004.

Delhaye, P. *Medieval Christian Philosophy, Volume Twelve*, trans. by S.J. Tester: *Twentieth Century Encyclopedia of Catholicism*. New York: Hawthorn Books, 1960.

Deme, D. *The Christology of Anselm of Canterbury*. Burlington: Ashgate Publishing, 2003.

Dillistone, F.W. *The Christian Understanding of Atonement*. Philadelphia: Westminster Press, 1968.

Dobbin, E. "Reflections on Wolfhart Pannenberg's Revelation Theology." *Louvain Studies No. 4.* 1972.

Douglass, D. "The Norman Conquest & English Feudalism." *The Economic History Review, Vol. 9, No. 2.* Glasgow: Economic History Society, 1939.

Eadmer. *The Life of St. Anselm, Archbishop of Canterbury* ed. by R.W. Southern. Oxford: Clarendon Press, 1962.

Evans, G.R. *Anselm.* Wilton: Morehouse-Barlow Publishers, 1989.

Evans, G.R. *Anselm & A New Generation.* Oxford: Clarendon Press, 1980.

Evans, G.R. *Anselm & Talking About God.* Oxford: Oxford University Press, 1978.

Evans, Joan. *Monastic Life at Cluny 910-1157.* Oxford: Oxford University Press, 1931.

Fairweather, E. *A Scholastic Miscellany: Anselm to Ockham.* Philadelphia: Westminster Press, 1956.

Feuerbach, L. *Das Wesen des Christentums.* 1841.

Feuerbach, Ludwig. *The Essence of Christianity,* trans. by George Eliot. Amherst: Prometheus Books, 1989.

Finlan, S. *Problems with Atonement: The Origins of, & the Controversy About, Atonement Doctrine.* Collegeville: Liturgical Press, 2005.

Foot, S. "Church & Monastery in Bede's Northumbria." *The Cambridge Companion to Bede* ed. by Scott DeGregorio. Cambridge: Cambridge University Press, 2010.

Forsyth, P.T. *The Work of Christ.* London: Hodder & Stoughton, 1910.

Frank, F.H.R. *Zur Theologie A. Ritschl's,* 1888.

Galloway, A. *Wolfhart Pannenberg.* London: Allen & Unwin, 1973.

Gilson, E. *History of Christian Philosophy in the Middle Ages.* New York: Random House Publishers, 1955.

Gilson, E. *A History of Philosophy: Medieval Philosophy.* New York: Random House Publishers, 1962.

Gilson, E. *Reason & Revelation in the Middle Ages.* New York: Charles Scribner's Sons, 1938.

Girard, R. *The Girard Reader,* ed. By James G. Williams. New York: Crossroads Books, 1996.

Girard, R. *Things Hidden Since the Foundation of the World,* transl. by Stephen Bann & Michael Metter. Stanford: Stanford University Press, 1987.

Gonzalez, J. *The Story of Christianity Volume I: The Early Church to the Dawn of The Reformation*, New York: HarperCollins Publishers, 1984.

Gouwens, D. *Kierkegaard as a Religious Thinker*. Cambridge: Cambridge University Press, 1996.

Graham, R. "The Intellectual Influence of English Monasticism Between the Tenth and Twelfth Centuries." *Transactions of the Royal Historical Society, New Series, Vol. 17*. 1903.

Grant, E. *God & Reason in the Middle Ages*. Cambridge: Cambridge University Press, 2001.

Green, J.. & M. Baker. *Recovering the Scandal of the Cross: Atonement in New Testament & Contemporary* Contexts. Downers Grove: Intervarsity Press, 2000.

Grenz, S. *Reason for Hope: The Systematic Theology of Wolfhart Pannenberg, 2nd Ed*. Grand Rapids: Eerdmans Publishing, 2005.

Gunton, C. *The Actuality of the Atonement: A Study of Metaphor, Rationality and the Christian Tradition*. Grand Rapids: William B. Eerdmans Publishing, 1989.

Hamilton, S. *The Practice of Penance: 900-1050*. Suffolk: St. Edmunsbury Press, 2001.

Henry, C. *God, Revelation, and Authority*. Waco: Word Publishers, 1976. Henry, D.P. *The Logic of St. Anselm*. Oxford: Clarendon Press, 1967.

Heyward, C. & E. Davis. *Speaking of Christ: A Lesbian Feminist Voice*. New York: Pilgrim Press, 1989.

Hodgson, P. *Jesus – Word & Presence: An Essay in Christology*. Philadelphia: Fortress Press, 1971.

Hogg, D. *Anselm of Canterbury: The Beauty of Theology*. Burlington: Ashgate Publishing Company, 2004.

Hollister, C. "The Irony of English Feudalism." *The Journal of British Studies, Vol. 2, No. 2*. Chicago: University of Chicago Press, 1963.

Holopainen, T. *Dialectic and Theology in the Eleventh Century*. New York: E.J. Brill Publishers, 1996.

Hopkins, J. *A Companion to the Study of St. Anselm*. Minneapolis: University of Minnesota Press, 1972.

Hoyt, R. & C.W.H. "The Iron Age of English Feudalism." *The Journal of British Studies, Vol. 2, No. 2*. Chicago: University of Chicago Press, 1963.

Hoyt, R. & S. Chodrow. *Europe in the Middle Ages, Third Ed*. New York: Harcourt, Brace, and Jovanavich Publishers, 1957.

Hume, D. *An Enquiry Concerning Human Understanding*, ed. by Tom Beauchamp. Oxford: Oxford University Press, 1999.

Illig, H. *Wer Hat an der Uhr Gedreht?* Neuss: Ullstein TB Publishers, 2001.

Irenaeus. *Adversus Haereses.*

Irvin, D. & S. Sunquist. *History of the World Christian Movement Volume I: Earliest Christianity to 1453.* Mayknoll: Orbis Books, 2003.

Jinkins, M. *A Comparative Study in the Theology of the Atonement in Jonathan Edwards and John McLeod Campbell: Atonement and the Character of God.* Lewiston: Edwin Melon Press, 1993.

Johnson, E. "The Ongoing Christology of Wolfhart Pannenberg." *Horizons* 9, No. 2, Villanova: College Theology Society, 1982.

Jüngel, E. *God as the Mystery of the World*, trans. by Darrell L. Guder. Grand Rapids: Eerdmans Publishing, 1983.

Kähler, M. *So-Called Historical Jesus and the Historic-Biblical Christ*, ed. by Carl E. Braaten. Minneapolis: Fortress Press, 1988.

Kaku, M. *Hyperspace.* Oxford: Oxford University Press, 1994.

Kant, I. *Religion Within the Limits of Reason Alone.* New York: Harper and Row, 1960.

Kantorowicz, E. *The King's Two Bodies: A Study in Medieval Political Theology.* Princeton: 1957.

Karfikova, L. *Anselm z Canterbury: Fides Quaerens Intellectum.* Prague: Kalich Publishers, 1990.

Kegley, C. *The Theology of Rudolph Bultmann.* New York: Harper & Row Publishers, 1966.

Klappert, B. *Die Auferweckung des Gekreuzigten.* 1971.

Klooster, F. "Aspects of Historical Method in Pannenberg's Theology." *Septuagesimo Anno: Festschrift for G.C. Berkouwer*, ed. by J.T. Bakker. Kampen: Kok Publishers, 1973.

Klooster, F. "Historical Method & The Resurrection in Pannenberg's Theology." *CTJ* 11/1, 1976.

Knowles, D. "The Cultural Influence of English Medieval Monasticism." *Cambridge Historical Journal Vol. 7 No. 3.* Cambridge: Cambridge University Press, 1943.

Knowles, D. *The Evolution of Medieval Thought.* Baltimore: Helican Press, 1962.

Knowles, D. *The Monastic Order in England: A History of Its Development From the Times of St. Dunstan to the Fourth Lateran Council.* Cambridge: The University Press, 1950.

Knowles, M.D. "Some Recent Advances in the History of Medieval Thought." *Cambridge Historical Journal, Vol. IX, No. 1,* Cambridge: Cambridge Press, 1947.

Künneth, W. *Theology of the Resurrection,* trans. by James W. Leitch. St. Louis: Concordia Publishing House, 1965.

LaMonte, J. *The World of the Middle Ages: A Reorientation of Medieval History.* New York: Appleton-Century-Crofts Inc. Publishers, 1949.

Lapide, P. *The Resurrection of Jesus – A Jewish Perspective.* London: SPCK Publishers, 1984.

Le Goff, J. *Time, Work, & Culture in the Middle Ages,* trans. by Arthur Goldhammer. Chicago: The University of Chicago Press, 1977.

Lewis, G. & B. Demarest. *Integrative Theology.* Grand Rapids: Zondervan Publishers, 1996.

Lorde, A. *Sister Outsider: Essays & Speeches.* Freedom: The Crossing Press, 1984.

Lottin, O. *Psychologie et morale aux XIIe et XIIIe siecles, 5: L'ecole d' Anselme de Laon et de Guillaume de Champeaux.* Paris: Publishers, 1959.

Luther, M. "The Freedom of a Christian, 1520." *Luther's Works, Vol. 31.* Philadelphia: Fortress Press, 1957.

Lynch, J. *The Medieval Church: A Brief History.* London: Longman Press, 1992.

Maitland, F.W. *Domesday Book & Beyond: Three Essays in the Early History of England.* 1897.

Marenbon, J. *Early Medieval Philosophy 480-1150: An Introduction.* New York: Routledge Press, 1983.

Marone, S. "Medieval Philosophy in Context." *The Cambridge Companion to Medieval Philosophy.* Cambridge: Cambridge University Press, 2003.

McDermott, B. "Pannenberg's Resurrection Christology: A Critique." *Theological Studies.* 1974.

McDonald, H.D. *The Atonement of the Death of Christ: In Faith, Revelation & History.* Grand Rapids: Baker Bookhouse, 1985.

McGrath, A. "Christology & Soteriology: A Response to Wolfhart Pannenberg's Critique of the Soteriological Approach to Christology." *Theologische Zeitschrift 42.* 1986.

McIntyre, J. *St. Anselm & His Critics: A Re-Interpretation of the Cur Deus Homo.* Edinburgh: Oliver and Boyd Publishers, 1954.

McKenzie, D. *Wolfhart Pannenberg & Religious Philosophy*. USA: University Press, 1980.

McNeill, J. & H. Gamer. *Medieval Handbooks of Penance: A Translation of the Principal Libri Poenitentiales and Selections from Related Documents*. New York: Columbia University Press, 1938.

Migliore, D. "How Historical is the Resurrection?" *Theology Today: Vol. 33, No. 1*. Princeton: Princeton Theological Seminary, 1976.

Molnar, P. *Incarnation & Resurrection: Toward a Contemporary Understanding*. Grand Rapids: William B. Eerdmans Publishing, 2007.

Moltmann, J. *Theology of Hope*. Minneapolis: Fortress Press, 1993.

Morgan, R. "Monastic Reform and Cluniac Spirituality." *Cluniac Monasticism in the Central Middle Ages*. Hamden: Archon Books, 1971.

Mostert, C. *God & The Future: Wolfhart Pannenberg's Eschatological Doctrine of God*. London: T & T Clark, 2002.

Murdock, W.R. "History and Revelation in Jewish Apocalypticism." *Interpretation 21*. 1967.

Murphy, George. "Prolepsis & The Physics of Retrocausality."
Theology & Science, Vol. 7, No. 3, 2009

Neelands, D. "Crime, Guilt, and the Punishment of Christ: Traveling Another Way With Anselm of Canterbury and Richard Hooker." *Anglican Theological Review Vol. 88 No. 2.*, 2006.

Neie, H. *The Doctrine of the Atonement in the Theology of Wolfhart Pannenberg*. New York: Walter DeGruyter Publishers, 1979.

Nietzsche, F. *Die fröhliche Wissenschaft*. 1882.

Obayashi, H. "Pannenberg & Troeltsch: History & Religion" *Journal of American Academy of Religion 38 no. 4d*. 1970.

Olive, D. *Makers of the Modern Theological Mind: Wolfhart Pannenberg*. Waco: Word Books, 1973.

Olsen, G. "Hans Urs Von Balthasar and the Rehabilitation of St. Anselm's Doctrine of the Atonement." *Scottish Journal of Theology Vol. 34*. Edinburg: Scottish Academic Press, 1981.

Osborn, E. *Irenaeus of Lyons*. Cambridge: Cambridge University Press, 2001.

Otten, W. "Medieval Scholasticism: Past, Present, and Future." *NAKG* Vol 81, 2001.

Oxford Latin Dictionary. Oxford: The Clarendon Press, 1968.

Pannenberg, W. *Anthropology in Theological Perspective* trans. by *Matthew J. O'Connell*. London: T & T Clark Publishers, 2004.

Pannenberg, W. *Basic Questions in Theology: A Collection of Essays (2 Volumes)*. Minneapolis: Fortress Press, 1970.

Pannenberg, W. "Constructive & Critical Functions of Eschatology." *Harvard Theological Review* 77, No. 2, 1984.

Pannenberg, W. *Faith and Reality*. Philadelphia: Westminster Press, 1977.

Pannenberg, W. *Jesus – God & Man, trans. by L. Wilkins & D. Priebe*. Philadelphia: The Westminster Press, 1968.

Pannenberg, W. *Grundzüge der Christologie*. Gütersloh: Mohn Publishers, 1966.

Pannenberg, W. *Systematic Theology, (Three Volumes), trans. by Geoffrey W. Bromiley*. Grand Rapids: William B. Eerdmans, 1991.

Pannenberg, W. *Revelation as History*. New York: The Macmillan Company, 1968.

Pannenberg, W. *The Apostles' Creed: In the Light of Today's Questions*, trans. by Margaret Kohl. Philadelphia: The Westminster Press, 1972.

Pannenberg, W. *Theology & The Kingdom of God*. Philadelphia: Westminster Press, 1969.

Pannenberg, W. *What is Man?* Philadelphia: Fortress Press, 1970.

Pearson, C. *The Early and Middle Ages of England*. Port Washington: Kennikat Press, 1861.

Pelikan, J. *The Christian Tradition: A History of the Development of Doctrine, Vol. 3: The Growth of Medieval Theology (600-1300)*. Chicago: University of Chicago Press, 1978.

Peters, T. *God: the World's Future*. Minneapolis: Augsburg Fortress Press, 1992.

Philosophy in the Middle Ages, ed. by A. Hyman & J. Walsh. Indianapolis: Hacket Publishing, 1974.

Pieper, J. *Scholasticism: Personalities and Problems of Medieval Philosophy*. New York: Pantheon Books, 1960.

Poole, R. *Illustrations of the History of Medieval Thought & Learning*. New York: Dover Publications, 1960.

Pourrat, P. *Christian Spirituality in the Middle Ages, trans. by S.P. Jacques*. Westminster: The Newman Press, 1953.

Radford Reuther, R. "Feminist Interpretation: A Method of Correlation." *Feminist Interpretation of the Bible*, ed. By Letty M. Russell. Philadelphia: Westminster Press, 1985.

Radford Reuther, R. *Sexism & God-Talk: Toward a Feminist Theology.* Boston: Beacon Press, 1983.

Rahner, Karl. "Jesus Christus, III B." *Lexikon für Theologie und Kirche, Volume Five.* Freiburg: 1957-1965.

Rashdall, H. *The Idea of Atonement in Christian Theology.* London, MacMillan Publishers, 1919.

Ray, Darby K. *Deceiving the Devil: Atonement, Abuse, and Ransom.* Cleveland: Pilgrim Press, 1998.

Readings in the History of Christian Thought, ed. Robert L. Ferm. New York: Holt, Rinehart, & Winston, 1964.

Rogers, K. *The Neoplatonic Metaphysics & Epistemology of Anselm of Canterbury.* Lewiston: The Edwin Mellen Press, 1997.

Rogers, K. "Anselm on Forgiveness, Patience, & Free Will." *Anselm Journal 6.2.* Manchester: The St. Anselm Journal, 2009.

Rogers, K. *Anselm on Freedom.* Oxford: Oxford University Press, 2008.

Round, J.H. "The Introduction of Knight-Service into England." *English Historical Review VI.* Oxford: English Historical Review, 1891.

Round, J.H. *Feudal England.* London: 1892.

Rule of St. Benedict in English & Latin With Notes ed. by Timothy Frye. Collegeville: Circleville Press, 1981.

Saint Anselm – His Origins and Influence ed. by J. Fortin. Lewiston: The Edwin Mellen Press, 2001.

Sayles, G. *The Medieval Foundations of England.* Philadelphia: University of Pennsylvania Press, 1950.

Schemiechen, P. *Saving Power: Theories of Atonement and Forms of the Church.* Grand Rapids: William B. Eerdmans Publishing Company, 2005.

Schleiermacher, F. *The Christian Faith,* ed. by H.r. Mackintosh & J.S. Stewart. Edinburgh: T & T Clark, 1928.

Schmitt, F.S. *S. Anselmi Opera Omni: Vol. II.* Edinburgh: Thomas Nelson Publishers, 1946.

Schufreider, G. *Confessions of a Rational Mystic: Anselm's Early Writings.* West Lafayette: Purdue University Press, 1994.

Schweitzer, A. *Von Reimarus zu Wrede.* 1906.

Segundo, J. *The Historical Jesus of the Synoptics*, trans. by John Drury. Maryknoll: Orbis Books, 1985.

Sonderegger, K. "Anselm, *Defensor Fidei.*" *International Journal of Systematic Theology* Vol. 9, No 3. Oxford: Blackwell Publishing, 2007.

Southern, R.W. *Medieval Humanism and Other Studies*. Oxford: Basil Blackwell, 1970.

Southern, R.W. *Scholastic Humanism and the Unification of Europe, Vol. I, Foundations*. Oxford: Blackwell Publishing, 1995.

Southern, R. *St. Anselm: A Portrait in a Landscape*. Cambridge: Cambridge University Press, 1990.

Southern, R.W. *St. Anselm & His Biographer*. Cambridge: Cambridge University Press, 1963.

Southern, R.W. *The Making of the Middle Ages*. New Haven: Yale University Press, 1953.

Southern, R.W. *Western Society and the Church in the Middle Ages*. Middlesex: Penguin Books, 1970.

Stenton, F.M. *The First Century of English Feudalism, 1066-1166*. Oxford: Clarendon Press, 1932.

Stephenson, C. *Medieval History: Europe from the Second to Sixteenth Century, 4th Edition*, ed. by Bryce Lyon. New York: Harper & Row Publishers, 1935.

Stricken By God: Nonviolent Identification & the Victory of Christ, ed. by B. Jersak & M. Hardin. Grand Rapids: William B. Eerdm. ans Press, 2007.

Swinburne, R. *Responsibility & Atonement*. Oxford: Oxford University Press, 1989.

Taylor, I. *Pannenberg on the Triune God*. London: T&T Clark Publishers, 2007. *The Atonement Debate: Papers from the London Symposium on the Theology of Atonement*, ed. by D. Tidball, D. Hilborn, & J. Thacker. Grand Rapids: Zondervan Books, 2008.

The Catholic Encyclopedia Volume I, ed. by C. Herbermann. New York: Robert Appleton Company, 1907.

The Glory of the Atonement ed. by C. Hill & F. James III. Downers Grove: Intervarsity Press, 2004.

The Legacy of the Middle Ages, ed. by C.G. Crump & E.F. Jacob. Oxford: The Clarendon Press, 1926.

The Modern Theologians, ed. by D.F. Ford. New York: Basil Blackwell Publishers, 1989.

The Theology of Wolfhart Pannenberg, ed. by C. Braaten and P. Clayton. Minneapolis: Augsburg Press, 1988.

Theology and Change, ed. by R. Preston. London: Student Christian Movement, 1975.

Tillich, P. *A History of Christian Thought: From Its Judaic and Hellenistic Origins to Existentialism*, ed. by Carl E. Braaten. New York: Touchstone Books, 1967.

Torrance, T. *Space, Time, & Resurrection*. Edinburgh: T & T Clark, 1976.

Trelstad, M. *Cross Examinations: Readings on the Meaning of the Cross Today*. Minneapolis: Augsburg Fortress Press, 2006.

Tupper, F. *The Theology of Wolfhart Pannenberg*. Philadelphia: The Westminster Press, 1973.

Visser, S. & T. Williams. *Great Medieval Thinkers: Anselm*. Oxford: Oxford University Press, 2009.

Von Rad, G. "Typological Interpretation of the Old Testament." *Essays on Old Testament Hermeneutics*, ed. by Claus Westermann. Philadelphia: John Knox Press, 1963.

Weaver, J.D. *The Non-Violent Atonement*. Grand Rapids: William B. Eerdmans Publishing, 2001.

Weber, O. *Grundlagen der Dogmatik, Vol. II*. Neukirchen Kreis Moers: Verlag der Buchhandlung des Erziehungsvereins, 1955.

Weinberg, J. *A Short History of Medieval Philosophy*. Princeton: Princeton University Press, 1964.

Weiss, J. *Die Predigt Jesu vom Reiche Gottes*. Gottingen, Vandenhoeck, & Rupert, 1964.

Williams, G. *Anselm: Communion & Atonement*. St. Louis: Concordia Publishing House, 1960.

Wood, L. *Theology as History & Hermeneutics: A Post-Critical Conversation with Contemporary Theology*. USA: Emeth Press, 2005.

Wood, L. *God and History*. USA: Emeth Press, 2005.

Workman, H. *The Evolution of the Monastic Ideal: From the Earliest Times Down to the Coming of the Friars*. Boston: Beacon Press, 1962.

Workman, H. *The Evolution of The Monastic Ideal*. Boston: Beacon Press, 1913.

Wright, N.T. *The Resurrection of the Son of God*. Minneapolis: Fortress Press, 2003.

Young, F. *The Making of the Creeds*. London: SCM Press, 1991.

www.ingramcontent.com/pod-product-compliance
Lightning Source LLC
Chambersburg PA
CBHW031312150426
43191CB00005B/189